Shop Drawings

for

Craftsman Interiors

Shop Drawings

for

Craftsman Interiors

Cabinets, Moldings & Built-Ins
for Every Room in the Home

Measured and drawn by
Robert W. Lang

CAMBIUM PRESS
Bethel, CT

Shop Drawings For Craftsman Interiors
Cabinets, Moldings & Built-Ins for Every Room in the Home

ISBN 1-892836-16-5

First printing: October 2003
Secnd printing: October 2004
Printed in the United States of America

Published by
 Cambium Press
 PO Box 909
 57 Stony Hill Road
 Bethel, CT 06801
  203-778-2782
  www.cambiumbooks.com

Library of Congress Cataloging-in-Publication Data

Lang, Robert W. 1953-
  Shop drawings for Craftsman interiors : cabinets, moldings & built-ins
for every room in the home / measured and drawn by Robert W. Lang
   p. cm.
  ISBN 1-892836-16-5
 I. Furniture -- Drawings. 2. Measured drawing. 3. Arts and crafts
movement. I. Title.
TT196.L3523 2003
749'.4--dc22

                        2003024084

DEDICATION

In memory of my parents

CONTENTS

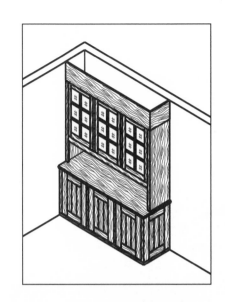

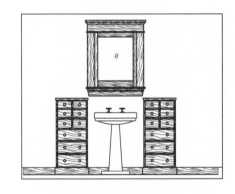

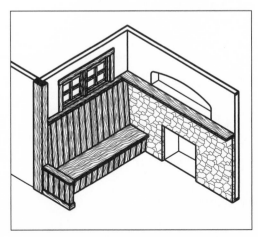

INTRODUCTION

Some of my favorite pieces of Craftsman furniture aren't exactly furniture at all—they are the woodwork built into Craftsman homes. Built-in bookcases, china cabinets and sideboards, stairways and doors are among the elements that make these houses special homes, and blend freestanding furniture and other decorative items in to a comfortable, integrated interior. Gustav Stickley is now well known as the leading furniture manufacturer of the American Arts & Crafts period, but he was also a leader in architecture and interior design, as well as in prosletyzing the philosophical foundation on which the Craftsman home is built.

There are many coffee table books about Craftsman homes, full of beautiful photos of completed interiors. Some of these contain useful information regarding structural elements, but few go to any depth. Some do an excellent job of telling the history of the period, while others fall well short of the mark. Very few, however, answer the questions I have: how were these things made, and why were they made that way? What is that made of, and how does that all go together? This work is intended to answer those questions, in enough detail to really benefit the owner of a period home doing a restoration, or the builder of a new structure attempting to recreate the look and feel of the period.

This book, like my previous books on Craftsman furniture, is a bit different. It is not a coffee table book, but more of an old-door-on-a-pair-of-saw-horses book. It is intended to guide homeowners, builders, designers, and architects with an interest in accurately reproducing the woodwork of the period. The drawings are based on the original designs that appeared in Stickley's *The Craftsman* magazine, and from original architectural drawings prepared by Stickley's firm. They are also based on my personal experience both in building and installing custom cabinets and other architectural millwork, and in preparing detail drawings for their construction. The drawings and text also take into account the many differences between then and now, both in the availability of materials and in methods of building.

While I have been able to take a very close look at what appears in this book, it should not be taken as the final word on Arts & Crafts period interiors. The sheer number of homes constructed, and regional differences in choice of materials and construction techniques prevent any book from being truly comprehensive. The reader should feel free to adapt the designs to fit his or her taste and budget. The many designs originally shown in *The Craftsman* were nearly always changed in one form or another as they were built, and Stickley's architectural drawings also show variations from the magazine designs, because the homes were tailored to suit individual clients.

What I have tried to do is give a general view of common elements, with a close look at how they are actually constructed, and how they relate to and fit into the building as a whole. Where the differences between then and now are great, I try to identify these differences, and present reasonable alternatives. Readers will need to make their own choices regarding historical accuracy and living in the modern world.

While the sources for this work are authentic, they often did not provide the same level of detail as these drawings do. I have based my details on what was shown or mentioned in *The Craftsman*, what Stickley's architectural drawings showed, what other sources for details of the period recommended, and lastly, my own judgment based on my practical experience.

The original architectural drawings were remarkably similar to architectural drawings of today. They show the designer's intentions as to the appearance of the finished product, but they don't really show all of the details

necessary for construction. Architects have always relied on the knowledge and experience of the various trades to build what they have envisioned. Bearing responsibility for the entire building, the architect cannot really be expected to know every detail of every item within it. Occasionally, an architect will venture into unknown territory and provide details that don't always make sense in the real world. The drawings I studied were prepared by a number of different draftsmen, and reflected different styles and levels of detail. In preparing my own drawings, I took the same approach that I take when preparing shop drawings for contemporary architectural millwork and cabinets: the finished work should look and function as its designer intended, plus it should be simple to construct, and efficient to install. I have tried to provide a method for constructing what the original designer intended, including the original details that made sense, while substituting my own details if following the original details would not provide sound construction or efficient manufacture.

The drawings in this book were prepared in the same way that I prepare drawings for fabrication in custom architectural woodworking (a fancy way of saying custom cabinets, doors, trim, and anything else made out of wood that might end up in a building), with a few differences. Generally in the trade, shop drawings are limited to plans (looking directly down on something), elevations (looking directly at something), and sections (looking directly at something that has had an imaginary slice taken through it). The three-dimensional views in this book are included to help the reader visualize the finished work, and to show the relationships between various elements that are not always apparent in two-dimensional views. These drawings are rendered as isometric or axonometric views: each direction in the drawing is in the same scale, rather than as a perspective drawing. Because of this lack of perspective, they sometimes appear to be distorted. On the other hand, they can be quite helpful because they can be scaled and measured. In some places in this book, the original illustrations from *The Craftsman* magazine have been included. These give a good idea of what the finished room should look like, but because they are artistic rather than practical in nature, they don't always show the true relationship between parts.

The plans, elevations, and section drawings show things from one point of view, and everything in the drawing is at its true size, in a scale small enough to fit on the page. All dimensions are given in inches and are actual, not nominal. If things don't seem to make sense at first, take some time to study the drawings, and look for each element in two different views. Learning to read a mechanical drawing is like learning a new language, without the pain of conjugating verb forms. The point of view of a drawing is from the center of the drawing, not from where it would be in real life, and one of the mistakes often made by architects and designers is to create a design that looks good on paper, but looks funny when built. The opposite can also happen—things don't look quite right on paper, but when built, and seen from the proper point of view, look in proportion, just right.

As in my books on Craftsman furniture, this book can't cover the material it needs to cover, and also be a basic instruction manual in finish carpentry, cabinetmaking, and restoration of old buildings. Along with the drawings, there is a good deal of information regarding techniques for fabricating and installing the woodwork shown. I am assuming that the reader has at least a basic knowledge of woodworking and woodworking tools, or the common sense to obtain that knowledge before proceeding with tools that can be dangerous, and materials that can be expensive. The bibliography lists some good written sources, and many vocational schools and technical colleges offer woodworking and carpentry instruction. Volunteering to work with Habitat for Humanity will also provide the novice with some practical experience, while helping a worthy cause. In many areas of the country, there are organizations based in historic neighborhoods for homeowners to share their experiences and advice. Don't be afraid to ask for help from those who have been through a project of their own.

In my opinion, the development of the Craftsman home, or bungalow, is one of the high points in American building history. At a time when our society was changing dramatically, we came up with a style of home building that had not been seen before, and much like jazz or blues music, uniquely reflected the best elements of our character. These homes also met the needs for shelter and comfort in a practical and efficient manner. In the early years of the Twentieth Century, we were able to build affordable housing for the middle class-homes that were well constructed, and exhibited a charm and grace that makes them truly homelike. These homes are enjoying a resurgence in popularity for many of the same reasons that made them popular when they were new. They are comfortable and relatively easy to care for, they provide a sense of home and neighborhood that positively affects the families that live in them, and the communities that surround them.

Between the early 1900s and the start of the Great Depression in 1929, thousands of these homes were constructed in nearly every area of the United States. In my own area, there are several neighborhoods with excellent examples that have aged quite gracefully. These neighborhoods have a character and charm that simply isn't present in buildings constructed before or since. They fit in with their environment visually, and they have met the practical needs of the families that have lived in them for nearly a century.

Since the end of World War II, building in America has little to be proud of. The ranch home of the fifties, which held some promise of continuing the growth of neighborhoods that the bungalow had begun, was stripped of all charm and warmth, and became little more than a series of sterile boxes, endlessly repeated. Today we now build generally the same cracker-box with two floors, energy efficient but built as quickly and cheaply as possible, with little or no thought to how living in such a house might affect its occupants. The wealthy get better quality, but the emphasis is more on size than grace, and instead of a comfortable style the emphasis is on imitating past periods of excess, with layer on layer of crown molding painted white. I have often wondered, while working on such houses, why the owners didn't just build a simple house and paper the walls with twenty-dollar bills. The house would be more livable, and the impression made on visitors would be about the same.

My hope is that with the return of the popularity of the Craftsman style, there will also be a return of the Craftsman ideal. Our children deserve to live in homes that reflect warmth and quality in all things. We deserve to live in homes and neighborhoods that make us comfortable, not just physically, but mentally and spiritually as well. While working on this book, my wife and I were recalling a home we once lived in that had a little dining nook—a spot just off the kitchen with high wainscoting and casement windows above. We realized that never before or since had we enjoyed the quality of conversation with each other that we had in that little nook. It was a spot that made us comfortable, and allowed us to focus on each other. Every home needs at least one such place.

As Gustav Stickley wrote in *The Craftsman* in November of 1912:

"For after all, the building of a home is a serious matter. Most people build but once, and then it means investing the savings of a lifetime. It means, too—or at least it should mean—the embodying in concrete form of their own ideals and aspirations, their feelings about home relationships, and household tasks; it means the reflection in their home of their own personality.

In the first place, the house should be itself, not an imitation of other houses; free from all false pretense or affectation of a luxury it cannot attain. In fact, style is the least important thing. If the house is built strongly and carefully, of suitable materials, to meet the owner's needs, with due consideration for beauty of proportion and detail, then it will be a law unto itself; it will have created its own style. And how much more permanent and wholesome an influence will such a dwelling have upon the lives of those within, and especially upon the children whose minds retain so easily the impressions of their early surroundings. They will unconsciously learn from it independence of thought, fearlessness of expressions, love of simplicity and beauty and the sincerity of a true home atmosphere."

In April 1914 he also wrote:

"The truth lies right here, that there are some things in the world that you cannot buy. There are good things that can only be created by the person desiring them. It is not enough to have walls to live within; to have an actual home which expresses your own life, you have got to contribute your own thought, your own effort to it. And the great result of this is not the house itself, but the development that you gain through your work; as a matter of fact it is seldom the material result of anything that counts, it is the spiritual result which is most significant, and the spiritual result of work done in the right spirit is character."

HISTORICAL CONTEXT

In 1900, Gustav Stickley was a successful furniture manufacturer, and like many successful men of his day, was the product of difficult beginnings and self-education. The eldest son of a family abandoned by its father, he accepted the burden of supporting the family at age 13, leaving school and going to work. In his late teens, he entered the furniture business in a chair factory owned by a relative. Over the next twenty years, in a variety of ventures, he perfected his skills in the trade, married and began a family. In the next few years he would expand his interests and become the pre-eminent figure in the American Arts and Crafts movement: not only as a designer and manufacturer, but also as a successful publisher, architect, and spokesman for the philosophy of the movement.

The period of time between the Spanish American War and World War I is largely passed over in the study of American history and decorative arts, but it marked some significant changes in the character of American culture. The United States in 1900 was in the midst of widespread change. New technology was moving the country from an agricultural society to an urban industrial empire. The Victorian era had brought new capabilities in manufacturing, but did not provide a clear vision of what to manufacture. Homes were cluttered both with machine made decoration, and all manner of things with no useful purpose. As cities grew, and the automobile and streetcar provided transportation, suburbs appeared, and with them the need for new housing and furnishings.

In England, the excesses of the Victorian age had been recognized by the likes of William Morris and John Ruskin, and the Arts & Crafts movement they started sought to make sense of mankind's place in the home and society, and the effects that life in the factories, and life surrounded by manufactured things, had on individuals and society. In America, we were getting good at making things like furniture, but lacking a sense of identity or style, we lived through revival after revival of past styles. Describing his motivations for developing a new style, Stickley wrote in 1909 (*Craftsman Furniture Catalog*, page 9):

" . . . I did so because I felt that the badly-constructed, over-ornate, meaningless furniture that was turned out in such quantities by the factories was not only bad in itself, but that its presence in the homes of the people was an influence that led directly away from the sound qualities which make an honest man and a sound citizen. . . . It seemed to me that we were getting to be a thoughtless, extravagant people, fond of show and careless of real value, and that one way to counteract this national tendency was to bring about, if possible, a different standard of what was desirable in our homes."

As Thomas Edison, Alexander Graham Bell and Henry Ford created entire industries based on new ideas, other creative people also began to look for new ways to meet society's needs. Architecture was one area where new ideas were embraced, and where a style that was distinctly American helped to change our society from a follower of European styles to a leader for the world. In the 1890s the Greene brothers in California and Frank Lloyd Wright established their practices, leading the development of the Prairie and Bungalow styles. In another ten years, Gustav Stickley would bring to the rising middle class what the Greenes and Wright had brought to their wealthy clients: a new form of the American home, one that made sense practically, aesthetically, and economically.

In the midst of this sea of change, Gustav Stickley took time off from his furniture business and toured Europe and England to see for himself the workings of the Arts & Crafts movement, and to develop a new form for American furniture and design. Upon his return from Europe, Stickley's first new designs were based on Art Nouveau forms: delicate tables stylized and named after the poppy and the lotus. Dissatisfied with these, he sought to "start from scratch" as he put it in the introduction to his 1909 furniture catalog:

" . . .I had no idea of attempting to create a new style, but merely tried to make furniture which would be simple, durable, comfortable and fitted for the place it was to occupy and the work it had to do. It seemed to me that the only way to do this was to cut loose from all tradition and to do away with all needless ornamentation, returning to the plain principles of construction and applying them to the making of simple, strong, comfortable furniture, and I firmly believe that Craftsman furniture is the concrete expression of this idea."

In July of 1900, Stickley first exhibited his designs at the semiannual furniture trade show in Grand Rapids, Michigan, then the center of the American furniture industry. His furniture quickly became quite popular, and Stickley was soon surrounded by a host of imitators. In October of the same year, he was featured in an article in House Beautiful magazine. On New Year's Day of 1901, the seventy workers in Stickley's Eastwood, New York, factory shared $2,000 in bonuses. By 1904, their number had grown to two hundred.

In the next few years tremendous growth occurred not only in Stickley's furniture business, but also in his overall interests and other business enterprises. Looking back, in 1913, Stickley wrote (*The Craftsman*, Oct. 1913 "The Craftsman Movement: its origin and growth"):

"Thus, unconsciously, a Craftsman style was evolved and developed, a style that gradually found its way into the homes of the people, pushing out a branch here, a branch there, first in one direction and then another, wherever it met with sympathy and encouragement. The next thing that naturally suggested itself was the need of a broader medium of expression for these ideas of craftsmanship and homemaking; the need of some definite, organized plan for reaching people who, I felt sure, would be interested in what I was trying to accomplish; some means of getting into direct communication with them, of entering, so to speak, into their very homes."

In October of 1901, the first issue of *The Craftsman* magazine was published, featuring articles on William Morris, and also including several pictures of Stickley's furniture. Stickley wrote in his foreword: (*Craftsman*, October 1901, p3):

"Thus, it is hoped to cooperate with those many and earnest minds who are seeking to create a national, or rather a universal art, adjusted to the needs of the century: that is, an art developed by the people, for the people, as a reciprocal joy for the artist and the layman."

In February of 1902, the first house plan appeared in *The Craftsman*, with drawings credited to Henry Wilhelm Wilkinson, illustrations of Stickley's furniture, and an article on the planning of the home as a dialogue between architect and client.

The magazine increased in size, scope and circulation in a brief period of time, covering an eclectic combination of topics. Interior design and decoration were mainstays, as well as articles on do-it-yourself projects

Early interior from *The Craftsman*

from woodworking to gardening. Also included were articles on social issues and education, indigenous arts and culture, and trends in design from Europe and England. House plans and articles on interior decoration were a regular feature of the magazine until it ceased publication in 1916.

In February of 1904, *The Craftsman* announced the formation of the Homebuilder's Club. For the cost of a year's subscription to the magazine, the subscriber could obtain, free of charge, detailed plans and specifications for any of the homes featured in the magazine. Many readers took Stickley up on his offer, and in the next few years articles written by readers about their experiences in building their Craftsman homes appeared in the magazine.

The Craftsman also featured articles on homes designed by other architects and designersof the time, including Charles and Henry Greene, Louis Sullivan, William Gray Purcell and George Grant Elmslie, Irving Gill, William Price, and Frank L. Packard. Harvey Ellis had articles and plans in *The Craftsman* during his brief tenure with Stickley, before his death in 1904. Louis Batchelder, the tile manufacturer, wrote a series about design. Frank Lloyd Wright was notably absent—his work was never mentioned in *The Craftsman* although he did travel to Syracuse to lecture in the Craftsman building.

In the early 1900s, most professionals, such as attorneys, doctors and architects, were the products of apprenticeships, not the lengthy schooling that we see today. In 1903 Stickley began listing himself as an Architect, and apparently directed a staff of draftsmen in the designs of the homes that appeared in *The Craftsman*, as well as editing and writing for his magazine, all the while running his successful furniture business. In 1905, he moved his offices and headquarters to New York City, while the furniture factory remained in Eastwood, near Syracuse, New York.

One of the changes that America went through at the turn of the century was the completion of a national railroad system that.allowed the regular, timely delivery of mail and goods from any location to any location. Businesses for the first time were able to deal efficiently in a national market. Sears and Roebuck, and J.C. Penney developed the mail-order catalog, and magazines with a national circulation began publication.

As American cities grew, and houses were built at an unprecedented pace, some new businesses came in to being to fill these needs. Several firms, notably the William A. Radford Company of Chicago, issued catalogs of house plans, offering at a price of $7 to $15 what Stickley was giving away as a premium for a magazine subscription. Going one step further were the kit home companies, such as Aladdin in Michigan. Sears also offered kit homes for many years. The order was placed and within a few weeks a railroad car delivered all the pieces of lumber and hardware, numbered for easy assembly. Many of these designs were similar to and derivative of designs that had been published in *The Craftsman*.

In 1908, Gustav Stickley added yet another branch to his interests, purchasing the land in rural New Jersey that was to become Craftsman Farms. In the October issue of

1908, he explained to his readers his dream of building a home of his own, putting in to practice the ideas of home design he had been expressing in the magazine. Detailed drawings and a lengthy article laid out his plan for an impressive structure to be built near the top of a hill on his new estate. This article also briefly mentioned Stickley's plans for a school, also to be constructed on the property.

In November of 1908, *The Craftsman* detailed plans for three cottages to be built for "the accommodation of students, crafts workers, or guests". In December, readers were given details of the log house, planned for a clubhouse at the estate. The following spring Stickley wrote an essay on the virtues of rural life, and his plans for establishing a school, in the hopes of developing a model that would be repeated at other locations. In 1909, Craftsman Homes, a compilation of plans and articles from *The Craftsman* was published. This book, and More Craftsman Homes, from 1912, are available in reprinted versions, and give a good idea of what was typically published in the magazine.

Stickley and his family moved to Craftsman Farms late in the spring of 1910, moving in to one of the cottages that had been built at the site. In August of that year, construction of the log clubhouse was begun, the original plan slightly modified as a residence for the Stickley family. It is not clear if Stickley intended this as a temporary home until the larger structure could be built, or if this was intended to be his permanent residence. The log home was completed the following summer and in the fall of 1911 it served as the site of the wedding ceremony between Stickley's eldest daughter, Barbara, who worked for her father, and Ben Wiles, Stickley's business manager. Even without the construction of the house originally planned, the expenses to purchase land and develop the estate were considerable:

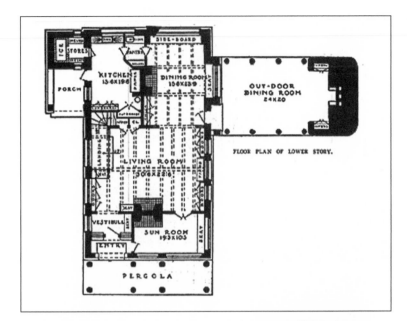

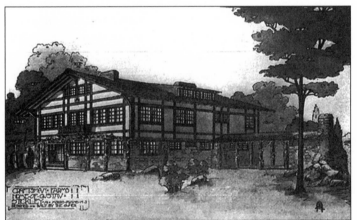

Log clubhouse at Craftsman Farms

between $200,000 and $250,000 at a time when the average cost of constructing a Craftsman home was between $2,500 and $3,500, and a subscription to the magazine was a few dollars a year.

During this period Stickley also constructed a few of his house designs, adding general contractor to his list of enterprises. He also invented a method of heating a home via ductwork from a fireplace. In 1912, he formed The Craftsman, Inc., a combination of all his properties and business interests.

In the summer of 1913, he announced the acquisition of the Craftsman Building, a 12-story building he leased in Manhattan around the corner from Tiffany and Bonwit Teller. Stickley envisioned it as a center for

home building and decorating, with his furniture and other decorative items shown on
the first three floors, the "Permanent Home
Building Exposition"—leased spaces to
manufacturers of other items— on the
fourth through eighth floors, and *The
Craftsman* design and editorial offices along
with club rooms, lecture halls, a library, and a
restaurant above. Ben Wiles, Stickley's son-
in-law and business manager, was against
this move, and failing to convince Stickley
not to make it, Wiles resigned and returned
to Syracuse.

When the Craftsman building was opened
to the public in the fall of 1913, Stickley was
still at his peak of popularity and influence,
but the American economy was starting to
slow with the approach of World War I. The
expenses of furnishing and decorating the
Craftsman Building must have been considerable, as the offices and public areas were
paneled and decorated in the Craftsman
Style. In addition to this, the cost of the lease
was $60,000 per year.

In addition to a slowing economy, the other
effect of World War I was a dramatic change
in the attitudes and tastes of the American
public. As John Crosby Freeman points out
in Forgotten Rebel, "The beginning of
World War I had changed perspective on
everything." The Colonial Revival came into
fashion, and America sought the comforts of
home in the designs of the past.

As sales of Craftsman furniture slowed,
Stickley tried to change with the times. His
1915 catalog and advertising introduced a
line of painted furniture called Chromewald
as well as Chinese Chippendale reproductions. In the spring of 1915 he was forced in
to bankruptcy. Within the next two years,
Gustav Stickley would lose everything that
he had established. *The Craftsman* ceased
publication in 1916, Craftsman Farms was
sold in 1917, and his brother Leopold would
take over his furniture factory in 1918.

According to Freeman, (Forgotten Rebel, pp.
25) Stickley could have survived financially
had he accepted orders for his Chromewald
line. His brother Leopold survived the
change of taste by jumping on the Colonial
Revival bandwagon, introducing a line of
reproduction furniture.

Gustav Stickley had described his involve-
ment with the Arts & Crafts movement as
"like a religion" to him, and it appears that he
chose to quietly retire, rather than return to
being just a furniture manufacturer. A read-
ing of *The Craftsman* shows that he truly was
concerned about the moral and spiritual values that were the basis for his designs. His
dream was not just to become a financially
successful businessman, but also to lead society, through the way people lived, worked,
and were educated, to a better way of life.
The Craftsman ideal is not just a set of
design criteria, but a way of living in harmo-
ny with what the world provides us. As
Stickley's designs return to popularity, hope-
fully the results of living with those designs
will have an impact on us all.

In spite of the collapse of the Arts & Crafts
movement at the time of the first world
war, the Craftsman home, or bungalow,
continued to be a popular style until home
building all but ceased with the stock market crash of 1929. In the next chapter, the
three Craftsman homes that Gustav
Stickley designed for his own family will be
discussed.

GUSTAV STICKLEY'S THREE HOMES

The tradition of lights on a Christmas tree began in Germany, and at the turn of the Twentieth Century these lights would have been candles. This is a scary tradition, and in practice, some one had to stand by ready to put out the flames should the tree itself ignite. Gustav Stickley, of German descent, and his family would have enjoyed this tradition. On Christmas Eve, 1901, a fire broke out in the Stickley home on Columbus Avenue in Syracuse, extensively damaging the interior. Almost a year later, an article in *The Craftsman* detailed the changes that had been made in rebuilding.

From the outside, the home looks much like the others in the neighborhood, except for the massive front door, wider than usual, constructed of oak with wrought metal hardware and ten amber glass lights above three oak panels. Inside, however, it is the first example of Stickley's interior designs, and one of the finest, showing a consistent vision of the ideal interior. As Samuel Howe described it in the magazine:

> "It contains evidence of serious thought and honest intent, with abundant freshness and wholesomeness, which are innovations in these days of machine carving and jelly mold enrichments. Here is a house that has qualities generally lacking in architectural schemes, where their details too often smack of the dust of the drawing office. Quiet harmony is the prevailing note of the composition, characterized by a singular uprightness and sturdy independence."

Perhaps the most striking change is the opening of the floor plan. The living room, hall, dining room and nook are all part of a continuous space, the different areas being divided by overhead beams supported by columns and panels. The trim at the top of the doors and windows continues throughout the space, wood panels below, and plaster above. Wood and plaster also alternate at the ceiling, where beams run in the long direction of the plan, drawing the eye to the next adjacent space. One of Stickley's talents was his ability to delineate an area without separating it from the rest of the house. These first-floor areas are each distinct, their purpose quite clear, but they are all a part of the unified whole. Point of view is also used effectively.

From the front entry, the space is private, until the visitor is invited inside and takes a few steps. From that vantage point the living area is seen as one large room, a great room, with distinct areas divided not by walls but by obvious indications of their intended use. At the front of the house is an informal living room, replacing the formal parlor popular at the time. The entry hall is not merely a traffic hub, it is part of the living area and is oriented at a right angle to the house, with a distinctive stairway at one end and a seat below casement windows at the other. At the far end of the house, past the dining room, is a small nook with a fireplace and window seats.

It is extremely rare in architecture to see a design that is entirely new, and most of the elements of Stickley's home had been seen in English Arts & Crafts designs, particularly in the work of C.F.A. Voysey and Bailey-Scott. Stickley's accomplishment was to bring all of the elements together in a nearly perfect combination of form and function. The

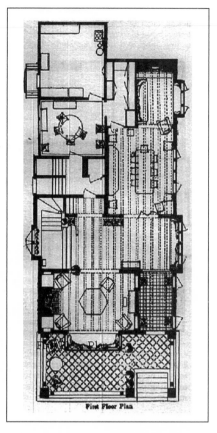

First Floor Plan

Floor plan for Stickley's Syracuse house

Interior renderings for Syracuse house

appearance is unified and congruent, yet there are distinct areas for different domestic activities. It is easy to imagine an evening in this home; conversation in front of the fire in the living room followed by dinner at the long table between a massive sideboard and a row of windows, ending in the nook beyond the dining room with the warmth of the fire.

It is interesting that Stickley's ideas were so well developed in this, his first attempt at designing an interior. Nearly all of the elements that make up a Craftsman home are present —the wide planked hardwood floors, the vee-grooved wood paneling, beamed and paneled room transitions, and built in cabinets, that would be seen in later designs published in *The Craftsman*. The design appears simple, it is comfortable and warm without any extraneous elements, yet it combines a number of intricate details. Wood meets brick at the fireplace, glass in the cabinet and passage doors, and plaster at the frieze and ceiling. Where the wood intersects other wood elements, there are lines and shadows, slight recesses and vee-grooves that keep the simple shapes quite interesting.

At the top of the stairs, on the second floor, the hall is also used as an extension of the adjacent living spaces. It has a small sitting area, a place to relax and wait, in a space that is rarely used effectively. It is a transition, but it is also a destination, a quiet place on the way from the public areas downstairs to the private areas of the adjacent bedrooms and study on the second floor. The illustrations of this area published in *The Craftsman* show a waist-high railing separating the space from the stairwell. A chair rail continues at this height, and the wall paneling and doors are integrated.

In March of 1913, an article in *The Craftsman* laid out the distinguishing features of the typical Craftsman Home, which had been established by Stickley in his first attempt, in 1902:

"The central thought in all Craftsman activities is the simplification of life and a return to true democracy. Accordingly the exterior lines of the Craftsman house are very simple and its interior divisions are few.

"Elaborate ornamentation is eliminated by our method of interior treatment. Post-and-panel construction replaces useless partitions. Native woods are used liberally. The fireplace is made an ornamental feature.

" . . . possibly the greatest economy of all is the permanent quality of the homes we design.

"The simple lines of the Craftsman house give it a beauty and a dignity which react most favorably upon the life and character of the family.

"Too large a house with unused rooms breeds a spirit of extravagance. The relation of every part of the interior of a house to the needs of the family should be direct and apparent. A Craftsman house is designed to meet these needs just as simply, comfortably and economically as possible.

"A Craftsman interior, with its built-in features, its cozy nooks, its fireplace and friendly atmosphere created by absence of separate rooms and overcrowded furnishings, affords real decoration without additional expense.

"The dining room is usually designed to be either almost or wholly a part of the living room. We believe this arrangement to be a constant expression of the spirit of hospitality—entertainment grows thus less elaborate and more friendly, and this phase of home life becomes less formal.

"Craftsman interior decoration is brought about by the proper use of woods and harmonious color schemes. "

These factors are quite different from a lot of popular notions regarding room arrangement and interior finishes. How a room felt, and the effect of an environment on its occupants are as important as materials and finishes that limit most schemes. I think that the current resurgence in popularity of the Craftsman home is due to our need for comfort, and desire to nurture good character. Most design schemes ignore these effects, speaking of how things look instead of how they feel, basing our designs either on irrelevant or erroneous historical periods. Craftsman designs look fresh and up to date because they speak to qualities in ourselves that are constant, not based on styles and trends that come and go.

The Craftsman article of 1902 ended on the following note:

"It is like hoisting a danger signal to speak out loud to Mr. Stickley of ornament, yet all people do not know this. "It is very grand," said one visitor, "but have you no ornament, carving or draperies in your house, Mr. Stickley?"

"No draperies, thank you, and as for ornament, have we not our friends?"

Three years later, Stickley moved his headquarters to Manhattan, while his family and manufacturing operations remained in Syracuse. He apparently divided his time between the two locations, sharing an apartment in New York with his daughter Barbara, who had left school to work in the family business. It was not until the summer of 1911 that he moved in to the log home at Craftsman Farms.

When the log home was first described to *The Craftsman* readers, it was intended to be used as a clubhouse for the estate, a place for meeting and entertaining. Construction was originally planned to start in the spring of 1909, but it was delayed a year, and its design had been modified slightly to become the Stickley residence.

The original entrance to Craftsman farms comes up a hillside, through woods between the property and the road beyond. Rounding a slight curve in the driveway, the log home comes in to view, its stone foundations rising above what was originally a rose garden. Although Stickley is known for his work in wood, he had apprenticed to his stone mason father at the age of twelve, and one of the most impressive things about Craftsman Farms is the fieldstone work in the log home foundation and chimneys, the retaining wall and pillars at the garden, and in the stables and other outbuildings. The log house rises up from the hillside, almost as if it had grown there. Craftsman Farms was much more than a residence—Stickley was interested in farming, and in the educational values obtained in growing up in an idyllic rural location. He was quoted in *The Craftsman* as saying:

"This is my garden of Eden. This is the realization of the dreams that I had when I worked as a lad. It is because my own dreams have come true that I want other

Log house at Craftsman Farms, as designed (top) and as built.

One of the biggest changes from the original design is the enclosing of the front porch, which runs the length of the downhill side of the house. The main entry to the house is actually to the porch, behind a massive door similar to the one in Syracuse. The porch commands a view of the property, now overgrown, but in Stickley's day would have shown the orchards and pastures of this working farm. At 14 feet by 52 feet, the porch is quite large, and was the site for the weddings of Stickley's daughters. The porch is connected by windows both to the farm fields below, and to the 20 foot by 50 foot living room behind it. The lower floor of the log structure is mainly two rooms, the living room and a dining room that is 12 feet-6 inches by 50 feet, with a 25 foot by 26 foot kitchen added at the back of the house. Despite the grand scale of these rooms, there is a feeling of intimacy in the space, made possible by discrete areas defined by groupings of furniture and the fireplaces at each end of the living room and in the middle of the dining room.

The original plan called for the kitchen to be roughly two-thirds of what is now the dining room, with a small sitting room in the other end. The change in plan leaves the first floor more open, and the kitchen in the addition would actually serve the purpose of entertaining better than the original plan. It was equipped with a massive restaurant-style stove, and an automatic dishwasher. At the opposite end of the kitchen, a door to a walk-in cooler is flanked by a pair of chestnut cupboards.

The freestanding furniture in the log home plays more of a role in defining spaces than in the Syracuse house, or in many other Craftsman designs. The log construction on the first floor prevents the use of built-ins; the spaces are neatly delineated by the arrangement and selection of the furniture, and the placement of the passages between the rooms, leaving each room with a sub-

boys to dream out their own good future here to themselves."

His dream of establishing a school never materialized, but the house he built is a wonderful example of a home suited to its site and its purpose.

Atop the fieldstone foundation, the first floor of the house is constructed of peeled chestnut logs, harvested from the site. The second floor is of frame construction, covered in shingles. The roof, originally intended to be covered with red slate, was instead covered with green Rubberoid, and a few years after construction, green terra cotta tiles were added. Massive fieldstone chimneys are centered at each of the gable ends, and the elevation from the downhill side is dominated by numerous windows on the porch, and in the large dormer above.

stantial area in the center and smaller areas at each end. The stairway anchors the middle of the wall separating the living room from the dining room, another change from the original plan, which had the stairway winding near one end of the living room. A high-backed settle, and large bookcases facing the fireplace at one end of the living room, form an intimate sitting area. An inlaid piano, library table, and tall-case clock are in the middle of the room, and at the opposite end, a hexagonal library table and bookcases form another discrete sitting area.

The dining room is also divided roughly into thirds. An immense sideboard, nearly the twin of one custom-made for the Columbus Avenue home, is centered on the long central wall opposite the fireplace. At one end two corner cabinets and a table create a nook for informal dining.

Upstairs, a ladies sitting room, centrally located at the head of the stairs, was in the original plan, but that space was reduced in size to become a hall with built in linen closets. Similar to the house in Syracuse, this hall is a distinct space with a long blanket chest in front of the rail. The woodwork in the hall is of gum, stained a rich reddish brown. In the bedrooms the walls were plaster bounded by wood trim. The second floor had the typical Craftsman treatment, well-defined spaces and a rich blend of wood, plaster, and tile at the fireplaces.

In most of the Craftsman home designs, we tend to see the built in furniture and other trim elements and don't realize how large a part the arrangement of interior spaces plays in the success of these designs. Because the log structure reduces the finish carpentry elements to a minimum, it becomes clear how the thoughtful use of space contributes to the feel of the home. The log home at Craftsman Farms is an excellent example of Stickley's design, although in a slightly different form. It was a compromise, driven by

Dining room (top), living room (middle) and bedroom at Craftsman Farms.

the financial impossibility of building the home the Stickley wanted to build for his family at the estate. Yet it is a testament to his architectural ability.

Had the construction of "The Craftsman's House" been possible, we would have a concrete example of Stickley's ideas played out without constraints. Just as Frank Lloyd Wright's personal residences let us see what the architect would do if he were also the client, Stickley's planned home gives us perhaps the best example of his design philosophy. The description, published in *The Craftsman* in October 1908, was lengthy and quite detailed. In addition to renderings showing the exterior at the crest of a hill, interior spaces, floor plans, and elevations, details were also published showing sections of the walls, foundation drains, ceilings and rafters. The original architectural drawings are not in the collection at the Avery Library, but from the material published in *The Craftsman* it is evident that Stickley had a near complete plan in place for what would have been his architectural masterpiece.

The Craftsman article begins with Stickley describing his move from approaching home design from a general "theoretical" approach, to a practical, personal one.

"I will not deny that I thoroughly enjoy telling my readers about this practical experiment I am making in the building of my own house. I never before realized how much pleasure was to be found in the building of a dwelling that as completely expressed one's own taste and individuality as the painting of a picture or the writing of a book. In fact, I can think of no creative work that is so absorbingly delightful as this creation of a home to live in for the rest of one's life. I have always felt that this must be so and have said and written it many times, but now the realization of the truth of it comes home to me a force that is entirely new, for this is the first house that I have

ever built for my own use, from the ground up to the last detail of the completed structure. So I give it as an object lesson and a suggestion to others who may find in it some incentive to devote as much thought and care to the building of their own homes instead of setting aside a specified sum and entrusting the whole pleasant task to an architect or builder, and so depriving themselves of the interest of sharing with him the work of evolving that which is as personal a possession as one's children or one's friends."

Stickley's vision of the home was so complete, that the article in *The Craftsman* reads more like the description of a completed structure than the outline of a proposed building. The three-story home was meant to be of timber frame construction, above a fieldstone first floor. The front of the house was to be 30 feet-6 inches wide, with a pergola extending the entire width, and approximately 5 feet deep. On the left side, the rustic front door, flanked by two casement windows, was in an enclosed niche and led to a vestibule. A second door led directly to a sunroom, designed so that the glass in the windows could be completely removed during the summer. A nearly identical sunroom, directly above this on the second floor, connected with a bedroom and an office. Three-quarters of the first floor was given to the living room and dining room with the kitchen occupying the remaining space. Also on the first floor, directly off the dining room, was an outdoor dining room, described by Stickley as "the expression of an individual fancy." A stone fireplace, complete with ovens and cupboards, were to be in a stone niche at the end opposite the house, and a tiled roof covered this area.

The second floor featured two bedrooms at the back, each with a small balcony, and one with a larger balcony that could be covered with canvas for use as a sleeping porch. At the front of the second floor, a sun room stretched across the entire width, connected to a bedroom and to another room labeled on the plan as "Mr. Stickley's Study". The third floor was dominated by a centrally located billiard room, and three additional bedrooms. Stickley's love of the fireplace was shown by the sheer number contained in this house: in each of the two sunrooms, the living room, the dining room, the billiard room, in two of the third floor bedrooms, and in the outdoor dining room. Built-ins, bookcases, seats, a sideboard and china closet of fumed chestnut were to be located in nearly every available space on the first floor, which was also to be paneled up to roughly half the height of the wall. The exposed structural beams and girders of the timber frame were to be cased in chestnut, finished to match the balance of the living and dining rooms. The kitchen was to have a Welsh quarry-tile floor, and walls of vee-grooved Georgia pine, in random widths with chestnut cupboards. The second-floor hall and staircase, as well as the billiard room on the third floor, were to be of straight-sawn oak, while the bedrooms were planned to be a showcase of different woods; Georgia pine, ash, hazel, maple, birch, beech, and California redwood.

The space in between the members of the timber frame were to be filled with two layers of hollow tile, arranged at right angles to each other to prevent the spread of fire. The roof was also to be of layers of tiles, to allow for the circulation of air. The house was planned without a basement, set on a solid foundation, with the heating plant and laundry located in an outbuilding nearby. Fruit cellars were also planned to be located separate from the main house, set in the hillside.

Stickley's plan was for a home that would showcase the ideals he had expounded in *The Craftsman*, and that would be his home for the rest of his life. The exact location planned on the Craftsman Farms site is not known, but there is a large open area uphill from the log house that seems to be the logical choice, based on his description and on the magazine renderings.

The article in *The Craftsman* was titled: "The Craftsman's House: A Practical Application of all the Theories of Home Building Advocated in this Magazine: by The Editor". He begins by saying, " I have always held the conviction that the first essential requisite for the development of a characteristic national style of architecture lies in the straightforward planning of a building to meet the need for which it is intended and to harmonize with the surroundings in which it is to be placed." In the abridged reprint of the magazine article that appeared in Craftsman Homes, Stickley wrote: "The dwelling shown here is perhaps the most complete example in existence of the Craftsman idea."

Stickley's role and influence in the architecture of the early Twentieth Century has largely been ignored. While he certainly wasn't the only person working to develop a new American style of architecture, his influence was profound and wide-reaching. While other architects created a few designs for a small number of individual clients, Stickley's efforts through *The Craftsman* and his related enterprises brought this new style to the common man, resulting in the building of countless homes across the country. In nearly any American town there can be found examples of homes based on the designs provided by Gustav Stickley. These homes were built to fit their sites, the needs of their residents, and their time. As we look at the state of building today, from the vinyl-wrapped cracker boxes of our suburbs to the oversized McMansions being built for the wealthy, it would serve us well to look back to the homes of *The Craftsman*. The quality of our lives and of our society is affected by where and how we live, and if we would have improvement in these areas, we need look no further than the examples that Gustav Stickley, the Craftsman, provided us.

THE BUILDING ENVIRONMENT

The drawings and text that follow show the finished elements that make the Craftsman home, but before any of these elements can be constructed the house, and individual rooms where they are going, needs to be examined, and the plans given herein will need to be adjusted. There will need to be some different approaches, depending on both the age of the structure and the care given to the quality of its construction. I am going to assume that the reader is looking for the highest quality possible, and the details and suggestions given will reflect that assumption. There are always ways to cut corners, or value engineer, but if you are going to live with the results of your work, you will find it is best to get it right the first time.

One of the first rules of quality architectural woodworking is to install all the woodwork straight, level, square, and plumb. There are a number of ways that the woodwork can be adjusted to fit in a building that is less than perfect, and these are detailed and discussed in the various sections of this book. If you are involved in the remodeling of a period home, make absolutely sure that all structural and mechanical issues have been addressed before worrying about the trim and cabinets. Cosmetic changes won't cure a leaky roof or a crumbling foundation, and will be the first things damaged if these other problems continue. It is normal, especially for houses constructed eighty to one hundred years ago, to have some settling or sagging, but the entire home should be gone over to determine if these are character marks of age, or warning signs of impending disaster. I hate to admit how many expensive remodeling projects I have been involved in, where large adjustments had to be made to the cabinetwork, in buildings that the owner

or contractor didn't want to admit were unstable.

Aside from shrinking and sagging, an older home is likely to be of far better construction than one newly erected. One of the reasons for this is that in the early 1900s there was not the distinction between rough and finish carpenters that there is today. Many of the articles published in *The Craftsman* submitted by readers relate how a few carpenters took the building from start to finish. Someone framing a rough opening for a door will have a different attitude about such things as location, size and plumb if he knows he will have to come back later to hang and trim the door. One of the biggest problems in the quality of building today is that rough carpenters or framers are now considered a distinct trade from finish carpenters. They are not taught or expected to work accurately, and are long gone from most jobsites when the finish carpenter or cabinetmaker says, "This isn't right and needs to be changed." At this point a choice must be made between compromising the appearance of the finished work, or bearing the expense of doing work a second time. The same is true of the differences between drywall hangers and plasterers. Generally, older plasterwork will be much flatter, and the corners especially will be neater, than with today's drywall work.

The homeowner doing his own work will have the ability to control the preliminary work, and thus make the installation of built-ins and trim much easier. If this work is contracted out, it should be carefully inspected to be sure it is correct, and while good trim work is often expected to cover up the short cuts of all the work preceding it, the final appearance will be greatly enhanced if the rough work is done properly.

While the finish work is the last thing to go into a house, it should be among the first things to be considered when planning. In the old days, pieces of wood called grounds were used wherever plaster met wood, providing a definite, straight surface for the plasterer to work to, and solid material for the fastening of trim. This practice forced the consideration of trim sizes and their relationships early in construction. Today, these relationships are often ignored until it is too late to correct in a cost-efficient manner. In quality work, blocking—pieces of solid wood between framing members—is provided behind the drywall to allow the solid attachment of trim and built-ins. This is usually shown in the detail drawings for built-ins and cabinets, and if in doubt, it doesn't hurt to have more solid material behind the wall.

It is always tempting to get the drywall up, so that it looks like progress is being made, but this should be delayed until it is certain that the framing is correct and all necessary blocking is in place. One place that is often troublesome is in the corner of a room or hallway, where two or more doors are adjacent to each other. Nothing looks nicer than to have all the casings come together neatly, and nothing is more frustrating to work with or live with than having a thin piece of casing on one side, and a narrow strip of exposed plaster on the other due to lack of foresight when laying out the walls and framing the doorways. It is wise to do a full size layout of the framing members, drywall, jambs, and trim before framing begins. In many of the details shown in the drawings in this book, all of the woodwork has a distinct relationship with other elements, and this relationship needs to be considered early on to achieve the desired effect.

When I measure a room for cabinets or trim, I first like to take an overall look around the room, and get a feel for how level the floors and ceiling are, and how plumb and square are the walls. Usually, out-of-level conditions are taken out of the baseboard, or lower trim of the cabinets. Horizontal trim, either at the ceiling, or at chair rails height, should always

be installed level, even if the ceiling is out-of-level. If the woodwork is very involved, or continues from one room to another, a benchmark should be established around the perimeter of the room, or even throughout the building, and all measurements regarding finished height should come off the benchmark, rather than the floor or ceiling. I also like to establish vertical benchmarks, usually at the midpoint of the walls. In laying out panels or cabinets, the final work will look nicer if you work from the center out to each end, rather than from one end to the other. I find that it is more accurate to take measurements from each direction to the benchmarks to obtain an overall width or height, than to try to accurately make an overall height or width measurement.

Laser levels have dropped significantly in price in the last few years, and make these layout tasks relatively simple. A unit that is self-leveling and shoots two horizontal lines at 90° plus a plumb line is now available for around $200, and will be well worth the investment, paying for itself in time saved and mistakes prevented. A surveyor's or builder's transit may also be used to establish a level line. A long horizontal line may be run with a 4-foot or 6-foot level, but the chance for error with this approach is considerably higher than if a laser or transit is used, and it will take considerably more time.

The condition of the walls also needs to be closely examined, both for plumb and for straightness. A plumb bob or long level may be used, or again, a laser that can shoot a plumb line is quite helpful. Measurements of spaces between walls will be of little help if you don't establish what you are measuring to, and where you are measuring from. If the walls are out of plumb, or out of square, there can be a significant difference in the measurements at different points, which must be considered. I generally measure at the floor, ceiling, and any points in between where my work will intersect the buildings walls. I also measure both at the wall itself, and out from the wall where the finished front of the work will be. Only after these measurements have been taken can the final sizes of the cabinet or panel parts be calculated. Drawing a layout at full size, either on a piece (or pieces) of cheap plywood, or directly on the walls and floor, can be quite helpful.

It is also necessary to determine if the walls are square to each other, but before this can be done with any reliability, the straightness of the walls must be determined. Usually this can be done by sighting down the length of the wall, and depending on the situation, a long straight edge, or the string from a chalk line, can be stretched from one end of the wall to the other. In new construction, I prefer to check for square after the drywall is in place, but before the wall is finished, as the "mud" often builds up in the first few inches from the corner. Measuring out from the corner with a 3-4-5 triangle, or in a larger room a 6-8-10 triangle, will be more accurate than placing a framing square in the corner.

In paneling work, it is critical that the finished wall be all in one flat plane, and the condition of the wall will play a large part in determining how the panels will be attached to the wall. If the wall is in good shape, the panels may be attached directly to the wall surface, or held on with metal clips. If the walls are out by more than an eighth or a quarter of an inch, then ledger strips, $3/4$ inch thick by $1\frac{1}{2}$ inch or 2 inches wide, nailed to the wall studs, should be provided for attaching the paneling and shimmed out to give a flat surface. French cleats (page 49) can also be shimmed from behind, and allow for holding the panels to the walls without a lot of fasteners showing. In any of these cases, it must be remembered that the final thickness of the wall will change, and this may affect door and window jambs as well as other trim elements.

Most of the built-ins and cabinets shown in the drawings in this book allow for a scribe, that is, some extra material to be fit to the wall upon final installation. The walls will not be perfect, and scribing is better than covering up any gaps with a small molding. Often a cleat is used at this same location for the purpose of attaching the front of the cabinet to the wall. Extra material may need to be added to the width of the cabinet part to ensure that there is enough room for both the cleat and for scribing. Depending on the conditions of the room, I will allow an extra $1/4$ inch or $1/2$ inch to the largest dimension I have recorded. On installation, the location for the cabinet is determined by locating the center of the cabinets or other millwork, and working from that point to each end. The end cabinet is set plumb and level as close to that mark as possible, with the edge touching the wall. A simple drawing compass is set to the distance of the widest gap between cabinet and wall, which should be equal to a mark on the opposite side, indicating the final location of the cabinet. The compass, held level, is run the length of the cabinet, transferring the variations of the wall to the face of the cabinet. On dark woods, masking tape on the face of the cabinet will make the pencil line easier to see. The scribe can then be trimmed with any number of methods, my preference is a jig saw and a block plane, but belt sanders, power planes, and angle grinders are often used to neatly fit the cabinet to the variations of the wall surface. Some makers prefer to back-cut the scribe at an angle so that the fitting in the field won't require the removal of as much material if the edge had been left square.

Another important consideration is the size of the various components of the cabinetwork. Built-ins are rarely "built in", that is, it makes more sense to assemble the cabinets in a shop than it does to cobble them together in their final location, although this was and is often done. I find it much easier to build complete boxes that can be fit in to place, rather than attempt to build and install at the same time. By building separately, cabinets can be clamped and screwed firmly together from behind or below, making for stronger and neater work. I also prefer constructing a separate base for cabinets to sit on. By doing this, I am assured of a straight and level surface for the cabinets to be installed on, making installation much easier, especially if the floor is low at the back of the cabinets, a condition that is quite difficult to correct if the base is an integral part of the cabinets.

The size of each unit must also be considered: it must be small enough to be carried in to the building, through doorways, and possibly up a flight of stairs. In many of the drawings in this book, I show distinct units that join together in the field, often with this joint covered by a stile that is attached to one cabinet in the shop, and to its neighbor in the field. These could be constructed as single units, but I would not do so. I pre-assemble an entire elevation of cabinets in the shop, using un-glued biscuits to hold the "field" joints in alignment.

Heat and humidity are also vitally important considerations. The building should be enclosed from the elements, and heat and air conditioning need to be operating before the beginning of any finish woodwork. The Architectural Woodwork Institute recommends that interior spaces be kept at a relative humidity of between 25% and 55%. Extremes of humidity, below 20% or above 80%, or changes in humidity of more than thirty percentage points, are likely to cause problems due to wood movement. Give the interior plenty of time to reach these conditions before bringing in finish wood materials. Remember that every drop of water used in plaster or drywall work will eventually evaporate, so all this work should be completed and allowed to dry before the wood trim work begins. Once the space has reached the optimum humidity, wood for trim, and finished cabinets and doors, may

be brought inside; they too should be given at least a few days to equalize to interior conditions. Theoretically, quality woodwork should be fabricated in an environment that is also maintained at these ideal humidity levels, but this is rarely the case. Depending on where you live, and the time of year, equilibrium moisture content between outside and inside—or between an unheated woodshed, or non-air-conditioned cabinet shop—may be enough to cause significant changes in the width of solid-wood material.

If you are doing your own fabrication you should be aware of both heat and humidity conditions in your shop, and the moisture content of your raw materials. Generally speaking, if the wood is between 5% and 10% you will likely not have problems in most parts of the country. A moisture meter will allow you to determine the exact moisture content of the wood. Without one, it is best to wait at least several days after bringing material into the house.

Trim work usually starts with the setting of the doors and windows, and then the door and window trim. This establishes definite lines that are straight and plumb for all of the work to follow. Paneling generally will follow next, and then any cabinets, seats or other built-ins. In a good deal of period work, if a room contained vee-groove vertical panels, the cabinets were constructed without backs, using the room panels for the cabinet backs. If the cabinet interiors are hidden from view, behind solid doors as opposed to glass doors, I would tend to use a plywood back for the cabinets, and run the panels to the edges of the cabinets. Each situation will likely be different, so planning the sequence of work to be performed is as important as planning the finished sizes.

All of the projects presented in these drawings have been drawn either at the original room dimensions, or at some standard increment, and will need to be adapted to the specific room for which they are intended. The easiest way to do this for width will be to consider the widths of vertical cabinet members as fixed, and the openings in between as variable. To adapt a design to a specific room, take the overall width of the room, and subtract the combined width of the fixed elements. Dividing that number by the number of variable elements, for example cabinet doors, will give the size of each opening. When figuring the doors, keep the stiles at the widths shown, and make the panels in between narrower or wider as needed. This is the best way to preserve the appearance of the designs, and in some cases, it will likely be necessary to increase or decrease the number of variable elements. I think it looks best to keep cabinet doors to a width between 12 and 18 inches; much wider than that introduces problems with hardware sagging, and the doors intruding upon the space of the room when open. Much narrower, and it doesn't look right. The other consideration is the width of shelves inside the cabinet. Shelves that are $3/4$ inch thick will begin to sag in the middle if they are made much wider than 30 inches, or 36 inches if they have a solid-wood front edge at 1 inch or $1^1/4$ inch wide. Also, bear in mind the intended purpose of the cabinets, and be certain that anything you intend to place inside actually will fit. If you have a special piece of period pottery that you are going to display in your new built-in china cabinet, make sure that the cabinet will be deep enough, and the space between the shelves tall enough.

Thorough knowledge of the building environment is essential to the successful completion of the type of work shown in this book. Once this knowledge is obtained, decisions can be made regarding what materials to use, and a plan developed for construction to proceed.

MATERIALS

In the first 20 years of the Twentieth Century, they types and sizes of wood that were commonly available were quite different than what is available today. This is in part due to the conditions of our forests, and in part due to the tragic decimation of one particular species, the American chestnut. At that time, there was still a tremendous amount of old-growth timber to be cut, although there were signs that supplies were not without limits. While wood is a renewable resource, and one that is reasonably well managed, it is doubtful that we will ever see the likes of lumber that was available eighty or ninety years ago. This difference between that day and ours may likely cause some difficulties in the duplication of the designs shown in this book.

Many of the solid wood trim pieces shown are quite wide, and obtaining wood in these widths can be difficult. While we are planting more trees than we cut, and most of our native species are available, the trees we cut today are mere youngsters of 60 to 80 years old, compared to the several-hundred-year-old giants that were being cut during the Craftsman period. It is possible to glue two or more narrow pieces together to get the necessary width, but great care must be taken to match grain and color, so that it appears to be a single piece of wood. Veneer over a man-made substrate can be a solution, but again, the leaves must be carefully matched to look like a single piece of wood.

The favorite wood of the period was clearly chestnut. With a grain structure similar to ash, it was durable yet soft enough to be easily worked. Stickley thought it to be a bit soft for furniture making, but an ideal wood for trim. His home in Syracuse had chestnut floors and paneling, and in his planned home at Craftsman Farms he intended to use chestnut extensively. In an article titled "Our native woods and the Craftsman method of finishing them," Gustav Stickley ranked chestnut as close to the equal of white oak: "Next in rank to oak for use in large rooms comes chestnut, which is equally attractive in fiber and markings, has a color quality that is even better, and is plentiful, easily obtained and very reasonable as to cost.

"One great advantage of chestnut—aside from its charm of color, texture and markings—is that it is very easy to work, stays in place readily, is so easy to dry that the chances of getting thoroughly dry lumber are much greater that they would be if oak were used."

At nearly the same time that Stickley wrote these words, the demise of the American chestnut was beginning. In New York City, in 1904, the fungus that caused the chestnut blight was discovered. At the time, one tree in four or five in our eastern forests was a chestnut, and the average size of a mature tree was about five feet in diameter, and up to one hundred feet tall. In places in the Appalachians, chestnuts were so abundant that the ridge tops in spring appeared to be snow covered by the blossoming trees. By 1950, the species had all but disappeared. In northeastern Ohio, where I grew up, great amounts of trees were harvested in the 1920s and 1930s in an attempt to save usable timber before the fungus destroyed the trees—the charm of "wormy" chestnut being a later invention. Much of this wood was used in WPA projects during the depression—there are still some buildings in the Cuyahoga Valley National Park made entirely of clear chestnut, including a dining hall at a Boy Scout camp considered to be the world's largest chestnut structure.

There are efforts being made to recover this species, crossbreeding with overseas varieties resistant to the blight, and from the few surviving trees that can be found occasionally. Ash, properly stained is likely the closest substitute for chestnut, and plain-sawn white or red oak will have a similar appearance. Chestnut can be found in existing structures and there are several companies throughout the country that specialize in recovering old woods. Many an old barn has a chestnut frame, and this timber can be recovered and milled into suitable lumber for restoring an older home. Wormy chestnut is from trees that have been infested with the fungus, and is often sold for quite high prices, even though it is punky and full of holes. This is not the same as the wood used in the period, which was clear and sound.

Plain-sawn white oak was also frequently mentioned as an interior wood in *The Craftsman*, and is probably the best choice for new work, although it is of a denser structure, and therefore a bit more difficult to work than chestnut. Width can be a problem, but generally, mills that specialize in white oak are willing to sort for size and width, at a premium price. Quartersawn white oak, the preferred wood for Stickley's furniture, is a bit too figured for trim and paneling, and is rarely available in suitable widths. Red oak could also be used, but because of its current popularity smaller trees are being cut, and the quality of available wood is not as good as white oak. Butternut is not commonly used today, but would also make a good choice. It is similar in appearance to walnut, but lighter in color, and softer. Unfortunately, the butternut population is beginning to suffer from a blight of its own, and its days as a commercially viable wood may be numbered. Walnut was occasionally used in the period, and even though it is not fashionable today, I think it would be a good choice if wide stock were available.

Mahogany was popular on the West Coast at the time, along with redwood. Mahogany is often available in good widths, but there is currently some controversy regarding its harvesting that can affect the international trade in it. There are also some environmental issues with redwood that may affect a decision to use it.

Red gum was used by Stickley in the second floor of the log house at Craftsman Farms, and it is quite attractive in that location. In *The Craftsman* article mentioned previously, Stickley described it: "It is a pity that this beautiful wood should have been so little used that most people are unfamiliar with it, because for woodwork where fine texture, smooth surface an delicate coloring are required, quarter-sawn gumwood stands unsurpassed among our native woods." His description fits pretty well today, as gum is not often used in interior work. It grows abundantly in the southeastern United States, usually sold as sweet gum when sorted for the darker heartwood, and sap gum for the lighter sapwood. Its interlocked grain makes it difficult to dry, and it has a reputation for shrinking and warping when plain-sawn. It is variously described as appearing similar to walnut or similar to cherry, and can be machined and stained easily.

Poplar is similar to red gum in that it is abundant, fast growing, inexpensive and relatively easy to machine and stain. Like gum, it also moves quite a bit in response to humidity changes. Its main use is as a secondary wood, and is often painted. It can be stained to look similar to just about anything, but like gum, it really doesn't have much character. Once in a great while an interesting piece will be found, but mostly it is rather bland and uninteresting. West of the Mississippi, alder is commonly used for the same purposes as poplar in the east. It shares many of the same characteristics and qualities as poplar and gum.

Eastern white pine and cypress are also possibilities, available in wide widths, not too expensive, and capable of good color and finish. These two species are quite soft, however, so be prepared for dents and dings from normal everyday use that would not appear if a harder wood were used.

Most of these woods are readily available, but you may need to do a little detective work to find a reliable, affordable source. If your local big box store or lumberyard has any, or can get any, the price will be ridiculously high compared to buying from a mill or distribution yard. If you can't find a source in the yellow pages under "Lumber," try looking under "Hardwoods." On the Internet, www.woodfinder.com lists sources for hardwoods around the country, and will enable you to search by species, quantity, or geographic area.

Hardwoods are usually sold in random widths and lengths, in the rough, and by the board foot, with the thickness designated by quarters of an inch, 4/4 being 1 inch thick, 8/4 being 2 inches. A board foot is a measure of volume, 1 foot wide, 1 foot long, and 1 inch thick, which is equal to 144 cubic inches. You can estimate the quantity you need in board feet by multiplying the thickness by the width by the length (all in inches) and dividing by 144. Add at least 15% for waste, and bear in mind that random widths may not provide the widths you will need. Ideally, you will be needing wood for both trim and cabinets, and can use the narrower stock and off-cuts from the trim for cabinet parts.

There are also different grades of hardwoods, FAS being the highest, although at many places Select and Better is the highest grade available. If you are looking for material for trim work, you will be looking for the highest-grade material available. If you are building furniture, or a cabinet project with small parts, you probably can use #1 common, which should yield approximately two-thirds of the clear material of FAS. If the price is less than two-thirds of the FAS price, you will save some money, but you will have more waste, and will spend some time cutting around defects.

A lot of people can be intimidated when buying hardwood, but you really need to ask a lot of questions before you purchase. If the person on the other end of the phone doesn't have time to answer your questions, look for another source. I've been dealing with lumber dealers for many years, and I always explain what I need the material for, any special size requirements I may have, and ask for their recommendations, and their interpretations of grading rules. Most places will surface the two sides of the lumber, and straight-line rip one edge, for an additional fee. This rarely will be the quality of surfacing needed for finished work, especially as the faces are usually just run through a planer without being flattened first on a jointer, but it will save some time in processing.

Most of these species are also available as sheet goods or plywood. I use the AWI definition for plywood, which is simply sheet material of three or more plys, the outer plys being veneer. This definition includes veneered sheets of particleboard or MDF (medium density fiberboard) under the broad term plywood. Materials are specified by the face veneer—species and grade—and by the core material. The term veneer-core refers to what is essentially a plywood core. This is admittedly confusing, but it makes sense to professional dealers and specifiers, as the different cores have different properties for various applications.

For paneling, the sheets should be at least $1/2$ inch thick for quality work. Material that is $1/4$ inch thick can be used for cabinet door panels and backs, but the quality of this thickness is generally quite poor, and it is usually somewhat thinner than its nominal size. For a nice cabinet door, I would use $1/2$-inch thick material, and mill a $1/4$-inch tongue on the edge.

Veneers can also be obtained in sheets, held together by a paper, veneer, or phenolic backing, ranging in size from two feet by eight feet up to five feet by ten feet in some species. These sheets can be laminated to your own core material, but there are some relatively common problems with using this material. Most users approach their first veneer project as if they were using plastic laminate, and use a minimal amount of contact cement to adhere the veneer to the core. If contact cement is used, it is better to use a water-based rather than solvent based contact cement, and to press the veneer in place, working from the center out to the edge, using the edge of a block of hardwood, rather than rolling it with a laminate roller. Better results will be obtained using wood glue instead of contact cement, and pressing the veneer with weight, clamps and cauls, or a vacuum bag. Caution must also be exercised when finishing these veneers—they are so thin that they can easily become saturated with finish, causing delamination or bubbling. It is best to finish with very light coats to build up the finish over time.

One of the big advantages of veneer is that the panels for an entire room or interior can be obtained from a single flitch, and will therefore match in grain and color. A good supplier of veneer or veneered plywood should be able to obtain sequence-matched material. This means that the individual leaves of veneer are kept in the order they were cut from the log throughout the manufacturing process. This will greatly improve the appearance of finished panels or cabinets, and should ensure even coloring around the room.

Many people are adamantly opposed to particleboard or MDF cores, but for most casework and for paneling I think it is a better choice than veneer-core material. Veneer-core is a bit stronger, but in most applications, this won't make an appreciable difference. My main objection to veneer-core material is the poor quality of the core, especially regarding flatness. Poplar or lauan are generally used for cores and any defects or movement of the core telegraphs through to the veneer, making a good finish nearly impossible.

For kitchen and bathroom cabinets, where the interior of the cabinet is not seen when the door is closed, there are some modern materials that are worth considering; the first being pre-finished maple-veneer plywood, and the second being melamine-covered particleboard. Both of these materials will save a great deal of time in finishing, as they will eliminate the need to finish the inside of the cabinets. In everyday use, I find it preferable to have the insides of the cabinets as light as possible in order to better see the contents. Both of these materials are also quite durable and easy to clean. The one disadvantage is that wood glue won't stick to the finished faces, so that joints must be made in order to glue to the core material.

Finishes for exposed woodwork should be chosen to maximize the appearance of the grain and character of the wood. Gustav Stickley preferred fuming—exposing the wood to the fumes of 26% ammonia to obtain a darkening of color through the chemical reaction with the tannic acid that naturally occurs in the wood. This is an effective technique, but may not give as good results with today's materials. Since this method is based on a chemical reaction, the tannic acid content of the wood will give different effects to boards from different trees, so it is likely that uneven results will occur, especially if solid woods and veneers are mixed. In the early 1900s, especially when working with chestnut, it would have been likely that all the material for one room or area came from a single tree.

It should also be remembered that 26% ammonia is a powerful chemical capable of causing permanent damage to eyes and lungs. A proper respirator and chemical goggles must be worn when working with it.

One of the reasons that chemical treatments were popular at the time is that available stains were nowhere near as predictable, reliable, or durable as their modern counterparts. Staining the woodwork is probably the best choice, both in terms of the results obtained and the ease of application. The appropriate colors are warm shades of brown, and it should be remembered that most hardwoods will naturally darken over time, and this natural coloring of aged wood was the look that was desired. I would apply any stain lightly, and wait for nature to take its course.

While old ways of coloring wood may not be the best choice, I think an old surface finish—shellac—makes more sense than modern acrylics, polyurethanes, or lacquers. It is easy to apply and repair, and protected with a final coat of wax, is quite durable in most interior applications. Orange or amber shellac will impart a bit of color over the stain, making the finished work look more like the old.

Any finish treatment should be tested on scrap, and viewed in the room itself before committing to any particular color on an entire project. Built-in woodwork can be pre-finished before being installed, but I prefer to install everything unfinished, and then stain and finish the entire room afterwards.

HARDWARE

There was a distinct difference in the type of hardware used in cabinets in kitchens and bathrooms—considered at the time to be "utility" rooms— and built-ins in more public areas. In living rooms, dining rooms, and studies, the hand-hammered copper or iron hardware seen on Stickley's furniture would be appropriate, as would the less expensive alternative—a round or pyramid-shaped wooden knob. In kitchens, the predominant pull of the period was the bin pull, which is still readily available. Upper cabinets often used a casement latch to hold the doors closed, and to serve as a pull. There is a trend today to treat kitchens and baths as more public rooms, and to dress up the cabinets with furniture style hardware. There really isn't anything wrong with this, and if the kitchen is actually part of a great room or family room area, this approach might look better than the historically accurate approach. Bathrooms and bedrooms were generally painted, and round wooden knobs were quite common.

Locksets for passage and entry doors could also be hammered copper. Reproduction hardware is available, but sit down before you ask the price. It is quite expensive, and being hand-made in small quantities, the price is justified. Many homes at the time used simple knobs and back plates in dull brass, which is the less expensive alternative.

MOLDINGS & TRIM

Most of the trim shown in these drawings is square, without the molded edges that we are accustomed to seeing. While it is plain, all of the interest in the finished work will come from careful preparation of the surfaces, allowing the figure and color of the wood to provide the desired effect. All trim should be sanded so there are no knife or machine marks visible in the finished work. Small, portable planers do an excellent job of surfacing, although they do tend to snipe at the ends of long stock. Small thicknessing sanders are now available for under $1,000, and the trimming of an entire house in the Craftsman style would justify the purchase of one.

Trim is usually relieved on the backside, that is, hollowed out $1/8$ inch or so, leaving edges $1/2$ inch to $3/4$ inch wide. The reasons given for this usually include making installation easier, and preventing warping or cupping of the finished stock. The first argument has a bit of merit, if there is a hump in the wall that requires planing off some material from the back, it is easier to plane just the narrow edges. However, if the walls and jambs are not in the same plane, or if the plaster is not flat and even, relieving the back of the trim won't help matters—the joints won't look right if the trim is not placed flat. The second argument, to prevent warping, only applies if a good deal of material is removed from the finished face, and the material is casehardened or otherwise improperly dried. For best results, do take the time before and during installation to seal the back and edges of every trim piece, then to make sure every piece seats flat and tight.

In recent years the trend in building has been to let the quality of all the work suffer in the name of speed, and to expect the last work to be performed—the trim—to cover up and magically fix all of the shortcuts and mistakes made in previous work. For true quality, all of the work, from the laying of the foundation to the finishing of drywall or plaster, needs to be held to the same high standard.

The overall quality of the job will benefit from pre-assembly, particularly of door and window casings. An assembled door casing is simply three pieces of wood, each of the correct size, neatly fastened together and attached to the jamb. I don't see the point of doing this in place, standing on a bucket or ladder, if it can be done faster and with better results on the bench. The size of the pieces won't be different, and neither will their relationship to each other. What will be different will be the methods of joining them, and the ease of doing that task.

Visible fasteners should be kept to an absolute minimum, and the detail drawings of jambs and trim show some examples. If trim is pre-assembled, joints may be reinforced with biscuits or splines, and either glued and clamped without nailing, or fastened from behind with screws in pocket-holes. Where nails must be used, pneumatic nail guns will give better results than hammering by hand, and will speed the work considerably. Pneumatic nails usually have a tee-shaped head, and the gun should be held so that the heads of the nails go with the grain, rather than across it, making the holes much less visible after filling.

SMALL CROWNS

Where the wall meets the ceiling is where the Craftsman style sharply departs from Victorian style, as well as from a lot of what is popular today. These profiles are all very small compared to the crown moldings we usually see, and most of the illustrations in *The Craftsman* and nearly all of Stickley's architectural drawings show no crown molding at all. Most of the photographs in *The Craftsman* of projects constructed by readers and other builders do show a small molding such as these. Where Stickley did show trim at the wall-ceiling line it was generally a flat board, or half of a beam. Stickley's scheme is visually striking, but framing and plastering need to be carefully done for this effect to succeed. Traditional crown moldings pull the transition away from the corner, where less than straight lines are less noticeable. Flat planks can be scribed to the ceiling, but one expects to see the top and bottom of these pieces parallel and straight. These little moldings can be used in conjunction with a flat molding, or just to please our modern tastes.

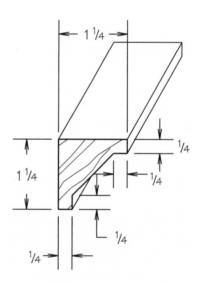

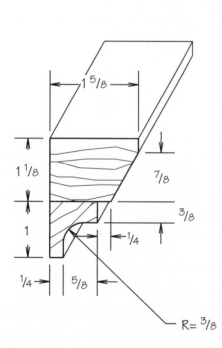

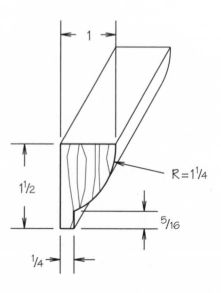

Small Crowns (*continued*)

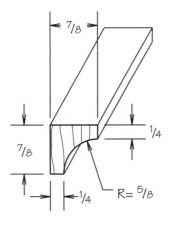

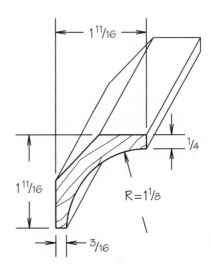

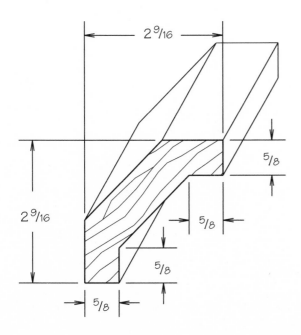

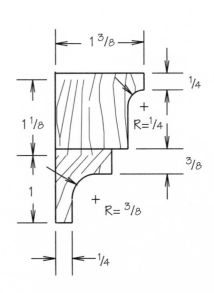

LARGE CROWNS

If you simply must have a crown molding, this example is typical of the period, and although not strictly Craftsman would be entirely in keeping with a home of the period. The drawing below suggests a treatment for ceiling beams from *Old House Measured and Scaled Drawings for Builders and Carpenters,* by William Radford, which was originally published in 1911. The matching crown at right can be used either with the ceiling beam detail, or by itself. While this is more in keeping with what we expect to see today, the frankness and bold structural statement of plainer designs are lost. As the Craftsman era moved in to the 1920s, the concurrent Colonial Revival favored moldings fancier and more decorative, even in Craftsman-style homes. Many of these profiles are still available, and still in use. The bibliography lists some resources for profiles of the period. Simplicity should be a key element in choosing any of these profiles, and a decision on whether or not to use crown molding can be put off until later if it turns out that the plain designs are just too plain.

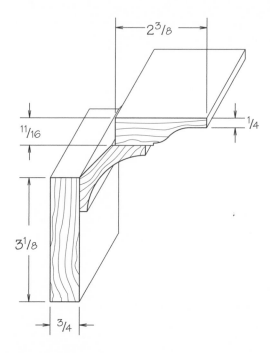

3-piece crown

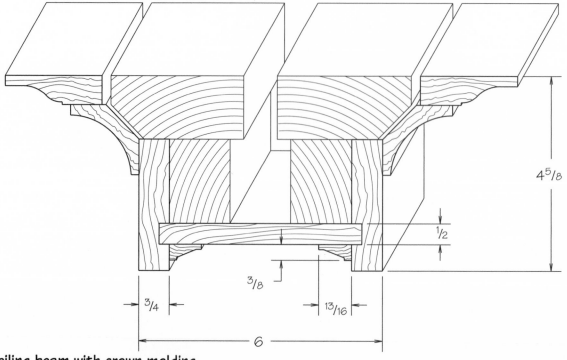

Ceiling beam with crown molding

BASEBOARD

These baseboard profiles, from Radford's *Old House Measured and Scaled Detail Drawings* book, are representative both of the period and of the Craftsman style. Most can be milled with standard router bits, and the smaller examples can be used either alone at the base of cabinets, or in combination with a larger, flat molding.

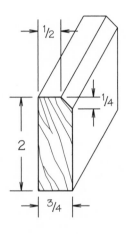

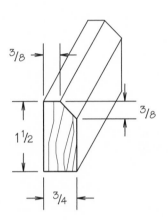

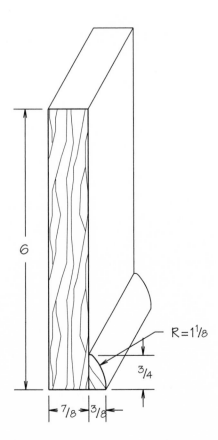

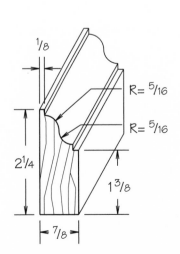

BASEBOARD (*continued*)

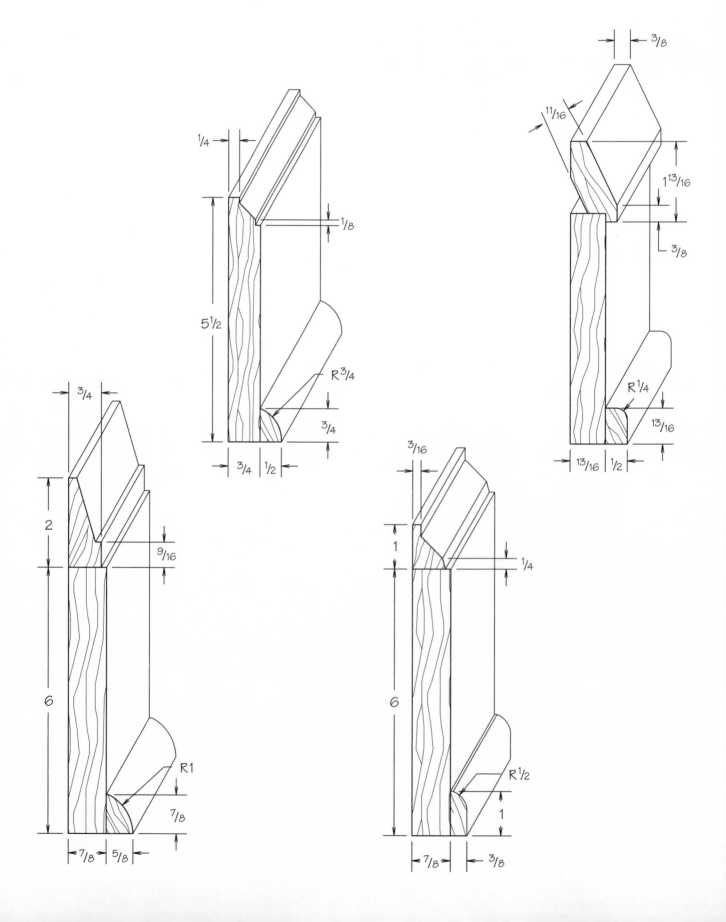

TALL BASEBOARD

This group of baseboard profiles comes from Stickley's architectural drawings, and his articles in *The Craftsman*. These wide, plain moldings appeared in nearly every house design presented by Stickley. Generally, the height of the baseboard matched the height of the lower rail on the doors, providing visual continuity through a continuous horizontal line. Today it can be difficult to obtain stock this wide, and there are not many alternatives to paying a premium for having baseboard this tall. It is possible to glue narrower boards together, but the grain must be carefully matched to preserve the appearance of a single, wide board.

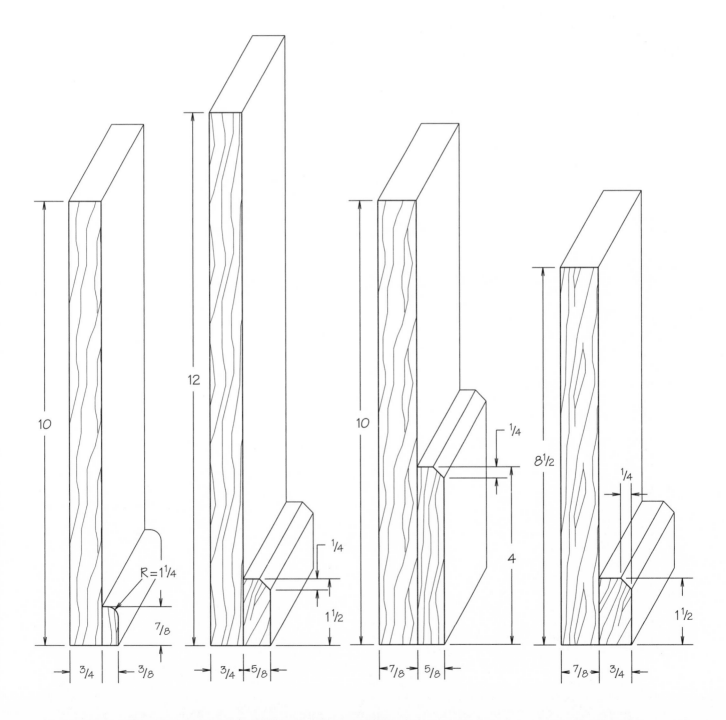

CHAIR RAIL

These chair rails, or perhaps more properly wainscot caps, were a common feature in Craftsman homes, either at the top of paneling, 4 feet or 5 feet above the floor, or by themselves as a horizontal design motif. Chair rails often were made wide enough for a groove to retain display plates or decorative platters, with the widest ones benefiting from the addition of corbels at regular intervals to help support the rail.

These same profiles were often also used as

moldings below windows, and in many cases the top of the wainscot would be aligned with the bottom of the window so that the molding would be continuous.

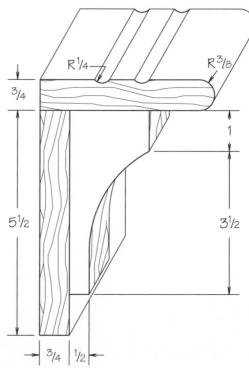

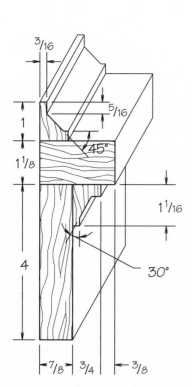

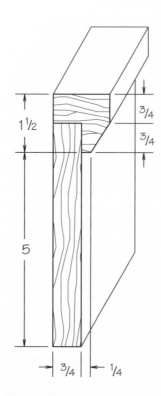

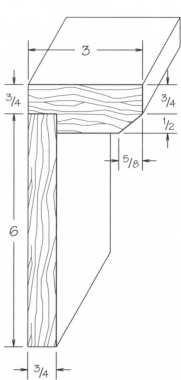

CHAIR RAIL (*continued*)

Depending on how the paneling is mounted to the wall, the rail may need to be made wider in order to provide the desired overhang, as seen in the example on the left. Any of the examples shown may be used with or without panels below.

The plate-groove example is a little busy, but the molding at the top of the rail does provide the advantage of hiding fasteners used to attach the rail to the wall studs. The molding below the rail is interrupted periodically by corbels, which reflect the molding profile at a larger scale.

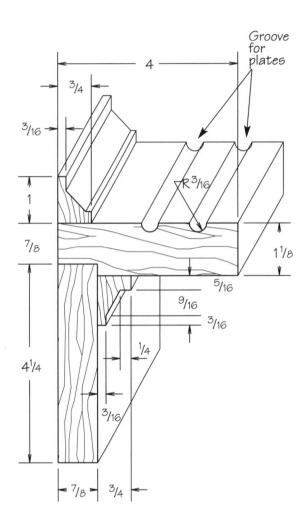

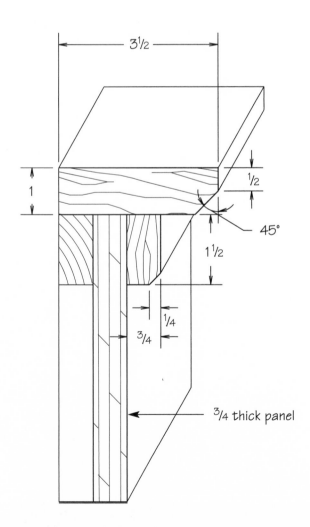

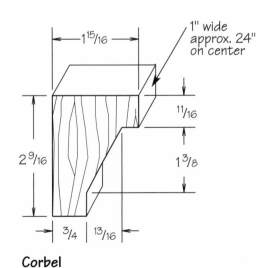

Corbel

HEAD CASING

The profiles shown here were common in the period for door and window head casings, usually combined with straight side casings. They are a bit fancier than pure Craftsman details, but are in keeping with the period and the style, particularly in bathrooms and bedrooms. The end should run past the vertical casing 1/4 inch or so, and be mitered on itself to return to the wall.

The smaller profiles can be used as crown or cornice moldings, or can be combined with flat stock for use as head trims. If used as crown, the corner that fits into the intersection of wall and ceiling should be trimmed off to make installation easier.

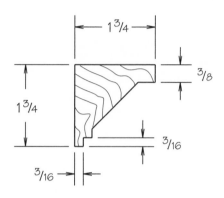

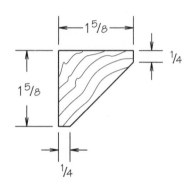

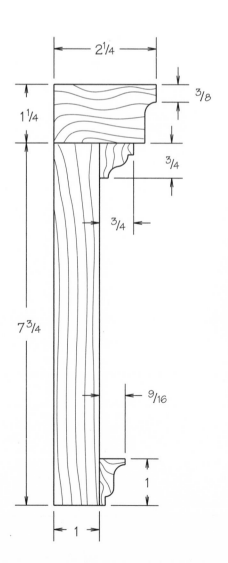

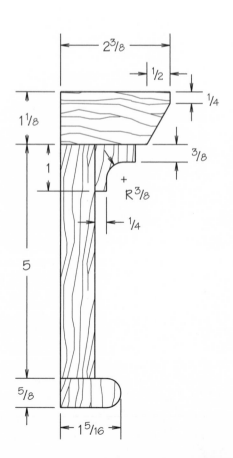

PICTURE RAIL

Picture rails dropped out of fashion as we stopped using plaster-and-lath for walls, and began to use drywall instead. If you have ever tried to drive a nail in a genuine plaster wall to hang a picture, or repaired a plaster wall after attempting to do so, you will appreciate the picture rail. In Craftsman homes they ran either at the same height as the door head casing, or 10 inches to 12 inches below the ceiling. Often the picture rail was incorporated into the door head casing, which commonly extended around the perimeter of the room. An example of this is the largest drawing at right. A double-ended metal hook fits over the top of the rail, with the lower part of the hook holding the wire that supports the picture frame. These hooks are still available from period hardware suppliers.

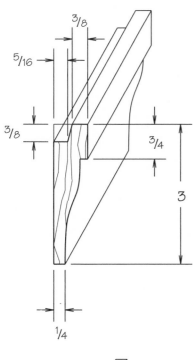

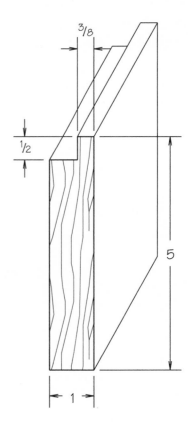

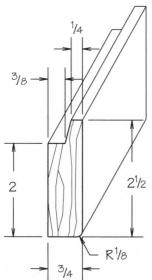

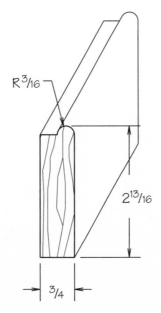

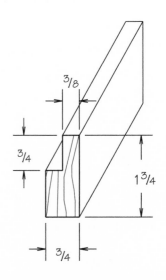

PANELING

For large vee-groove panels, Stickley preferred grooves milled in both edges of the board with loose splines. The example at the top is similar, but instead of the loose spline, the tongue is cut on one edge of the board. Both styles are easily milled, and readily available, however in the early 1900s it was much easier to find wide boards than it is today. Depending on the species used, it may take a great deal of hunting to find 10-inch or 12-inch wide stock. Narrower widths can be substituted, but it will change the look by adding more vertical lines.

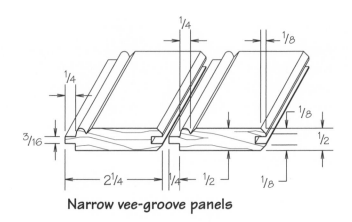

Narrow vee-groove panels

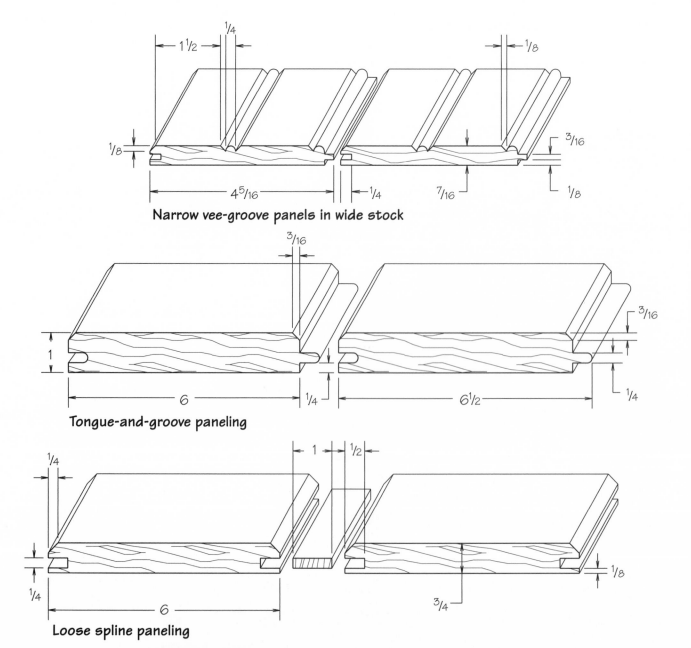

Narrow vee-groove panels in wide stock

Tongue-and-groove paneling

Loose spline paneling

BEAMS

Beams were made in various heights and widths, often within the same room, with a half-beam commonly used at the outer perimeter. Usually beams were aligned with some other element, such as door or window openings. For this to work out, the location of these other elements, and their relationship with the beams, must be considered early in the construction process, so that they really do line up at the end.

Sometimes these beams were structural, but more often than not they were decorative. In any case, they need to be well made, and securely fastened to the structure of the building. They look structural, so the builder must consider that some day in the future someone will attach something heavy to the beam. While making a box out of 2x material and covering it with finished wood may seem to be overkill, it is good practice. The blocking should be attached to the joists overhead if they cross the beam or to blocking between the joists if the beam is parallel.

The detail drawings show three methods of constructing the finished beams, with the rabbeted miters having the neatest appearance. This construction will appear more like a solid piece of timber than the other two examples. The method at center is likely to show the joint from below, if the wood shrinks after installation. The bottom example lets the joint show by introducing a reveal, that is, moving the bottom piece up a little from the sides. In some cases the reveal was deep enough for a small molding.

Molding where the beam meets the ceiling was rarely shown in architectural drawings, but was usually included in actual construction. If the ceiling is less than perfect, it is difficult to scribe the beams. A small molding not only covers gaps, but also hides screws.

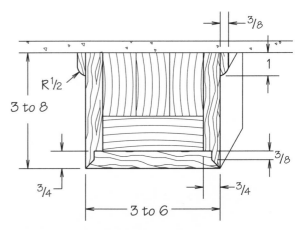

Beam with rabbeted miter

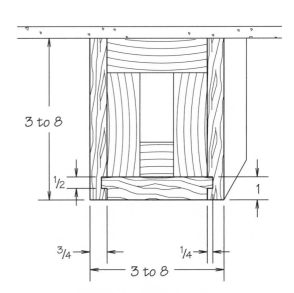

Beam with tongue-and-groove

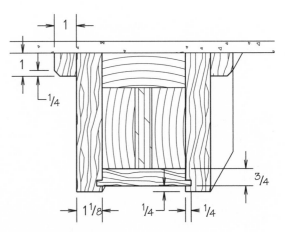

Beam with reveal

PANELED WAINSCOT WITH CHAIR RAIL

The rail and stile wainscot can be assembled in sections, and either attached directly to the walls, or hung with french cleats, as shown in the detail drawings on the next page. The panel sections should be sealed on the back and bottom sides before installation. Panels that are ¼ inch thick could be used, but ½ inch thick is not much more expensive and will yield a stronger, more stable panel. The baseboard should be installed first taking care to keep its top edge level. If there is much variation in the floor, the baseboard will

either need to be scribed to fit, or a shoe molding added to cover the gaps.

The french cleats can be ripped from an inexpensive grade of plywood, and if need be they can be shimmed to create a flat surface for the paneling. The chair rail should be made about ¼ inch wider than the finished dimensions shown in the sections, so that its back edge may be scribed to the wall.

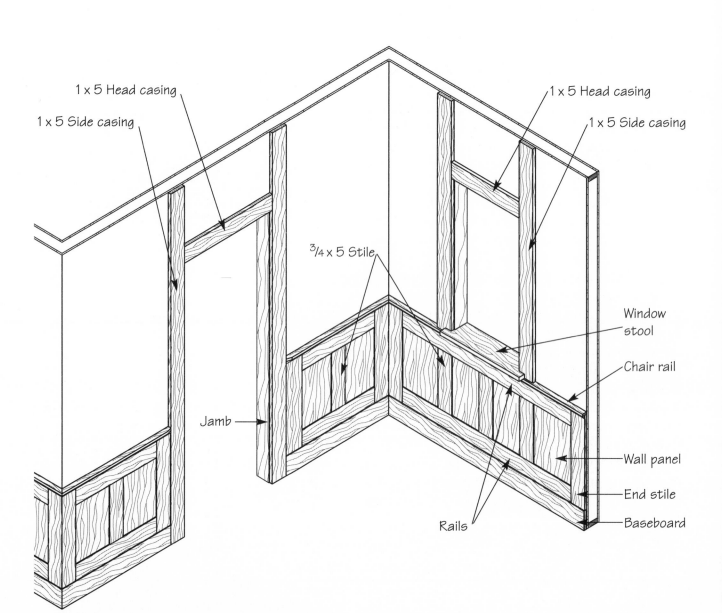

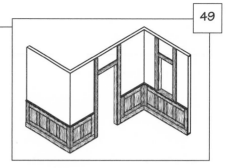

PANELED WAINSCOT
WITH CHAIR RAIL (*continued*)

Panel directly attached to wall

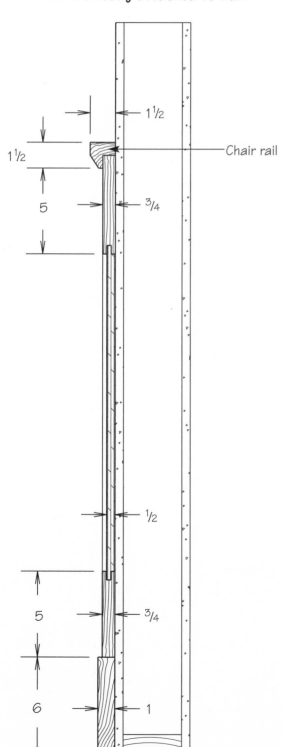

$1\frac{1}{2}$

$1\frac{1}{2}$ — Chair rail

5

$\frac{3}{4}$

$\frac{1}{2}$

5

$\frac{3}{4}$

6 — 1

Panel attached with french cleat

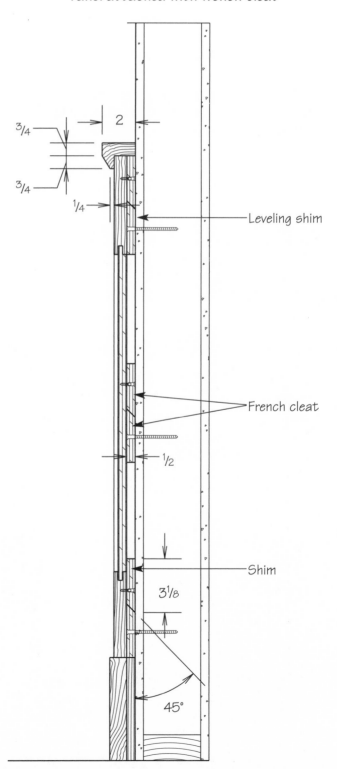

$\frac{3}{4}$ — 2

$\frac{3}{4}$

$\frac{1}{4}$ — Leveling shim

— French cleat

$\frac{1}{2}$

— Shim

$3\frac{1}{8}$

45°

TALL WAINSCOT WITH NARROW PANELS

A favorite Stickley device was panels much narrower than usually seen, occasionally smaller in width than the adjacent stiles. Construction and installation is practically the same as with the shorter wainscot shown on the preceding pages. Chair rails were often made wide enough to serve as a display shelf, sometimes with a shallow groove routed near the front edge to retain displays of plates. If the width of the chair rail becomes visually too deep, triangular or curved corbels can be added on centers of 16 inches to 24 inches between the top rail panel and the chair rail.

Note that the $1\frac{1}{8}$-inch thick door and window casing extends to the floor, with the 1-inch thick baseboard placed in between the casings. Trim pieces of different thickness is a hallmark of the period, providing visual interest in the form of small steps or reveals between the various trim elements, and shadow lines that help conceal the joints.

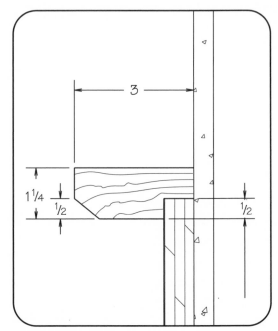

Chair rail: section

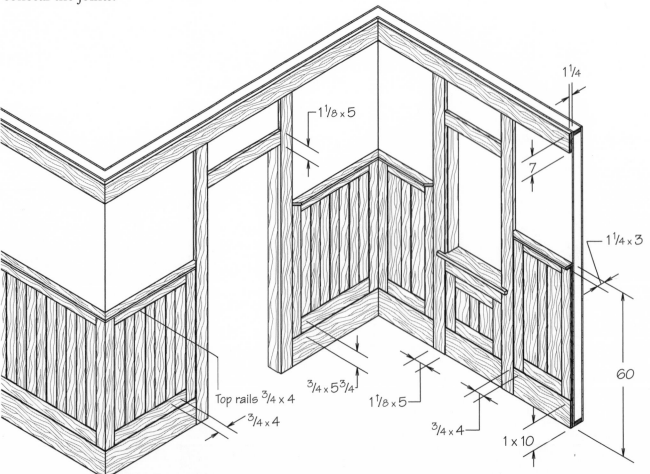

PICTURE RAILS

Here the space is defined by the vertical door casings and trim at the corners, and unified by the extension of the door head-trim around the perimeter of the room. This horizontal element is actually a picture rail, as detailed in the section at right. On true plaster walls it can be nearly impossible to drive a nail to hang a picture, so pictures were suspended by wires from special hooks that fit over the top of the rail.

The spaces in between the wood elements could be plain plaster, textured plaster, or covered with burlap or grasscloth. The narrow horizontal band above the picture rail was often decorated with stenciled or painted patterns similar to those used in Stickley's linen designs, or in the inlaid furniture of Harvey Ellis. Many of *The Craftsman* illustrations by Ellis show these decorative treatments at this location in the room.

The trim elements vary in thickness, creating shadow lines at their intersections. While *The Craftsman* illustrations and architectural drawings rarely showed a shoe molding at the base, or anything but a flat board at the ceiling, small moldings commonly were installed to cover gaps there.

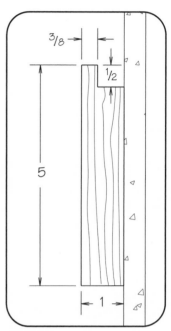

Section

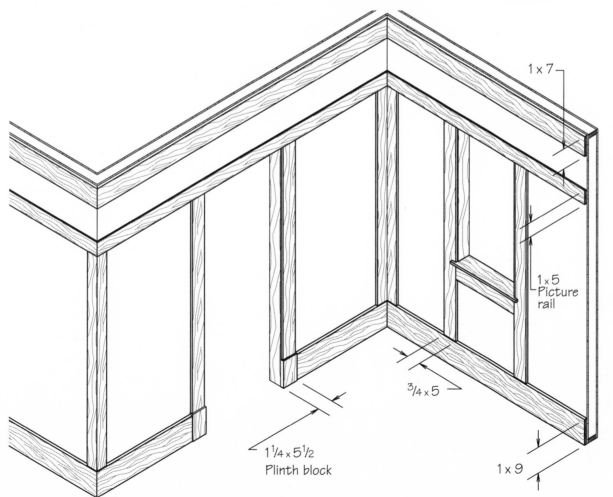

TRANSITIONS BETWEEN ROOMS

Transitions between rooms often were made not by traditional walls but by beams, columns, and panels as shown here. Occasionally the beams and columns concealed structural elements, but more often they served only as a decorative way to define a space without completely closing it off. Even without a structural function, these elements should be stoutly constructed. The blocking shown inside the beams and columns in the section views is 2x material, which should be selected for straightness, and given plenty of time to acclimate to the house. If need be, these pieces can be dressed with a jointer and planer to ensure that they are indeed straight and flat. It is essential that the column blocking be accurately located and installed plumb so that there is no visible gap where the intermediate panels join the columns.

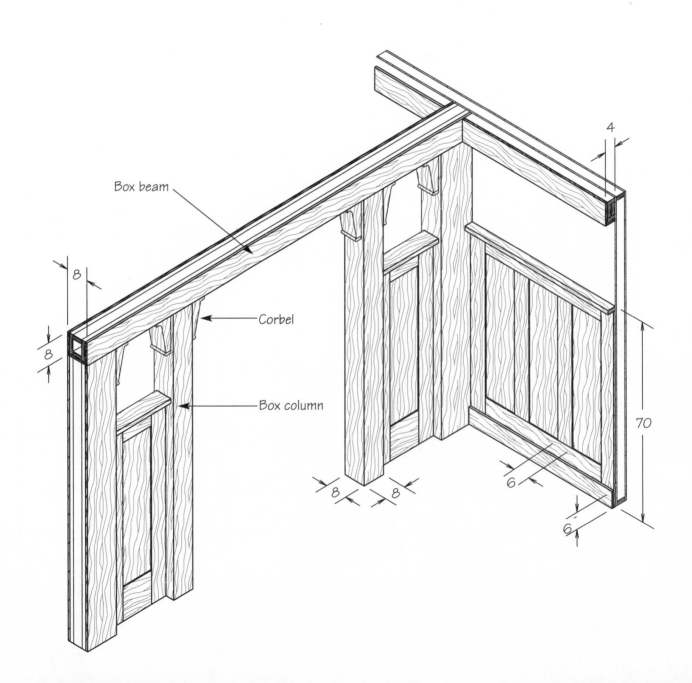

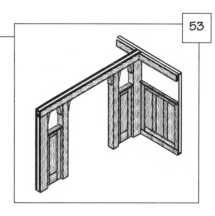

TRANSITIONS BETWEEN ROOMS (*continued*)

Columns can be pre assembled in two L-shaped halves, which minimizes fussy joints to be assembled in the field. The joint at the long corners is shown as a rabbeted miter. The rabbets could be eliminated, but these joints will be much easier to assemble if it is retained, or replaced with biscuits. A plain miter will tend to slide open, which the rabbet or biscuits will eliminate. Note that the columns and the panel extend all the way to the floor, with the baseboard terminating at the column that extends from the wall. The beam across the top and the floor at the bottom must be flat and level for this detail to work as shown. The alternative would be to run a small shoe molding around the bottom of these elements, and possibly a small scribe or cornice molding where the beam meets the ceiling. These small moldings should also be rectangular in section.

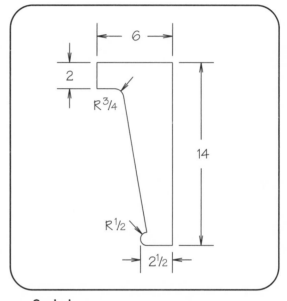

Corbel

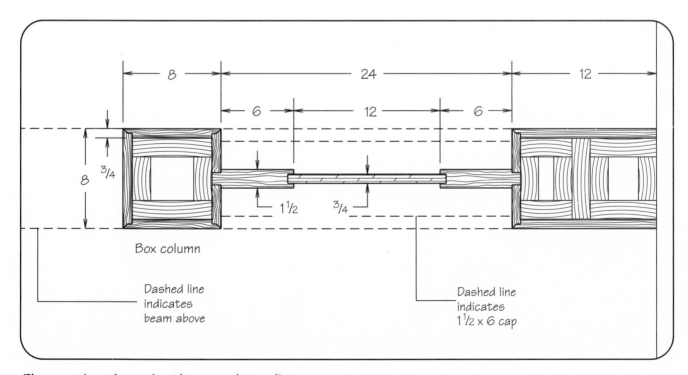

Plan section through column and paneling

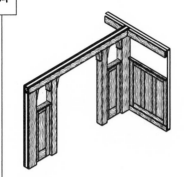

TRANSITIONS BETWEEN ROOMS (*continued*)

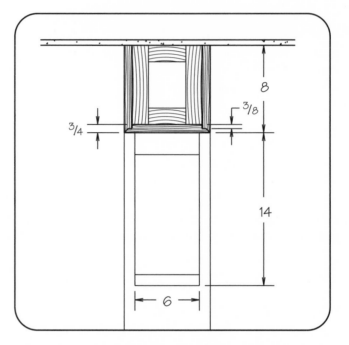

Section through beam

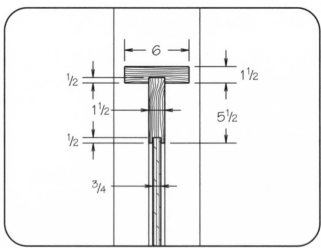

Section through panel

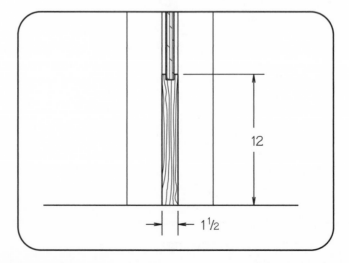

Section at base

VEE-GROOVE WALL PANELS

Vee-groove panels typically extend from floor to ceiling, set off by vertical casing at the doors and windows, and applied trim at the corners of the room. These vee-groove boards can either be held together by loose splines as shown on the following page, or may have the tongue milled in one edge, and the groove milled in the other. The planks shown in this drawing are 8 inches wide, which, depending on the species of wood used, might be a difficult width to obtain today. In the period, these were often specified to be 10 inches to 12 inches in width. The numerous vertical lines make the walls appear to be taller and narrower than walls with strong horizontal lines.

The trim at the top of the wall is shown as being half-beams. Full width beams would also cross the ceiling, aligned with the casing for the door and windows. If beams are not used across the ceiling, the trim at the top could be a single wide board, placed directly on the panels. The lower detail shows the condition at the floor, where the casing, base, and shoe molding, all of different thicknesses, come together.

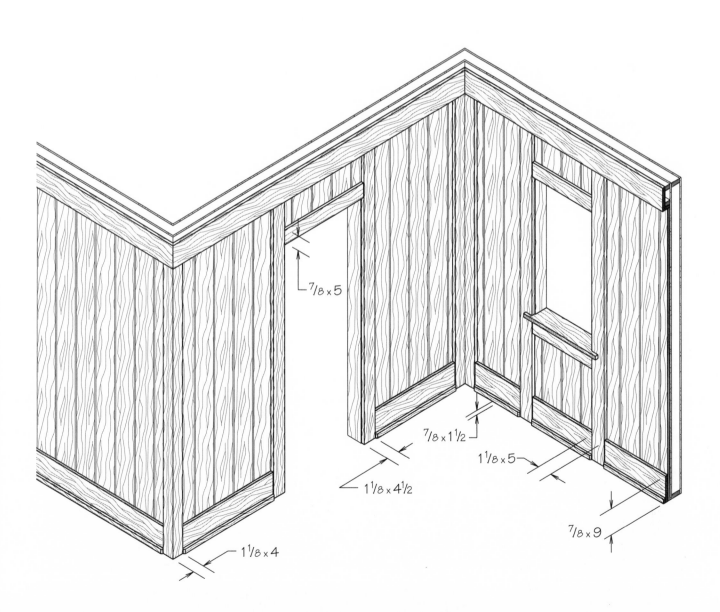

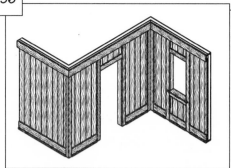

VEE-GROOVE WALL PANELS

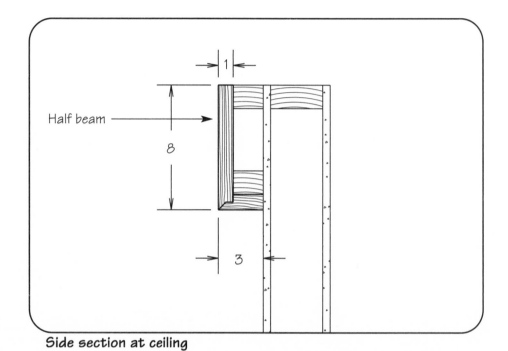

Half beam →

1

8

3

Side section at ceiling

Vee-groove panel   Loose spline

3/4

1¹/8

5

7/8   7/8

Base   Shoe

Window casing

Plan section

DECORATIVE CEILING BEAMS, BUILT-IN SEAT

The detail shows typical construction of ceiling beams, for decorative effect. The 2x material is for attaching the finished trim pieces to the ceiling above, and should be solidly secured to a structural element. Structural steel beams or wood beams may also be wrapped by finished material in the manner shown. More details on constructing beams is given on page 47. In this example, the beams are supported by columns at the corners, and by intermediate columns. The short dividing wall between the two columns is of standard 2 x 4 stud construction, covered with wide vee-groove planks. The vertical studs are shown placed directly behind the joints of the planks. Details are given on the next two pages.

The built-in seat could be made in nearly any

width, and is shown here constructed of the same vee-grooved boards used in the dividing panel. Such seats often appeared in the Craftsman home adjacent to stairs or near an entry. Without the back, these seats could be installed below windows.

The method of construction shown (next page), using framing material to support the front panels and seat, is likely more than necessary, seats were often detailed with a 2 x 4 cleat supporting the back, and 2 x 2s reinforcing the joint where the panels meet the seat and floor. I would build this detail as shown, however, in the belief that someday someone will see the solid look of the seat, and push its structural limits.

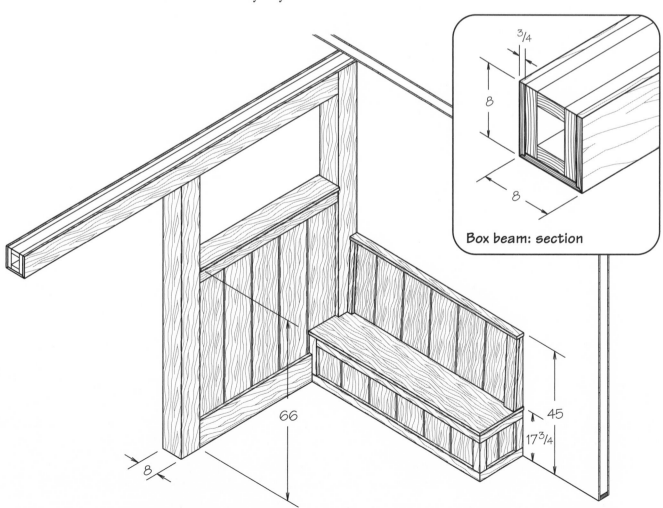

Box beam: section

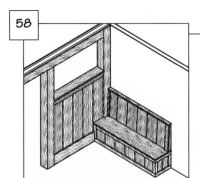

DECORATIVE CEILING BEAMS, BUILT-IN SEAT

The Craftsman seat can easily be made without the back, and placed below a window. The panels on the front of the seat often contained a grill for a heating and cooling register, or to conceal a low radiator. All or part of the seat may be hinged, to allow the space below the seat to be used for storage. Another option, if storage space is desired, is to build drawers below the seat.

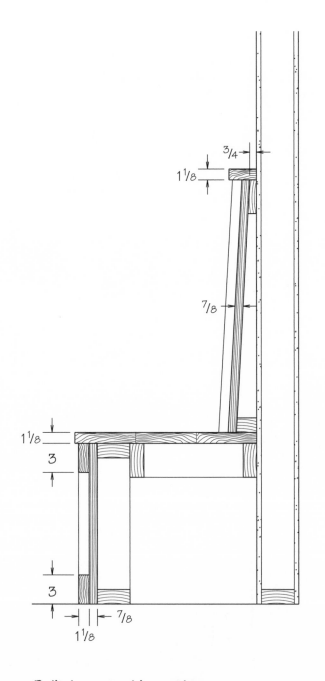

Built-in seat: side section

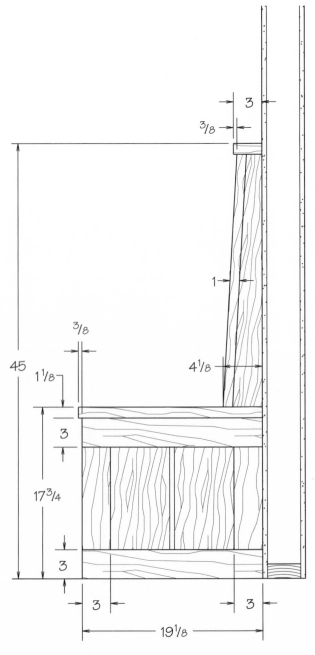

Built-in seat: end view

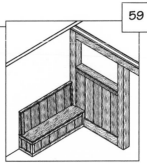

Dividing Panels for Built-in Seats and Half-Wall

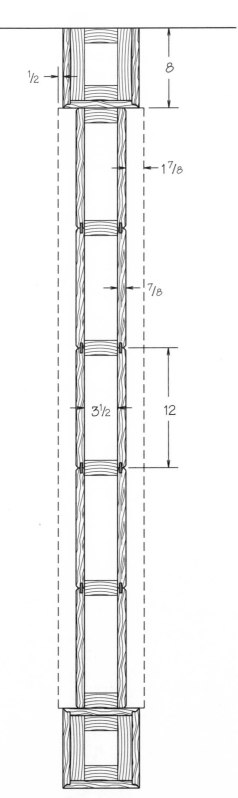

1/2

8

1⁷/₈

7/₈

3¹/₂

12

Columns and wall: plan section

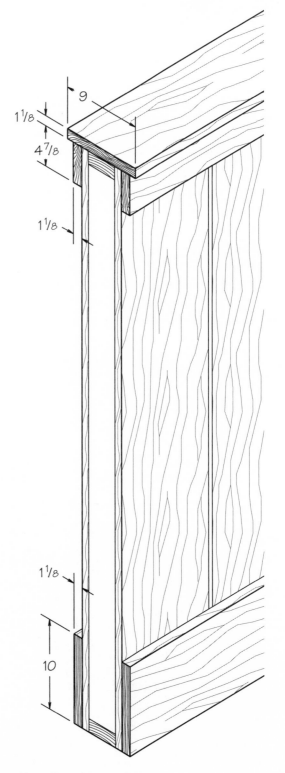

9

1¹/₈

4⁷/₈

1¹/₈

1¹/₈

10

Half-wall: side section

BEADED WAINSCOT

Kitchens and baths were often shown with a wainscot up to a height of 5 feet, and less often 4 feet, above the floor, capped with a simple molding. Many of the designs suggested ceramic tile both for the floor and the wainscot, but this represented the sanitary ideal, and most wainscot was actually wood beadboard. This material is currently available in the form of narrow boards; the profiles detailed on the next page give two typical examples. It can be applied directly to the wall, if the surface of the wall is flat. If the wall is not in good condition, then it would be better to run ledger strips horizontally, shimming as needed to make a flat plane for attaching the beadboard. One could purchase a pseudo-beadboard in the form of $1/4$ inch thick, 4-foot by 8-foot panels with the beaded design pressed in, but it just doesn't look right, and will never replace the real thing.

If the beadboard is applied directly to the wall, it can be attached with a bead of construction adhesive down the back of each piece, with small nails securing the boards while the glue dries. If ledger strips are used, they should be placed on 12-inch to 16-inch centers horizontally, and the beadboard secured by nailing, either through the face, in which case the nail holes will need to be filled, or by running the nails through the back portion of the groove. A pneumatic nail gun is highly recommended.

Generally, kitchens and baths had the woodwork painted white, but the wood could be given a clear finish instead. In either case, especially since kitchens and baths tend to be damp, the back side, and the top and bottom edges of the boards, should be finished before installation.

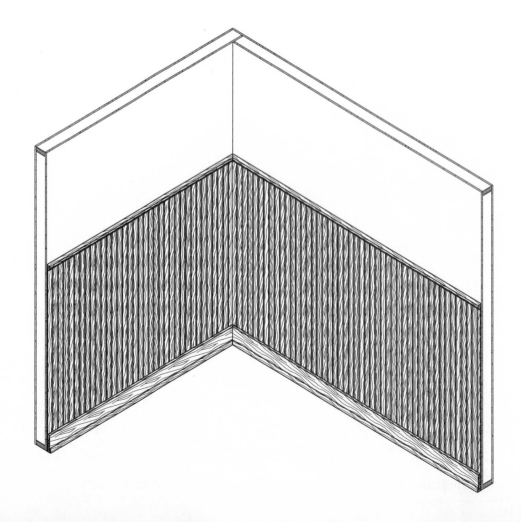

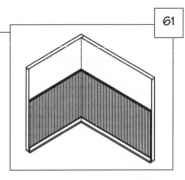

BEADED WAINSCOT INSTALLATION

Installing beadboard is more tedious than difficult, and care must be taken to keep the pieces plumb. Establish a vertical benchmark in the center of each wall, and a horizontal benchmark at the line of the top of the boards. Keep the level handy, and check each piece as you work. Plan the work from the corners, so that you don't end up with a bead or vee-groove hitting either an inside or outside corner joint. Ideally, you should have equal widths exposed at opposite corners of the room. This means either the center of a board or the center of a groove would be at the vertical centerline of the room.

Inside corners will likely need to be scribed, and the less common outside corners should be mitered. If needed, the vertical corners can be trimmed out with a thin flat molding, such as the shoe molding shown at the baseboard.

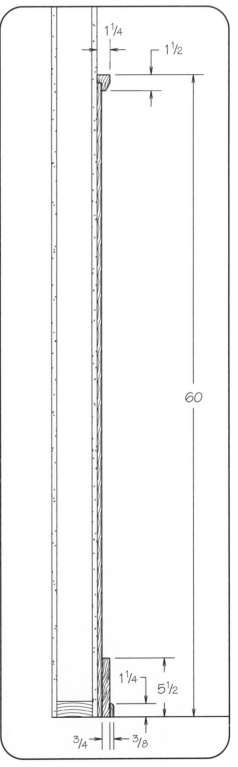

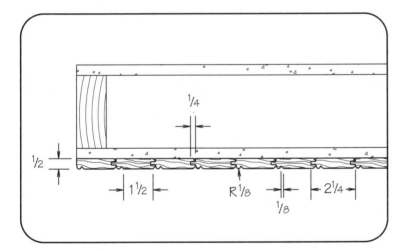

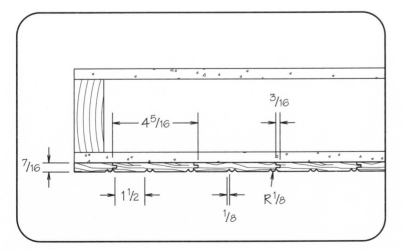

Sections at corner

Side section

DOORS & WINDOWS

Doors intimidate many woodworkers, and in the trades, doors are usually made by those who specialize, rather than by general cabinetmakers and mill workers. There really isn't anything special about door construction; except for scale, there isn't much difference between a cabinet door and a passage door. The text accompanying the drawings on the following pages gives most of the fine points, especially regarding specific designs.

Generally, the most important factor in making a good door is the ability to work accurately, and the wise selection and treatment of the material. A good door consists of good parts, for any twist, bow, or deviation from size will result in a door that doesn't function or look as it should. Today, many doors are built up from laminated stock, veneer over cheaper wood. This is usually sold as a better method than solid-wood construction, although the main advantage is lower material costs for the manufacturer. Well-seasoned, properly milled solid hardwood will be just as stable as laminated stock.

Wood to be used for doors should be carefully selected and properly dried. Thick stock takes longer to dry and to acclimate to new conditions, so it is wise to give the material plenty of time to adjust to the conditions of the shop, and to monitor its moisture content with a moisture meter. I usually mill door material oversize in width and thickness, and allow a week or two between rough and finish milling in case the material decides to move. A good jointer, of sufficient size, is essential for making straight, flat stock.

Joinery for doors is straightforward, as detailed in the drawings, and again the differences in door construction and cabinet construction are mainly of scale. Careful assembly is crucial, so that the flat, straight parts become a flat, straight door. Clamps

DOOR ANATOMY

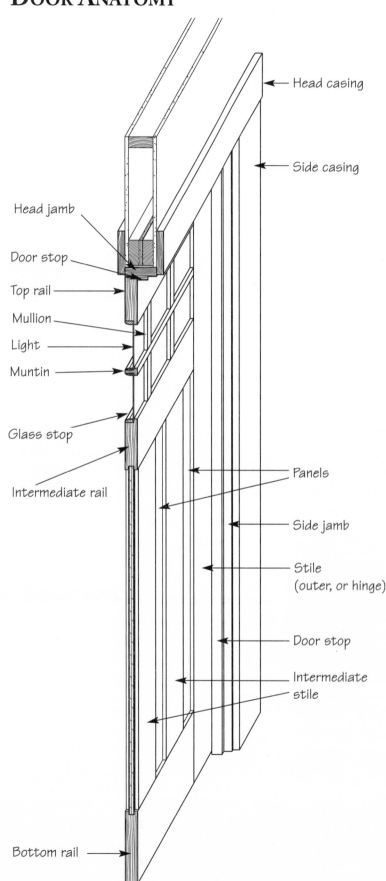

Head casing

Side casing

Head jamb

Door stop

Top rail

Mullion

Light

Muntin

Glass stop

Intermediate rail

Panels

Side jamb

Stile
(outer, or hinge)

Door stop

Intermediate
stile

Bottom rail

should be placed on both sides of the door during glue-up so that unbalanced clamps don't pull the joints to a slight angle. A good straightedge should be used to check that the joints are flat, and cauls are often clamped across the faces of the stiles and rails to be certain that the joints are in line. Doors and their jambs can be machined and fit for hardware when flat on the bench. As long as everything is accurately made, and the jambs installed plumb, they will fit and function better than if this work is done in the field, with the jambs in place.

Doors are sized in feet and inches, unlike cabinetwork, usually described in inches only. Dimensions given are to the finished opening between the jambs, with the actual size of the door being slightly smaller, with the gaps coming out of the door. This makes figuring and laying out the rough openings easier than if the door were made to the nominal dimension, and the jambs made slightly wider. Some old texts suggest leaving the stiles long, called ears, trimming to final length when hanging. While this will prevent damage to the corners during moving, it is better to trim the ends square and to length in the shop, when the doors are made.

Jambs also need to be carefully made, and the same cautions and techniques mentioned for the fabrication of doors apply. The side jambs are usually made long, allowing for trimming neatly to the floor at installation. The back sides of the jambs should be given at least a coat of sealer, to retard movement of the wood. Doors should be finished on all surfaces; all too often, the top and bottom edges are forgotten.

THE TYPICAL CRAFTSMAN DOOR

This configuration of an interior door occurs numerous times in the illustrations of *The Craftsman*. This particular example, a 2'-8" by 7'-0" interior door, is from House #13 of 1904, listed as "typical second story doors." Stickley's New Jersey home had doors similar to this on the second floor, leading from the hallway to the bedrooms. The lights at the top of the door were of amber-colored glass, translucent so that light could pass while maintaining privacy in the bedrooms. Although this is an unusual feature, it does allow someone outside the bedroom to know if the occupants are awake or sleeping. During the daytime, it also filters light into the hallway.

The original doors were specified to be 1½ inches thick with ½ inch panels. These have been drawn at 1¾ inches thick, with ¾ inch panels. 1½ inches is a little thin for a quality door (AWI standards call for 1¾ inches) and since either size would likely be made from 8/4 stock, this change makes better use of available material while providing a higher quality door. The other deviation from the original drawings is in the width of the outer stiles. In this example the original specifications called for 6 inches, but these have been reduced to 5½ inches so that a modern lockset with a 2¾ inch backset can be centered on the stile. Photographs of the originals often show the lockset to be off-center, but to our modern eye that doesn't look right.

Construction of these doors is straightforward, although the lights at the top complicate things a bit. A ¾ inch wide by ½ inch deep groove is machined on the inside of both outer stiles, and on one side of the top and bottom rails. The intermediate rail and two inner stiles are grooved on both sides to fit the panels. Since the panels are not very wide, making them out of solid wood shouldn't present problems with seasonal movement. The panels could be veneered, either cut from sheet goods with a veneer or MDF core, or veneered by the door maker. In any case, the

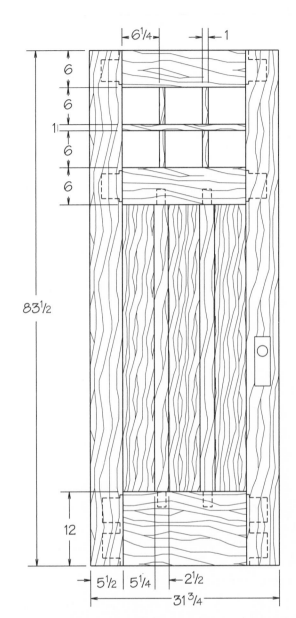

exact thickness of the panel stock should be used for the width of the grooves. Details of this are shown on the next page.

The dashed lines on the ends of the rails in the drawings indicate the tenons, which are haunched to fill the panel groove. This groove becomes a rabbet around the perimeter of the glass opening, and this can easily be done by routing off the inside cheek with a flush-trim bit. These cuts go the full length of the rails, but stop and start on the stiles. It would be prudent to pre-assemble the door, then run the router around the opening and clean up the corners with a chisel.

THE TYPICAL CRAFTSMAN DOOR (*continued*)

The section drawings show the details of the joints where the panels meet the stiles and rails, and details of the glass lights. If the panels are made of solid wood, they should be slightly smaller in width than the openings, to allow for expansion and contraction due to seasonal wood movement, and should not be glued in place. If the panels are veneered, they should be the same size as the openings, and may be glued.

The details on the next page show the mullions, muntins, and glass stop. The original drawings detailed the mullions and muntins, but did not show a detail at the perimeter of the opening for the glass. I have added the 1/4 inch thick spacer underneath the glass stop so that all of the stop material can be fabricated to the same dimensions. The muntins and mullions should be half-lapped where they cross, and joined to the rails and stiles with mortise and tenon joints, as shown in the exploded drawing on the next page. After the door is assembled, the spacers are butted to the muntins or mullions, and mitered where they meet at the corners of the glass opening. The beveled pieces of glass stop are then mitered at all four corners of the individual openings.

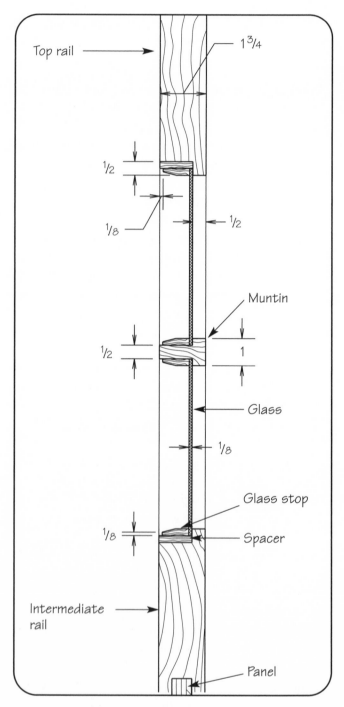
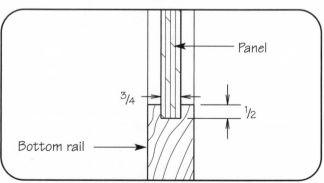

Typical Craftsman door: side sections

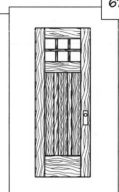

TYPICAL CRAFTSMAN DOOR (*continued*)

If there are several doors to be made in varying widths, the differences should occur in the width of the panels, and the width of the openings for the lights. The height and width of the intermediate stiles should be the same throughout the house. Not only will this facilitate a consistent appearance, it will also simplify construction of the various doors, since the intermediate stiles will be a common component. The light openings should be laid out so that they are square (or nearly so) in the most common size of door. All of the horizontal lines on the doors should be consistent, and the height of the bottom rail should be the same as the height of the baseboard.

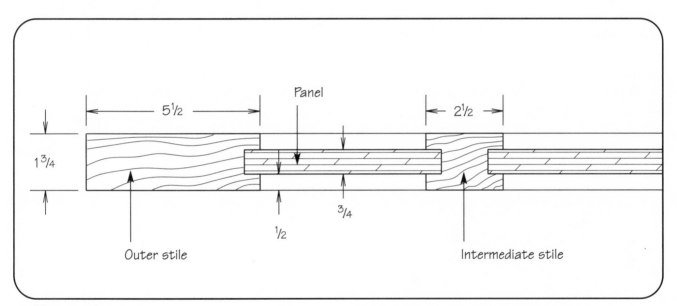

Plan section

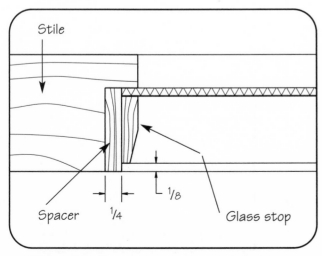

Glass detail

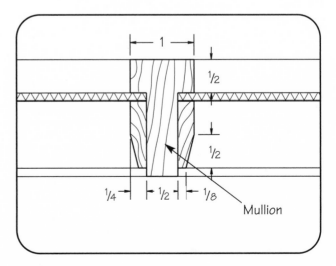

TYPICAL CRAFTSMAN DOOR (*continued*)

The exploded view shows the half-lap joints between the mullions and muntins, as well as the tenons for joining them to the rails and stiles of the door. This lattice of muntins and mullions should be assembled as a unit, and then joined to the top rail and intermediate rail. This drawing also shows the haunches on the rail tenons. The haunches on the top and bottom rail extend to the edge of the rail so that they are flush with the ends of the stiles after assembly is complete. Final assembly of the door should proceed from the inside out, the intermediate stiles and lower panels joined to the intermediate rail, and finally to the two outer stiles. It is best to do this in stages, to avoid trying to clamp too many pieces in different directions at one time.

The elevation shows the glass stops in place, from the loose-stop side of the door. Note that the flat pieces around the perimeter of the opening for the lights is butted when in between two mullions, and mitered at the outside corners. The loose glass stops are mitered and held with brads.

Stile detail

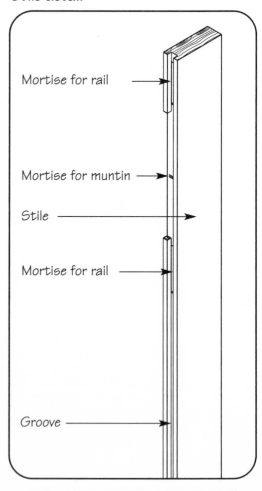

Rail and muntin joints

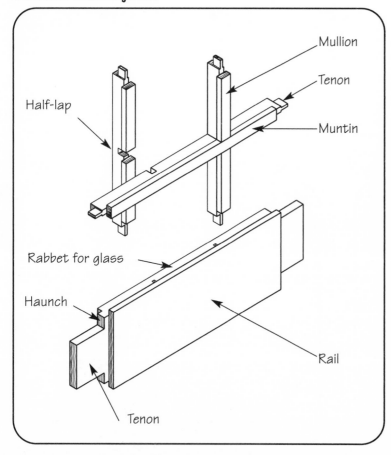

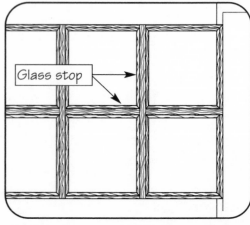

DOORS WITH WIDE RAILS AND STILES

These two doors were detailed in the drawings for house #13 of 1912 and are similar to the earlier door except for the width of the intermediate stiles, which are actually wider than the panels of the narrower door. Gustav Stickley liked this juxtaposition and used it not only in doors, but also in wall panels and built-in casework. The original drawings showed the two outer door stiles to be 5 inches wide, but these have been widened to 5½ inches to accommodate modern hardware with a 2¾ inch backset. The adjustment could just have easily been made in the opposite direction, reducing the stiles to 4¾ inches for 2⅜ inch backset hardware. At the original width, the lockset would be off-center.

The door on the left, at 2'-6" x 7'-0", is seen from the side with the loose glass stop. Note that the edges of the stop are aligned with the edges of the stiles and rails. The wider of the two doors, at 3'-0" x 7'-0", is seen from the opposite side. In this door, the intermediate stiles and panels are nearly equal in width.

Also notice that the tenons on the bottom rail are divided. This is good practice when the rail is this wide. A single, wide tenon would be more likely to become loose over time due to seasonal wood movement. With the divided tenons, the overall movement in width of the rail remains the same, but the risk of failure is much reduced.

2'-6" Door: side with loose glass stops

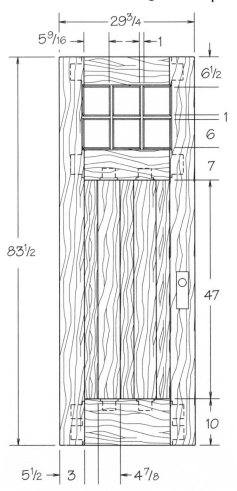

3'-0" Door: opposite side

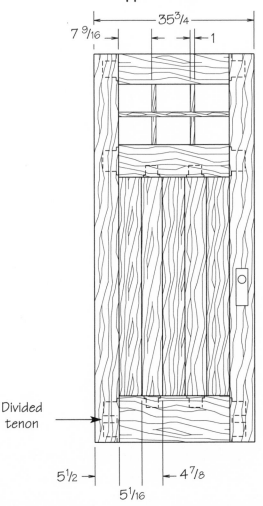

FRONT DOOR—1904 HOUSE

This front exterior door at 3'-6" x 8'-0" is larger than usually seen today. If the interior ceiling height allows for it, a front door of this size makes sense for both practical and aesthetic reasons. Visually, it makes quite an impression both from inside or outside, whether flanked by lights or panels, or by itself. Practically it is nice to have one entrance to a house big enough for moving large items. You may not be able to get the grand piano through any of the interior doors, but at least you will be able to get it off the front porch.

At this size, it might be prudent to construct this door at $2\frac{1}{4}$ inches thick rather than $1\frac{1}{2}$ inch or $1\frac{3}{4}$ inch. The extra thickness would make the door stiffer, and would allow sandwiching some insulating material between the wood panels. The bottom edge of the door should be carefully finished, and likewise the exterior side. While a varnish finish is generally frowned on in a Craftsman home, I would recommend a marine varnish if the door is exposed to the weather. If the door is exposed to direct sunlight, you can expect to refinish the outside every few years.

This door is also shown with the rail and tenons going completely through the stiles, and held in place with wedges. The previous doors have all been shown with stub tenons, about 3 inches in length. Both methods were used during the period, the through tenons being a bit more difficult to make, since the sloped top and bottom of the mortise must be chiseled by hand and the edges of the mortise will show on the finished door, where you can point them out to visitors. Although current Architectural Woodwork Institute quality standards allow dowel joints, I would not use them in an exterior door.

EXTERIOR GLASS DOOR

Exterior doors such as this were used between bedrooms and sleeping porches or balconies. The size of 2'-8" x 7'-0" could be widened to 3'-0", but the height of the intermediate rail and the panel below it would also need to change to keep the lights square. It would probably be best to eliminate one row of lights rather than to lower the rail and panel. This would also make a good kitchen exterior door, or even a front door. Doors like this sometimes were used as interior doors—as a study or library door, or as a pair of doors separating a dining room from a living room or hall.

One of the difficulties in making this door is that the stiles and rails at the panel have a square profile, but the perimeter around the lights has a beveled profile with a $1/8$ inch reveal. The section drawings on the following page show the details. This is not an insurmountable problem; there will be some handwork where the transition occurs.

The detail drawing below shows the wedged through tenons and mortises. The slope of the mortise starts at the midpoint of the stile, and it is $1/4$ inch wider than the tenon at each end.

Perhaps the biggest benefit of this joint is bragging rights. While it will hold the tenon in place, it really isn't any stronger than a non-wedged tenon, providing that both are well made. It doesn't add enough strength to compensate for a poorly made tenon.

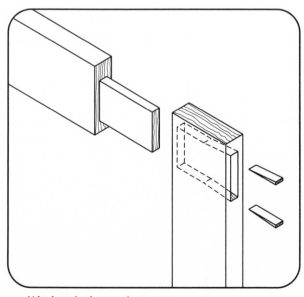

Wedged through tenon

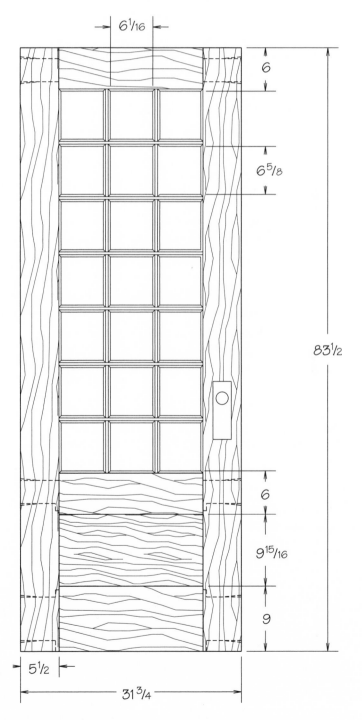

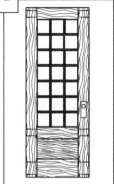

EXTERIOR GLASS DOOR *(continued)*

Mullion details are shown as glazed for exterior use. For interior use the profile of these pieces should be made with loose wood stops on one side, as shown on the detail drawings for the true French door on page 73. This detail differs slightly from the doors with small glass lights shown earlier, in that the profile is seen from both sides of the door. It also differs because the profile is added to the exposed width of the stiles. The dimension of 5 ½ inches refers to the flat portion of the door stile. The actual width of the stiles is $5^{13}/16$ inches before the profile is machined into the edge. The doors shown are square in section on the fixed side of the lights, and only show the beveled profile on the loose-stop side. Full-size details of each profile are shown with the French door details on page 74.

The glass may be clear, or amber, yellow, or cream colored, and is shown as $^{1}/8$ inch thick. Thicker glass may be used, either art glass, or double-layered insulating glass. In that case, take the adjustment out of the flat part of the mullion, rather than trying to adjust the beveled portion.

The transition between the lights and the panel presents a problem in machining, particularly for the exterior door. Normally the joints at the ends of the rails where they meet the stiles would be

coped in the reverse pattern of the profile. In this case, the pattern on the stiles should stop at the back edge of the profile of the intermediate stile. If working these joints on the shaper, stop an inch or so above the intermediate rail and complete the bevel by hand. Without a shaper, temporarily assemble the door to rout the bevel and quirk, leaving rounded corners to square up by hand.

Where the mullions and muntins cross, the joints should be half-lapped, as shown on page 68. This is simpler on the profile shown for interior use, as there aren't any bevels to be worked into the lapped joints. The loose stops should be mitered wherever they intersect.

Side sections

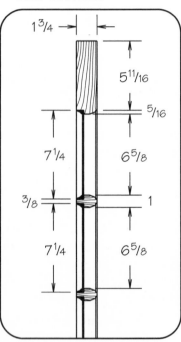

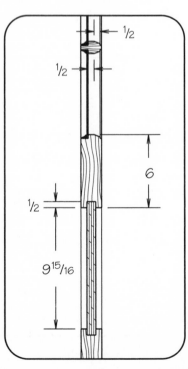

Plan section

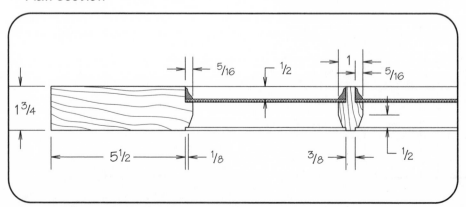

"True" French Door

Usually used in pairs, the "true" French door is simpler to construct than the door with the paneled bottom shown on the preceding page, even though there are more parts. Generally an exterior door leading from a dining room or study to the garden or porch, or from a bedroom to a sleeping porch or balcony, pairs of French doors also were sometimes used between interior rooms, particularly dining rooms and studies, where noise could be shut out without blocking light and vision.

The sectionbelow shows a rabbeted joint between two door leaves, which provides a clean, uncluttered joint. An astragal (a thin strip applied to the face of one door to cover the joint) is often used in doors with fancier profiles, but would look out of place in this circumstance. For interior use, ball catches would hold the secondary door closed, with the primary door latching into it. For an exterior door, the primary door should have a long deadbolt latching at the top and bottom, with the secondary door secured by a surface bolt.

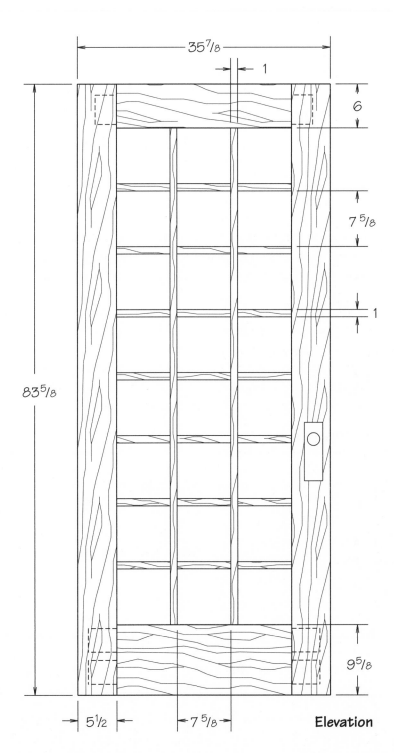

Elevation

Joint between doors: plan section

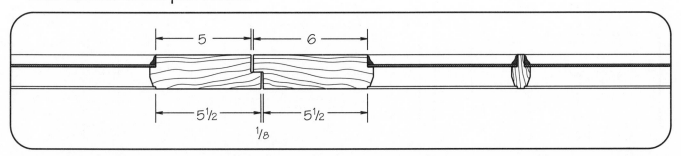

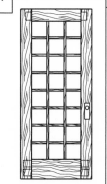

FRENCH DOOR GLAZING DETAILS

The sections show the French door glazed for exterior use. The full-size detail at the bottom left of the page shows the profile of the mullions. The second full-size detail shows an alternate mullion profile for interior applications. The first profile could be used inside, with a beveled removable wooden stop instead of the glazing compound. Thicker glass may be used, the adjustment in size coming from the flat portion of the mullion. The mullions and muntins should be half-lapped where they cross, and mortise and tenon joints should be used where the ends of these pieces meet the stiles and rails.

While these doors are drawn at $1^3/4$ inches thick, the original doors of the period were often made at $1^1/2$ inches. If making them thinner than drawn, it is simplest to take $1/4$ inch out of the flat part of the mullion, keeping the bevel the same dimensions as shown. The tenons on a thinner door should be reduced to $1/2$ inch in thickness from the $3/4$ inch on the thicker doors.

Top rail: section

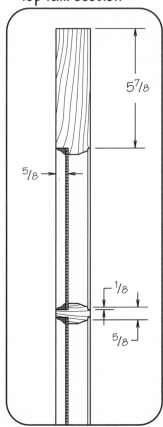

Stile and glass: plan section

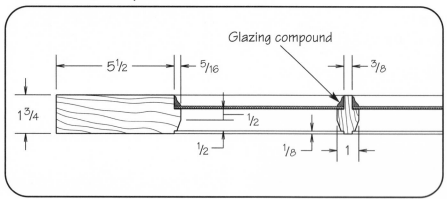

Glazing compound

Bottom rail: section

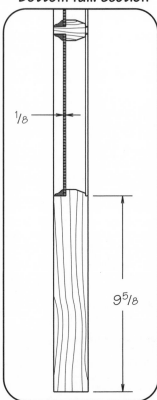

Exterior mullion: full size

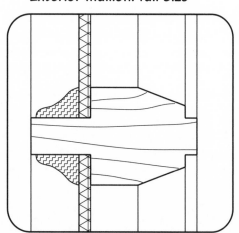

Interior mullion: full size

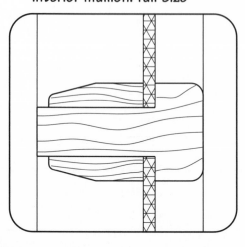

PASSAGE DOORS

Doors with wood panels and no glass lights were generally specified as "first floor doors" and were also used for bathrooms and closets on second and third floors. They follow the same general configuration and construction as the doors with glass lights. Construction is simpler because the same profile is used for both the top and bottom panels. These doors were specified at both $1\frac{3}{4}$ inch and $1\frac{1}{2}$ inch thick, and the difference in thickness between the panels and stiles and rails was either $\frac{1}{2}$ inch or 1 inch overall.

Doors with a relatively thick panel and the smaller $\frac{1}{4}$ inch reveal have a more subtle, elegant appearance, but present construction hurdles. The two detail drawings show both variations in panel thickness for a $1\frac{3}{4}$ inch door. With the thicker panel, the groove for the panels in the stiles and rails will be wider than the mortise and tenon

joint. Therefore, the tenon needs to be haunched not only in its width, but also in its thickness. In doors with the thinner panel, the panel groove and mortise and tenon joint match, so the tenons need only be haunched in width.

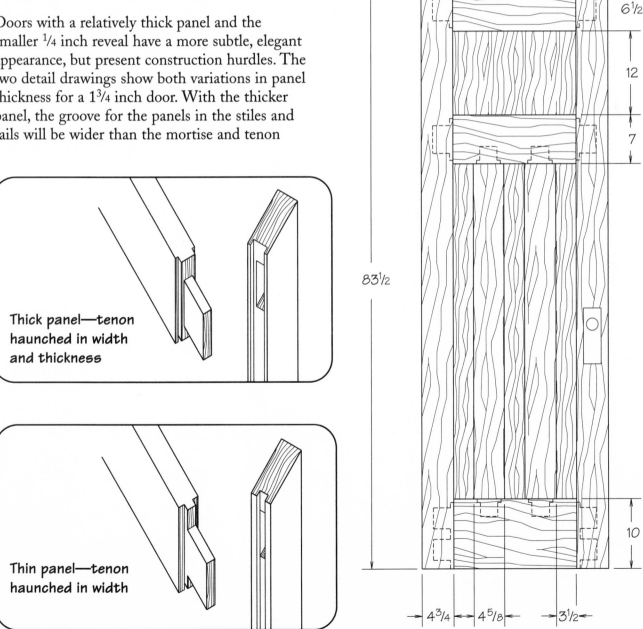

Thick panel—tenon haunched in width and thickness

Thin panel—tenon haunched in width

Elevation

PASSAGE DOORS: PANEL VARIATIONS

These sections show panels with ¼ inch reveals in both 1½ inch and 1¾ inch thick doors, the difference being in the thickness of the panels themselves, and consequently in the thickness of the joints. The original drawings note wide panels as "veneer," but did not note a core, which was likely to be veneer-core plywood. The panels below the intermediate rail were likely to be solid wood, and given their narrow width, I would use solid wood today.

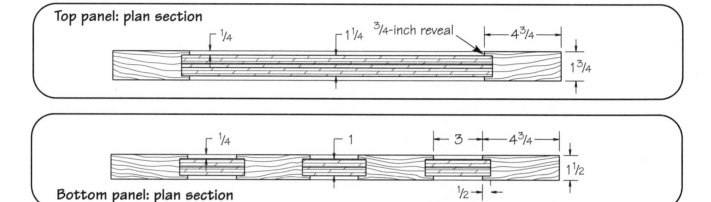

Top panel: plan section

Bottom panel: plan section

Panels: side section

For veneer panels I would use a single thickness of medium density fiberboard (MDF), and either press the veneer with a vacuum bag system, or with a lot of weight on a flat surface such as a cast-iron table saw table. Because so many people will not use particleboard or MDF in any circumstances, I have shown in the drawings two or more layers of veneer-core plywood. If I were to use this material (against my better judgment), I would be extremely careful in laminating these pieces together, and would not use a water-based (white or yellow) glue because that introduces a great deal of moisture to the lamination. Contact cement should not be used for laminating two pieces of plywood together. Reactive polyurethane glue is probably the best choice, although urea resin or resorcinol would also be good.

Hardwood plywoods are available with nearly any possible veneer, but most sources with a good selection deal with commercial customers, and may not make a retail sale unless you are building a lot of doors. Look in the yellow pages under "Hardwood Plywood", or search online at www.woodfinder.com for a local source.

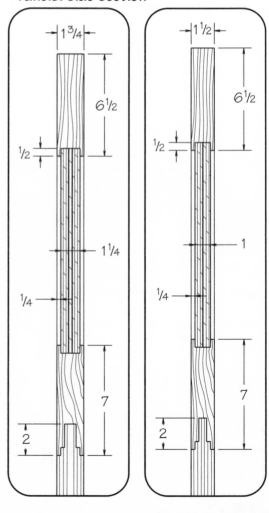

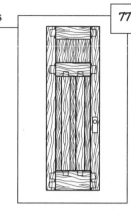

PASSAGE DOORS: PANEL VARIATIONS

These sections show the details of panels with a 1/2-inch difference between the stiles and rails and the panels on each side of the door. This version is more common than the doors shown on the previous page, and is easier to construct. The thickness of the groove for the panels matches the mortise-and-tenon joint, so that the extra haunch of the preceding door is not necessary. To make these doors 1½ inches thick instead of the 1³/4 inches shown, simply substitute 1/2 inch plywood for the 3/4 inch plywood shown, and reduce the thickness of the tenons to 1/2 inch.

If veneering your own panels, hardwood veneers are available in sheet form, in sizes from 2 feet by 8 feet and up. These veneer sheets have a Kraft paper, phenolic, or veneer back, and are much easier to use than individual leaves of veneer. The veneer should be cut slightly larger than the core, and trimmed flush with the core after it has been laminated. While contact cement can be used, it is safer to press the veneer using a glue that forms a more rigid bond. If contact cement is used, be sure to cover both the core and the back of the veneer, with two coats of cement. After the contact cement has dried completely, place dowels or thin slats of wood on the core to keep the sheet of veneer off the surface. When the veneer is in the right position, carefully remove the dowels and press the veneer down, working from the center of the panel out to the edges. A laminate roller does not generate enough pressure to thoroughly press the veneer to the surface. Some veneer suppliers sell a plastic squeegee, but I usually use a block of hardwood, such as teak or walnut, to bear down on the surface. Work with the grain, from the center of the panel out to the edges. The edges of the veneer may be trimmed with a router and flush-trimming bit, or with a very sharp knife.

Care must be taken when finishing these panels with a lacquer, because the solvent in the lacquer can loosen the contact cement. Seal first with very light coats, and under no circumstances saturate the surface with lacquer.

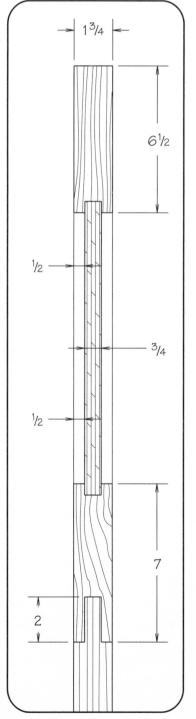

Side section

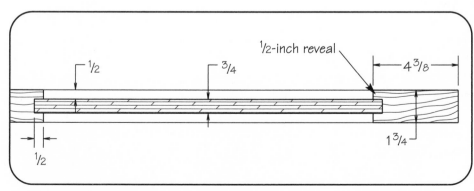

½-inch reveal

Plan section

SIMPLE CRAFTSMAN DOOR

This example is the simplest of the Craftsman doors, and was illustrated in the April 1910 issue in an article on "Mr. Hill's House." It has much in common with other doors of the period, but also some significant differences. First is the absence of any molded profile where the inside of the stiles and rails meet the panels. As seen in the previous section drawings, these edges remain square corners, though with the edges slightly eased. The other difference is the width of the bottom rail at 12 inches, to match the tall baseboard in the house; 8 inches or 9 inches would be about the usual size. Also, the intermediate rail is positioned much higher than its usual height of the doorknob. Structurally, it doesn't make much difference where this rail is placed, and putting it above the lock keeps the lockset from interfering with the rail mortises. Some old carpentry books went to great pains to detail splitting the rail tenons in thickness, so that a full mortise lockset could be placed in between.

This illustration also shows the door stiles at the originally specified 6-inch width. Because of the standard back set of $2^{3}/4$ inches, the doorknob is $1/2$ inch to the right of the center of the stile. Most of the photographs in *The Craftsman* showed this offset, so the choice must be made whether to be historically correct, or to center the door knob by reducing the width of the stile. Unless I was making a door to fit in with a group of existing doors, I would choose to center the knob, reasoning that to the modern eye an off-center knob would be bothersome. When replacing an existing door, or fitting a new door in an existing house, I would follow the example and size the door parts to match what is already there.

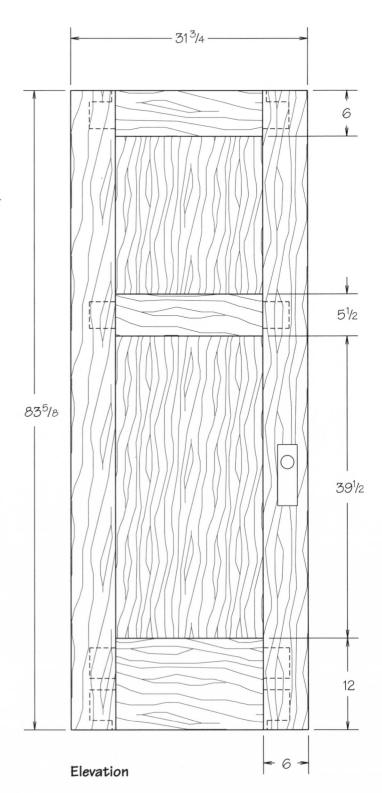

Elevation

Four-Panel Door

In a June 1905 *Craftsman* article, this form of door was illustrated several times as a bedroom door. In most cases it was painted, rather than with a clear finish. Many doors of the period had several small horizontal panels, but the more common form was five equal panels instead of the version shown here with a large bottom panel and three smaller ones above.

If it is to be painted, then the grain of the panels can run horizontally, instead of vertically as drawn. That would be the direction in the more typical five-panel door. The bottom rail, at nine inches, is also shorter than many other Craftsman doors.

Personally I think this door has too many horizontal lines to really have the Craftsman feel, unless the treatment of the wall picks up one or more of the intermediate rails, such as a chair rail about three feet from the floor, or a wainscot cap 4 feet or 5 feet up.

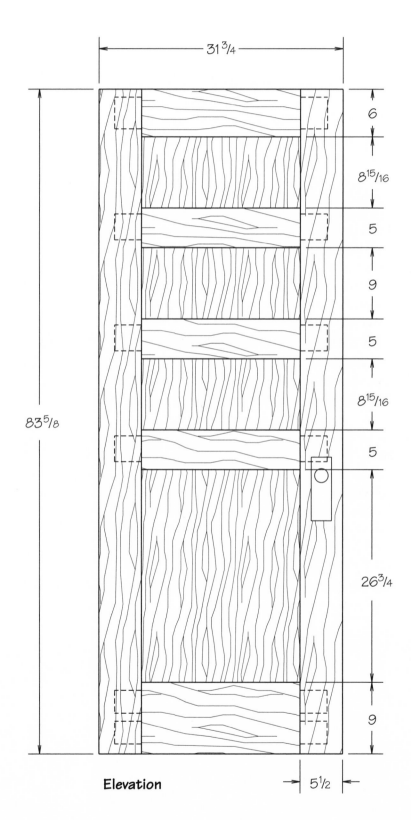

Elevation

VERTICAL DOOR

This door was listed in the drawings for Magazine House #10 from 1904 as a "typical first floor door." At 2' -8" by 7' -6", it is taller than a typical door of today. If ceilings are 9 feet or 10 feet high, this height should be used; with a typical ceiling height of today, it can be shortened to 6'-8" inches or 7'-0" inches, and the strong vertical lines will make the room appear higher. Although House #10 was rather large, the typical door only occurred in a few places, such as a coat closet, lavatory, and kitchen stairs to the basement. The simple form tends to downplay the door as opposed to the door with two intermediate stiles on page 73 or the doors with glass lights at the top that occurred at the front entry and second floor bedrooms of this same house.

In a paneled room, this door would blend in with the paneling. Against a plastered wall, it would have a commanding presence. As with the other paneled doors, this was originally detailed as 1½ inches thick with a ½ inch thick panel. In other cases, the thickness was listed as 1¾ inches, a better thickness, especially if it is made at the 7'-6" height or even taller.

The joints are shown as wedged through tenons, but this detail was not shown on the original drawings. Stub tenons could also be used.

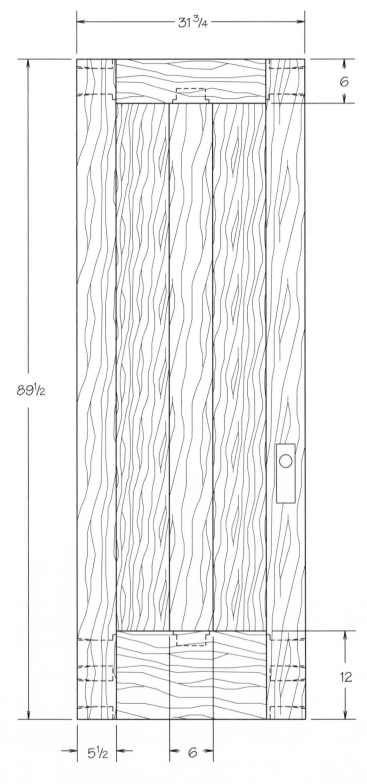

Elevation

LEDGER DOOR

The ledger door, shown here at 2'-8" x 7'-0" is another common form of Craftsman door, usually seen in rustic structures such as camps, cottages, and country houses. Its simple, gothic form exhibits a certain charm, and is an excellent way to showcase attractive wood. The planks making up the door should be equal in width, and there may be more or fewer than shown depending on the width of the door and of available wood.

The individual planks are chamfered at the joints, held together with separate splines that fit in ploughed groovest. The dashed lines in the elevation indicate dovetailed ledgers that brace the door horizontally, and help to keep it from sagging and warping. This tendency to sag and warp or twist is the biggest drawback to this form of door, and is the reason why paneled doors were developed.

These doors can be successfully made, if great care is taken during construction, and provided that the wood is stable and carefully seasoned. Wood used in these doors should be given plenty of time to acclimate to the shop or house environment before any milling is done. After the wood has reached equilibrium moisture content, it should be rough-milled—surfaces flattened and straightened, but larger than the finished size. After rough-milling the wood should again be given a week or two of "second seasoning" to ensure that it will stay straight and flat. Once it has been determined that the pieces are stable, final milling may take place, and the doors can be assembled.

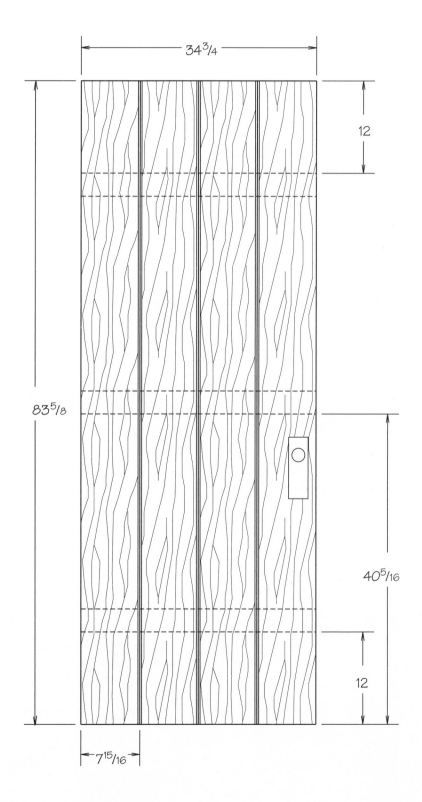

Elevation

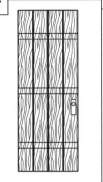

LEDGER DOOR *(continued)*

The thickness of the ledger door could be reduced to 1-$\frac{1}{2}$ inches, but the thicker stock shown would be preferable. The splines should be made from the same material as the planks, and the grain should run in the same direction. These could be milled as tongues milled in the edges of the individual planks, but it is likely that the maker will be needing all or nearly all of the available board width. It is possible to glue up for width to achieve the proper size planks, but the final appearance must be considered. If the glued-up planks don't look like a single board, then the effect of this door will be lost.

I think it is simpler to machine grooves in both edges rather than to set up for milling tongues and grooves. The grooves can be milled with a dado head in a table saw, though care must be taken when working with these long, heavy boards. Adequate support must be available on both the infeed and outfeed ends of the saw, and a tall fence should guide the stock past the cutter.

The individual planks must be perfectly straight and flat, or there will be variation in the grooves, and the joints will be compromised.

The grooves might instead be cut with a bearing-guided, slot-cutting router bit. This would allow the base of the router to rest on the wide face of the plank, rather than on the narrow edge. It would be wise to make a pass with the router from each face of the planks to ensure that the grooves are centered. The splines should be carefully milled to the precise width of the grooves; they should be a snug fit without being forced. If the splines have to be forced into place, they are quite likely to split the groove pieces. The splines can be cut to finished size on the table saw, but it would be better to saw them oversize, and then reduce them to finished thickness with a planer. The smooth surfaces produced by the planer will not only be uniformly sized, but also will provide for better glue joints.

Ledger door: plan section

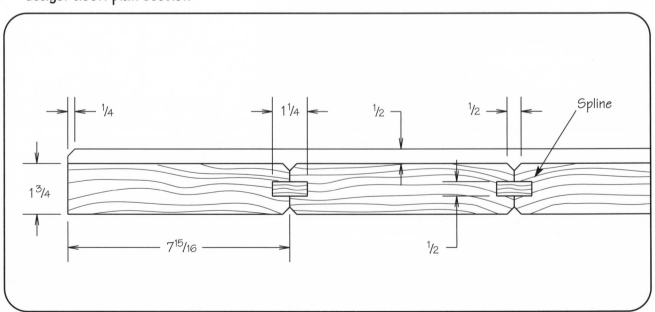

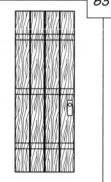

LEDGER DOOR *(continued)*

The planks and splines should be dry-fit and clamped together before the ledgers are laid out, and the housings for them milled. Great care must be taken to keep the parts flat during clamping, and to set the clamps evenly so that the door does not cup or twist. The assembled door must also be kept square. The planks can be made long, and trimmed later, but the fitting of the ledgers will depend on their dovetailed dados being square and straight across the width of the door.

The middle ledger should be centered in height on the door, with the top and bottom ledgers equally spaced as shown. The dovetailed edge is best cut on a router table, and again, the importance of the stock being stable and true cannot be over-stressed. The bulk of the waste can be removed with the router and a straight bit, but the edges of the dados will need to be routed to the proper angle. I would rout the angled edges with the door clamped together, and the router guided by a straight edge clamped square to the door. The remaining waste could be removed by any number of methods, but the simplest would be to take the door apart, and remove the waste from the individual planks with a dado head in a radial-arm saw.

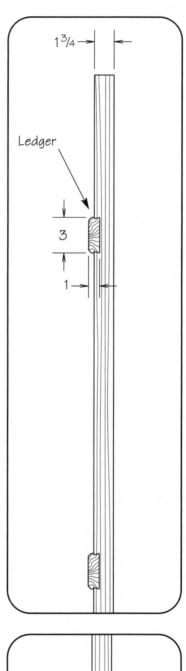

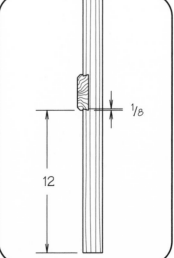

Ledger door: plan section

Ledger Door with Lights

Final assembly of the ledger door should take place in two distinct stages. First, the planks and splines should be glued and clamped together, being certain that the assembly is flat and square. The ledgers should then be driven in from one edge of the door. The ledgers really should not be glued, except at one end, since their grain is at right angles to that of the planks. Placement of the ledgers will be much easier if both the ledger and its dado receive a very slight taper in width. This is achieved in the planks by setting the guide for the router at the desired distance angled $1/16$ to $1/8$ of an inch across the width of the door, then slightly tapering one edge of the ledger itself with a block plane. This way there will be room for the ledger to slide across the width of the door, tightening in the dado at the very end of the assembly.

The elevation at right shows a variation of the ledger door with three glass lights at the top. This detail was used for the exterior door at the kitchen entrance of Stickley's own New Jersey home. Each light is four small squares of colored leaded glass to provide visual interest and to transmit light into what would otherwise be a dark interior.

Construction is similar to the previous ledger door, but the top ledger has been moved up, centered in the space between the opening for the glass and the top edge of the door. The planks are naturally wider, because the openings for the glass would be too small on the four-plank version of this door.

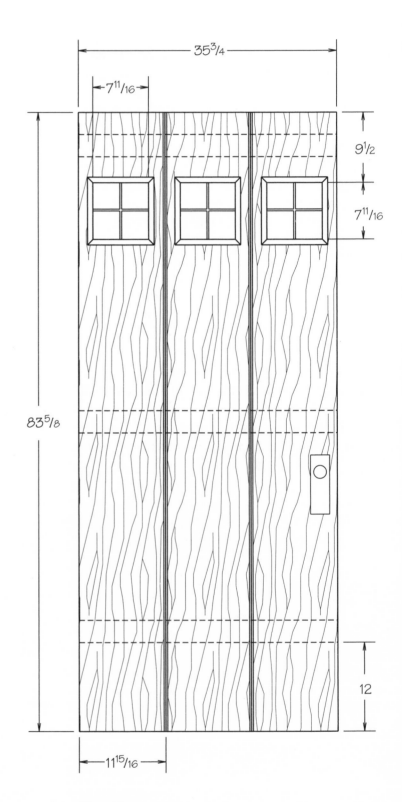

Elevation

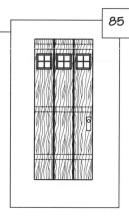

Ledger Door with Lights (*continued*)

Construction of the ledger door with lights is identical to the plain ledger door, except for the location of the top ledger, and of course, the cutout for the lights. The cutout for the lights should be located with the planks clamped together, but before the ledger is in place. Make a template to the finished size of the opening, rough-cut, then use a flush-trimming bit in the router to obtain a clean edge at the finished size. The corners will need to be squared with a chisel. The 3/4 inch deep by 1/2 inch wide rabbet for the glass and glass stop can be made with a bearing guided rabbeting bit. Again, the corners will need to be squared by hand.

The glass stop is rabbeted as shown in the section drawings, and is mitered at the corners. The glass is shown at 1/4 inch thick to accommodate the lead came, but it could be any practical thickness.

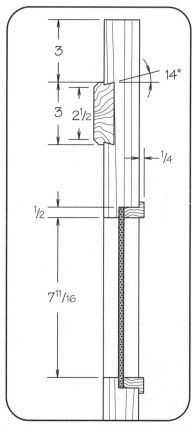

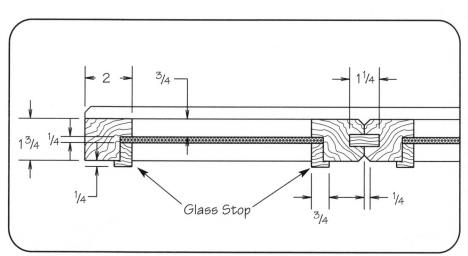

Plan section

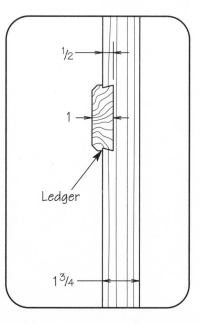

Side section

DOOR JAMBS

Door jambs, as commonly made today, are usually only ³/₄ inch thick, which is on the thin side for quality work, especially with a large and heavy solid-wood door. Pictured at left below, it is also common to angle the edges of the jambs slightly, theoretically to make the casing easier to fit to the wall. This approach causes more problems than it solves, because it makes it hard to fit the jamb flush with the wall surface, and tends to tilt the casing. The joint between the side jamb and head jamb is usually a rabbet, which should be glued together and reinforced with two screws. The drawing at left also shows the common practice of relieving the back of the casing, which is somehow supposed to prevent warping, and make the trim easier to install. The only real advantage to this practice is that it makes it easier to plane of the back of the casing if there is a hump in the wall surface.

The rabbeted jamb at right is considerably stronger, more likely to stay straight, and easier to set plumb and level in the door opening. Usually trim work starts with the setting of the door jambs, and they must be set properly both for the door to swing as it should, and for the balance of the trim work to be correct. It should be remembered that the jambs are not just trim, they are also part of the mechanism of the door, and they need to be attached firmly to the structure.

Contemporary jamb

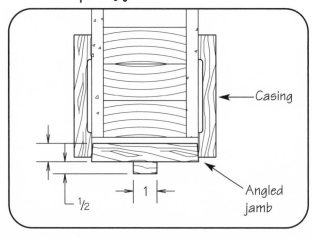

Casing

Angled jamb

½

1

Rabbetted jamb

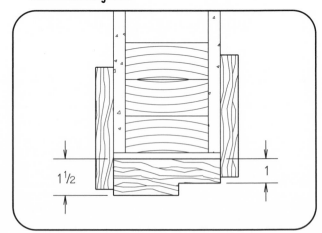

1½

1

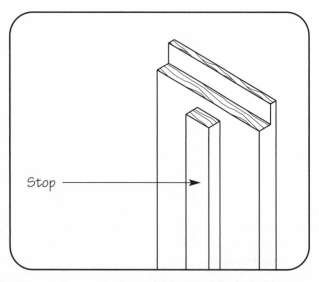

Stop

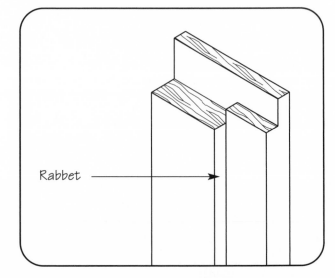

Rabbet

DOOR JAMBS (*continued*)

The drawing at left shows an improved method of fabricating the jamb, and an installation that does not reveal visible fasteners. The thicker jamb contains a groove in which screws used to attach the jamb may then be hidden by the placement of the door stop. This also creates a stronger stop, as opposed to one that is merely tacked on. The casing is shown as being attached to the jamb with biscuits, one side may be glued and clamped to the jamb before the jamb is set, and the other side glued and clamped after setting. This procedure will make for much neater joints in the casing, but the wall surfaces at the door opening must be in good condition.

The drawing at right is a variation of the rabbeted jamb in which the jamb is made in two pieces. This makes better use of raw material, and again the casing may be pre-assembled to the jamb. This method does not, however, provide for attaching the jamb without visible fasteners. Jambs are generally held in place with finish nails, but it is wise to also use a few screws behind the hinges, and to make sure at least one screw per hinge is long enough to reach through the jamb to the studs.

Improved jamb

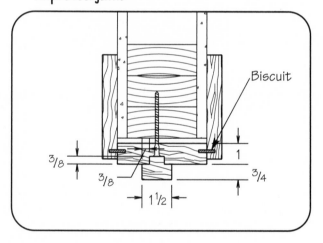

Two-part jamb

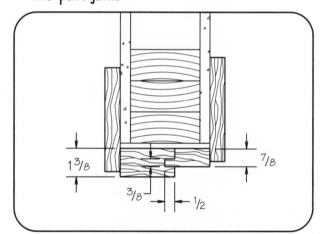

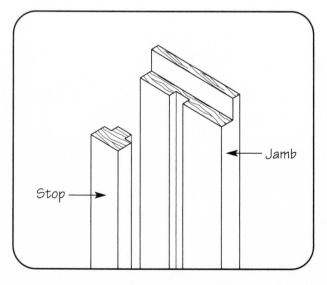

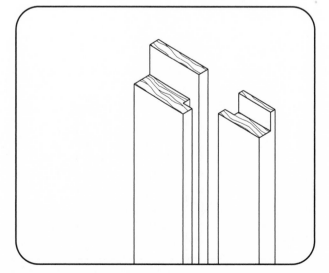

DOOR JAMBS (*continued*)

If panels are added to an existing wall, the existing jambs will not be wide enough to attach the casing. This is also a common problem with windows, in new construction as well as in remodeling. The left-hand drawing shows a method of extending the jambs, attaching the extensions to the jambs with long screws in counter-bored holes, the holes then being hidden by the casing. The joint between the two may be stepped as shown, or it can be flush. The stepped joint will make finishing easier, if new work must be matched with old, or if the jamb and the extension are of different materials, a situation more likely with windows than with doors.

The right-hand drawing shows a variation of the rabbeted jamb, particularly useful if the jamb must be deeper than normal. The rabbet may be made extra-large, to allow for the hidden fastening of the extension. In some cases the extension may actually be paneling, rather than a single piece of trim.

Extended jamb

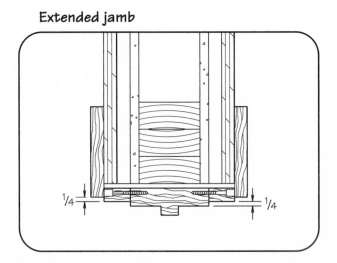

Deep rabbetted jamb

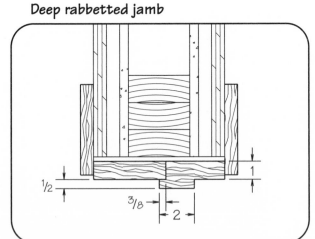

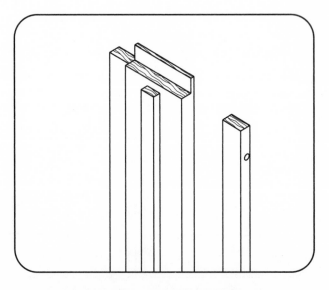

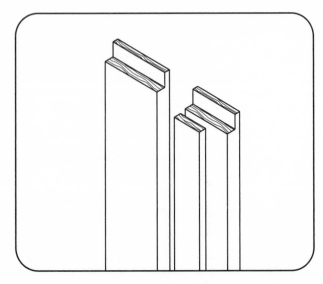

DOOR TRIM WITH TOP BAND

The side casing and head casing are both 1 inch thick, with the side casing extending to the top of the head. The top band across the head extends past the side of the casing a distance equal to its 1¼-inch thickness, and past the face of the casing a full inch. This creates an interesting shadow line and gives the door an elegant look. Note that the top band is rabbeted to fit over the casings. This provides a neat joint even if the casing shrinks.

The baseboard is ¼ inch thinner than the casing, but the shoe molding protrudes beyond the side casing. The portion of the shoe molding that extends is trimmed back at 45°. This isn't the most elegant solution, but Stickley did recommend it.

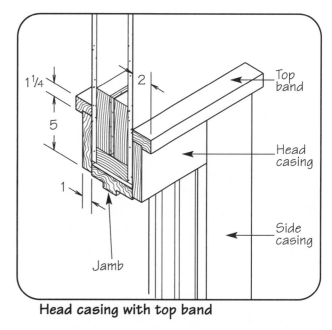

Head casing with top band

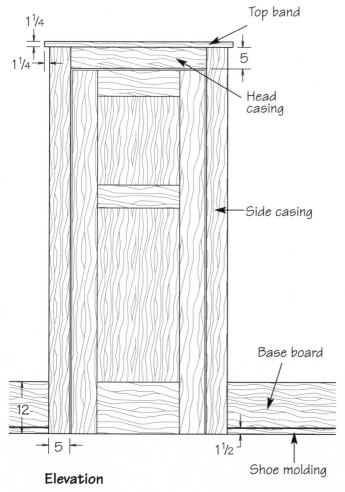

Elevation

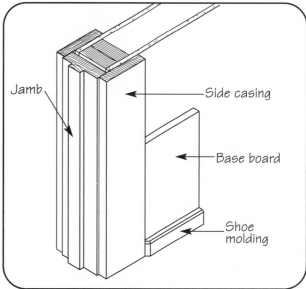

Base and shoe

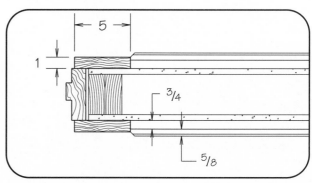

Plan section

DOOR TRIM WITH PICTURE RAIL

In this example, the head casing is actually a picture rail that extends around the perimeter of the room. It is ⅛-inch thicker than the side casing, creating a shadow line at the joint. Note the rabbet on the backside of the picture rail, which allows for a hook to be placed any where along its length.

The baseboard is ⅛-inch thinner than the casing, creating another shadow line where the two meet. The shoe molding extends slightly past the casing, and the corner is mitered back where the shoe and casing intersect.

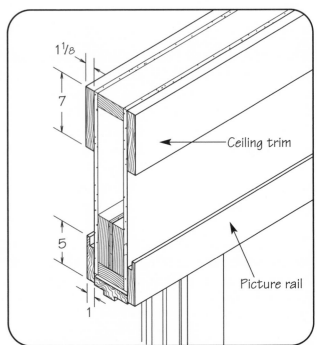

Picture rail and ceiling trim

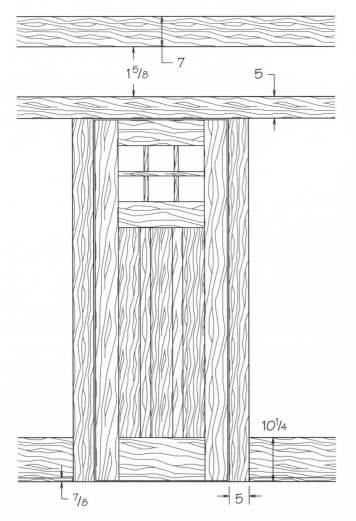

Elevation

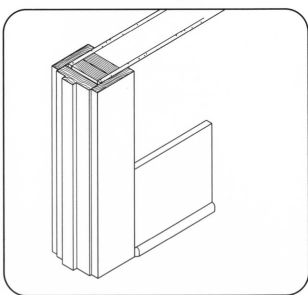

Base and shoe

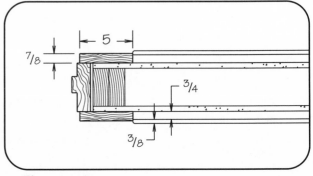

Plan section

DOOR TRIM WITH CROWN MOLDING

This example also has the head casing extending around the room, but capped with a thicker piece to create more visual interest. The trim at the ceiling is similar to the previous example, but a small, angled crown molding has been added. Crown moldings were rarely shown Stickley's *The Craftsman* magazine or in his architectural drawings, but I believe that they were used more often than not.

The side casing and baseboard are each stepped down 1/8 inch from the adjacent piece of trim. At the intersection of the side casing and baseboard is a plinth block, which terminates the shoe molding without extending beyond the casing.

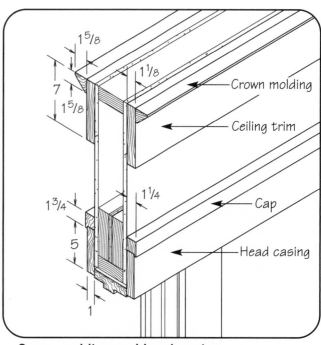

Crown molding and head casing

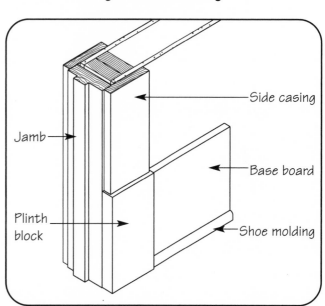

Base and shoe

Elevation

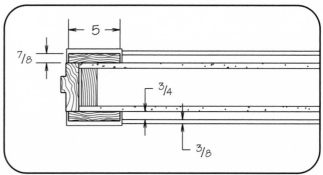

Plan section

DOOR TRIM WITH HALF-BEAM

This trim reverses some of the details given in earlier examples. The side casings are the same thickness as the head, but extend past them to the bottom of the half-beam at the ceiling. This half-beam detail sometimes occurred alone, but usually the ceiling detail also included full-beams extending across the ceiling.

The baseboard is considerably thicker than the casing, and the shoe molding extends even farther. To my eye this detail is awkward, but Stickley showed it this way in his "Practical Points . . ." article in 1913.

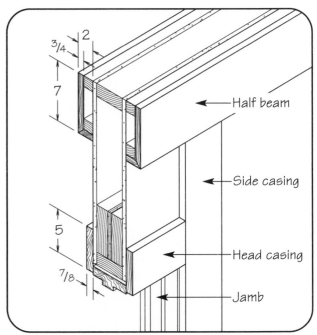

Half-beam and casings

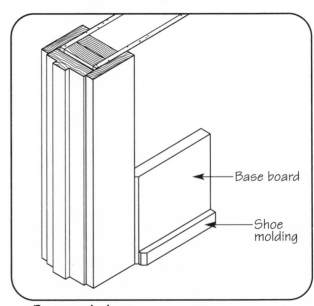

Base and shoe

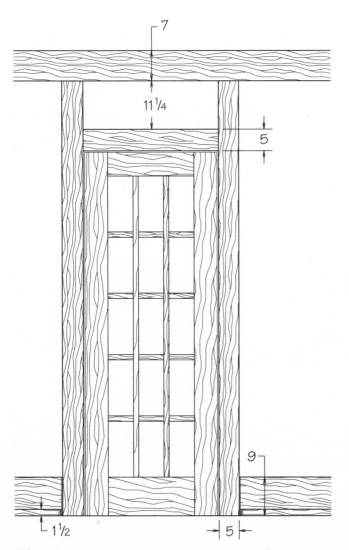

Elevation

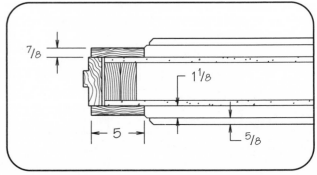

Plan section

DOOR TRIM WITH HEAD CASING

In the absence of other horizontal trim at the top of the wall, this is an effective way to trim a Craftsman door. The head casing is thicker than the sides, and extends ¼ inch beyond the sides.

If the baseboard and casing are the same thickness as shown here, then the shoe molding can extend to the middle of the casing, and can terminate with a mitered return. This is more refined than simply back cutting the shoe, but care must be taken that the casing and baseboard lie in the same plane.

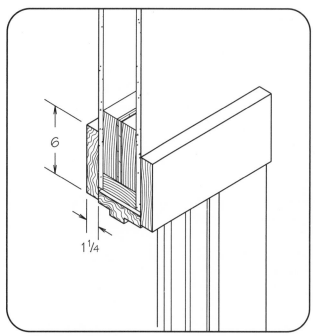

Head casing

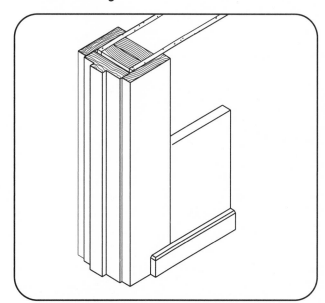

Base and shoe

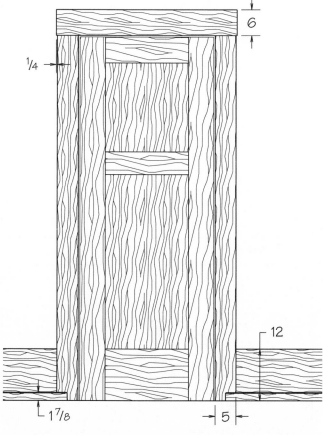

Elevation

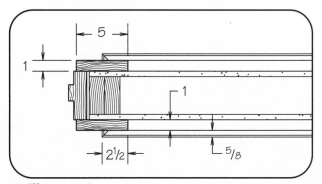

Plan section

DOOR TRIM WITH MOLDINGS

To some people, Craftsman trim is too plain and severe. This example is taken from *Radford's Old House Measured and Scaled Drawings*, originally published in 1911. The basic lines and proportions of the Craftsman trim are softened by the addition of some simple molding profiles. The head and side casings are the same thickness, but the wider head casing appears even larger with the addition of molded pieces top and bottom.

The baseboard remains as a rectangular piece, and the shoe has a simple bevel on its top edge.

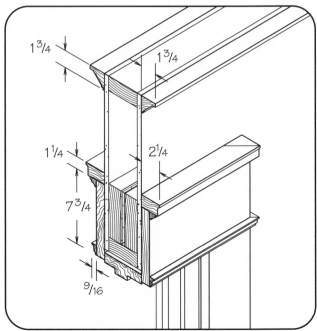

Head casing with moldings

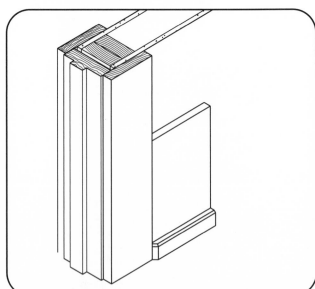

Base and shoe

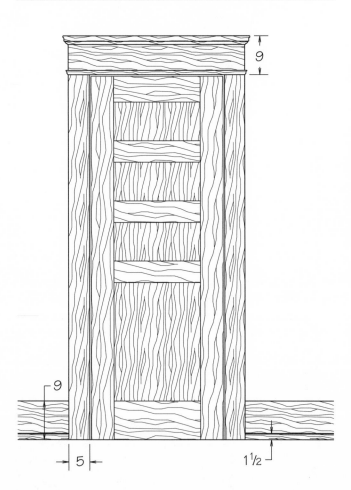

Elevation

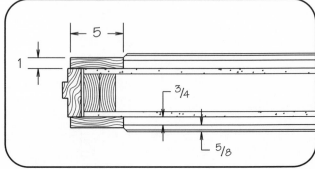

Plan section

DOOR TRIM WITH MITERED CASING

The addition of the back band around the
mitered casing is also a detail adapted from
Radford. It adds depth to the detail while
maintaining the straightforward Craftsman
profile. It can be adjusted by deepening the rabbet
and scribing to the wall, if the wall is not true
where it meets the side casing.

The back band also extends beyond the baseboard
and shoe, allowing those pieces to terminate
neatly at the casing.

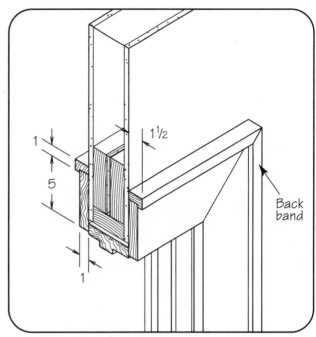

Mitered head casing

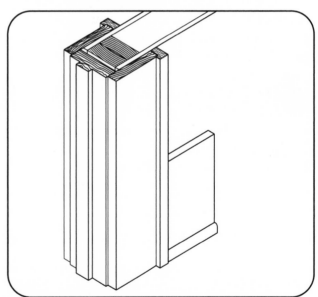

Base and shoe

Elevation

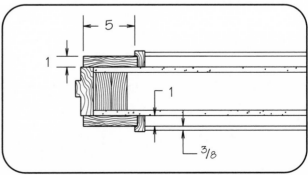

Plan section

CASEMENT WINDOWS, IN-OPENING

Gustav Stickley preferred casement windows over double-hung windows, and in many of his designs, small casements were mounted high in the walls. This detail is from his architectural drawings for Magazine House #6A, which appeared in *The Craftsman* in June of 1905. This window swings into the room, a feature that can cause difficulties with hanging curtains or drapes, and requires vigilance in making sure that it is closed in inclement weather. The advantage of opening inward is that a screen can be placed on the outside of the sash.

Casements could occur as single windows, in a variety of sizes, or in groups. These drawings show the basic details, and the plan view shows a typical method of grouping casements. The treatment of the bottom rail and the groove at the bottom edge of the sill allows water to bead up and drip off, rather than wicking up to adjacent woodwork. This is always a concern in building a good window—it will get wet. The trick is to help the water run off, rather than build up and cause damage.

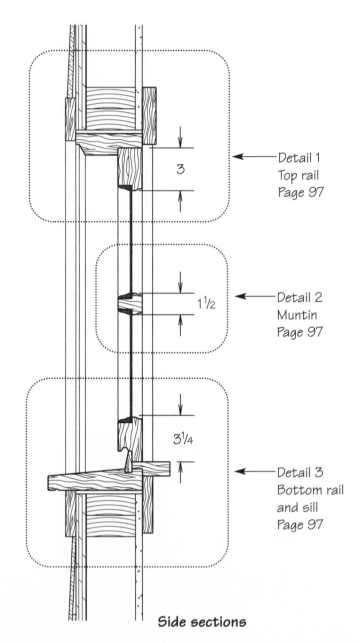

Detail 1
Top rail
Page 97

Detail 2
Muntin
Page 97

Detail 3
Bottom rail
and sill
Page 97

Side sections

Plan section

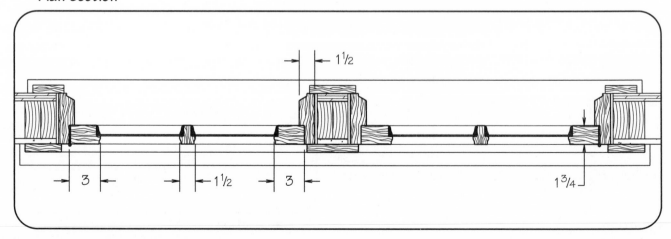

Casement Windows, In-Opening (*continued*)

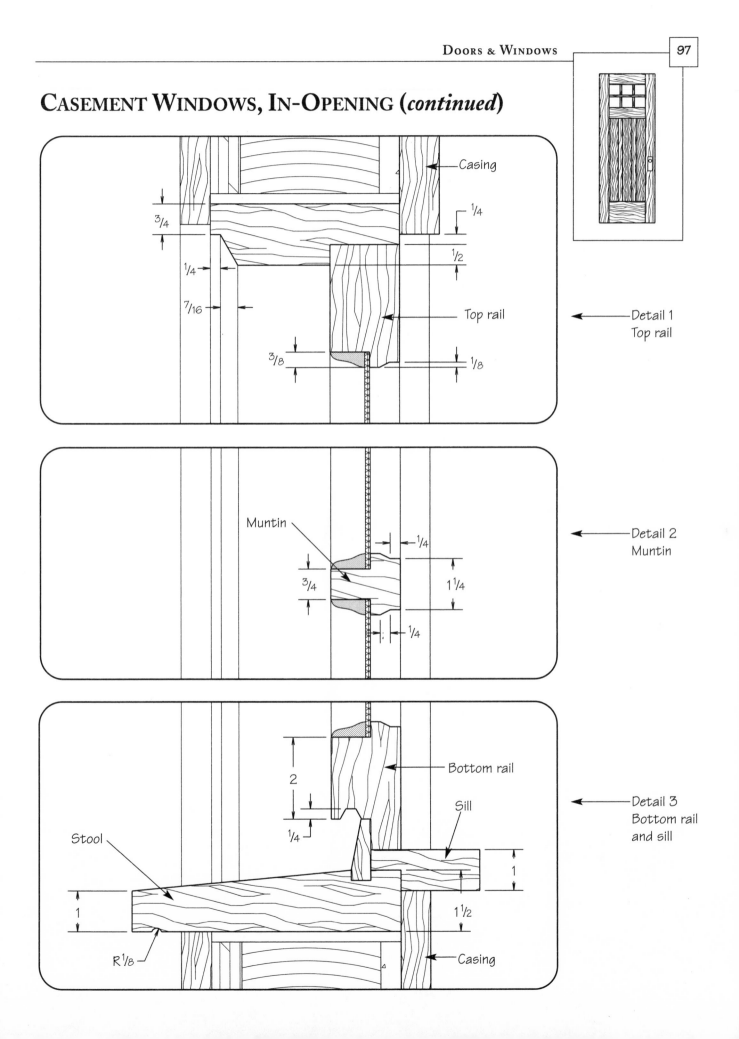

Casing

3/4

1/4

1/4

7/16

1/2

Top rail

3/8

1/8

Detail 1
Top rail

Muntin

3/4

1/4

1 1/4

1/4

Detail 2
Muntin

Bottom rail

2

1/4

Stool

Sill

1

1 1/2

1

R 1/8

Casing

Detail 3
Bottom rail
and sill

CASEMENT WINDOWS, OUT-OPENING

The other option is to swing a casement out, which solves the problem with curtains and drapes, but makes the placement of a screen difficult. This drawing is based on other examples of windows of the period. One of the advantages of the outward-swinging casement is that in can, depending on the direction of the wind, be left partially open in a light rain without soaking the interior of the house.

The plan view below demonstrates a method of joining two windows in one opening, and this design can also be used for a single window. Note that the vertical elements of the window also have grooves running their length, in order to allow any water that may build up to be carried away. The side sections also show copper flashing above the exterior window trim, a detail that should be included in any window application.

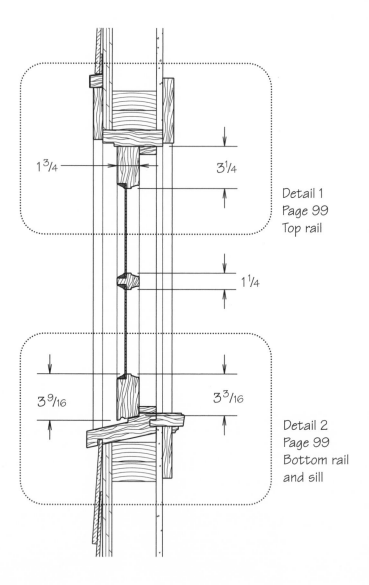

Detail 1
Page 99
Top rail

Detail 2
Page 99
Bottom rail
and sill

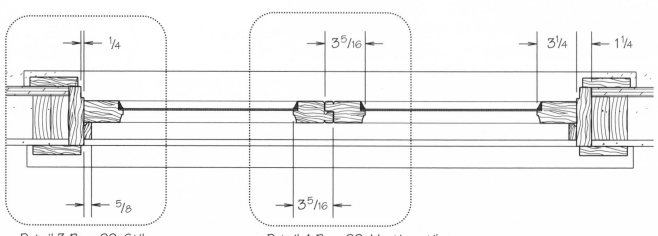

Detail 3 Page 99: Stile

Detail 4 Page 99: Meeting stile

Casement Windows, Out-Opening (*continued*)

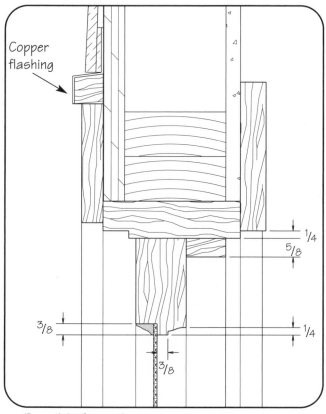

Copper flashing

Detail 1: Top rail

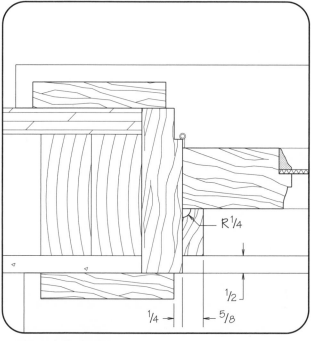

Detail 3: Stile

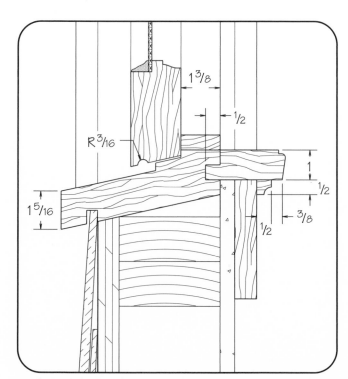

Detail 2: Bottom rail and sill

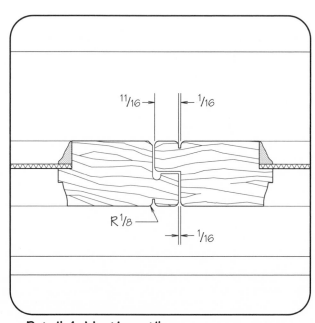

Detail 4: Meeting stile

CRAFTSMAN KITCHENS

Kitchens in the early 1900s were moving into the modern age, but they were still a long way from the standards we are familiar with today. Cabinets and appliances are the two places where it can be difficult to reconcile historical accuracy with modern life. The drawings in this book reflect this, but I will leave it to the reader to decide which course to follow. The kitchen, is after all, mainly a functional room and in this area especially, form should follow function.

Most of the kitchen cabinet drawings show first the details of the original cabinets as they were constructed, followed by examples that are in the same style adapted to the sizes in common use today. In a kitchen in a new home, or an addition to an existing one, I can't think of any good reasons to follow old dimensions. If you were undoing a 1950s or 1970s remodel, there might be an argument for new cabinets at the original dimensions, but there would need to be some compelling reason for the historical significance of the house, or a tremendous desire for authenticity. However, if there are original existing cabinets, they should be restored if possible, or replaced with accurate reproductions.

In the typical original kitchen, the cabinets would be limited to one or two dressers, and perhaps a counter at the sink. Most of the counter space would be in the form of a

freestanding table. Pantries were common, either for the purpose of storage, or as a butler's pantry—a transitional room between the kitchen and dining room. Either form is worth having either in new construction, or in a restoration. Many original pantries have been sacrificed, either to add a downstairs bathroom or an expanded kitchen plan, but they do serve to store a great many things in a small amount of space.

The cabinets in Craftsman homes followed a common style and were quite functional in design, but there is a considerable variation in height and depth of the individual cabinets. The biggest difficulty that will arise from following the original examples will be in how the cabinets function with modern appliances, both built-in and counter top. Modern stoves and dishwashers are designed to fit next to cabinets that are 24 inches deep, and under counters that are 36 inches high. Most counter-top appliances function best if there is 18 inches of space

between the top of the counter and the bottom of the upper cabinets, although this distance can be as little as 16 inches when necessary.

Because the original kitchen cabinetry was nowhere near as extensive as what we expect to see today, it is entirely possible to keep the original cabinets, and to add another elevation or two of modern cabinets in a complementary style. It will be much easier to fit the appliances into these elevations, rather than trying to force them in next to original cabinets.

The drawings on pages 104 to 118 compare and contrast some of the differences between period and modern cabinets. Aside from the differences in size, one of the most significant differences is the absence of a toe-kick where the base cabinet meets the floor. The 3-inch deep, 4-inch high space lets one stand closer to the cabinet while working at the counter, and allows mopping of the kitchen floor without damaging the finish on the cabinet itself. Original cabinets without the kick almost always show a great deal of wear on the baseboard, due either to cleaning the floor with harsh solutions, or from the physical wear of shoes rubbing against the baseboard. As a practical matter, I would include a toe-kick in new kitchen cabinets, and treat it as part of the floor, continuing the floor material up on the vertical surface of the toe-kick, or else use a vinyl or rubber cove base at this location. Many people will finish the kick as part of the cabinet, but it really isn't very visible, and if made of wood and finished with the same material as the cabinets themselves, won't look good for very long.

The exploded views on pages 106 and 107 show the basic elements for constructing modern cabinets, reflecting my preferences for making high quality cabinets that will have an appropriate look for a Craftsman home. The base cabinets can be made with an integral base rather than the separate base shown, but this complicates construction of the cabinets, and makes it much more difficult to level the cabinets on installation. The key element to a successful installation is getting the base set level in the room. The cabinet boxes are shown as individual units behind a common face frame. This detail not only simplifies construction, but also it is much easier to install several cabinets of manageable size as opposed to wrestling one giant cabinet in to place.

Base cabinets, and wall cabinets with wood doors, can be constructed from a number of materials. Birch or maple plywood is a good choice, and I prefer a clear finish on the interiors, which makes it easier to see inside the cabinet. This material is available pre-finished with a very durable coating that will eliminate the need to finish the inside of the cabinets. If using unfinished plywood, it is easiest to finish the cabinets and cabinet backs separately, and then attach the backs to the finished cabinets. Particleboard with a melamine coating is also a good choice for the cabinet boxes; again the interiors don't need to be finished, and the inside is light and easy to clean.

Frameless or European style cabinets can be used, with doors and finished end panels made in the styles as shown in the drawings on pages 125 to 133. The look of the finished kitchen won't be quite as authentic, but the cabinets will be slightly more functional. European style concealed hinges can also be used with face frame cabinets, but blocks need to be added behind the hinge-mounting plates to get the doors in the right position. Although this will encroach on the interior space of the cabinets, the big advantage is the ease of mounting and the adjustability of this hardware.

Wall cabinets with glass doors should have the same material and finish inside and out, and European hinges will be visible through the glass doors. Lights may be added inside these cabinets, and if they are used, then the shelves should be glass to allow the light to pass through.

Wall cabinets are nominally 12 inches deep, but with inset doors, this can be too small for dinner plates to lie flat on the inside of the cabinet. Making them an inch or two deeper will make

them much more functional. The bottom of the wall cabinets is shown with the bottom rail of the face frame extending down. This space may be used for mounting fluorescent or halogen light fixtures underneath the wall cabinets. If lights aren't used, the cabinet bottoms may be brought down flush with the bottom edge of the rail.

The original cabinets would likely have been made entirely of solid wood—of pine or whatever the inexpensive local species was. In today's market, this could be much more expensive than using plywood. If a solid wood was used, a hardwood such as poplar would likely be a more cost-effective solution.

The cabinets on page 114 are closer in configuration to typical modern cabinets, although the base cabinets are taller, and the space between the counter and the upper cabinets is smaller. The original architectural drawings did not show details or sections, but the elevations did show a detail around the doors and drawers of the base cabinets, which I interpret as a bead around the frame. The wall-cabinet elevations did not show this detail, so I have not included the bead in my drawing of the original cabinets. Since this is a popular detail today, I have included it in my drawing for the upper cabinets built to today's standard sizes.

Running the bead itself on the face-frame stock can be easily done on a router table. The real work in using this detail comes in making the joints where the parts of the face frame meet. The flat faces of the face-frame stiles and rails butt together, preferably with a mortise-and-tenon, and the beads are mitered where they meet. This can be done in a number of ways, but I prefer to make templates in the exact shape and size of the rail ends, and use a router with a top-mounted guide bearing to mill the joints in the stiles. This makes a clean, precise joint, but leaves the corners rounded. The corners are then cleaned up by hand, with a chisel.

TYPICAL CRAFTSMAN KITCHEN CABINET

The typical Craftsman kitchen only had one, or perhaps two, elevations of cabinets. The sink was separate from the cabinets, and was not enclosed. A separate table was usually used for work that today takes place at the kitchen counter, with pantries, or butler's pantries, for additional storage and work areas.

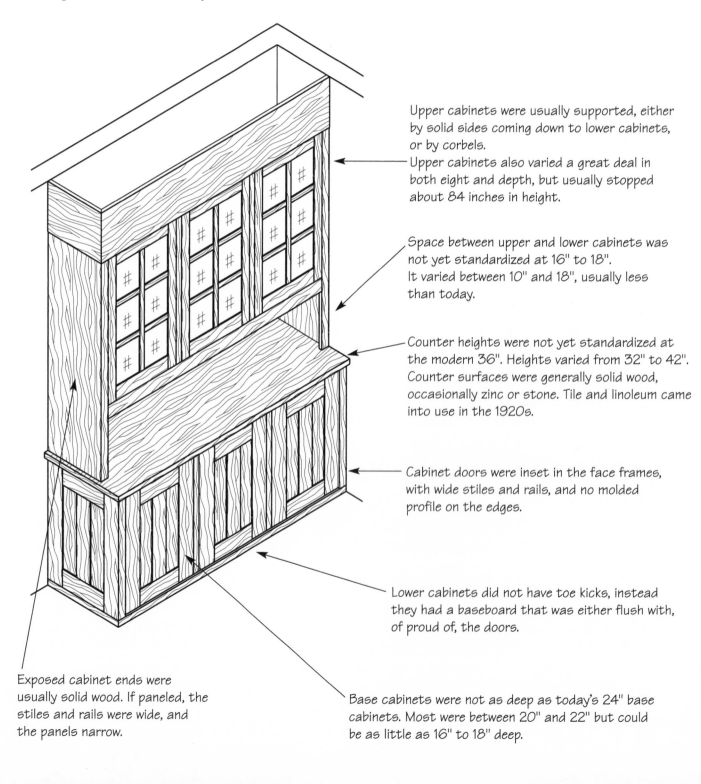

Upper cabinets were usually supported, either by solid sides coming down to lower cabinets, or by corbels.
Upper cabinets also varied a great deal in both eight and depth, but usually stopped about 84 inches in height.

Space between upper and lower cabinets was not yet standardized at 16" to 18".
It varied between 10" and 18", usually less than today.

Counter heights were not yet standardized at the modern 36". Heights varied from 32" to 42". Counter surfaces were generally solid wood, occasionally zinc or stone. Tile and linoleum came into use in the 1920s.

Cabinet doors were inset in the face frames, with wide stiles and rails, and no molded profile on the edges.

Lower cabinets did not have toe kicks, instead they had a baseboard that was either flush with, of proud of, the doors.

Exposed cabinet ends were usually solid wood. If paneled, the stiles and rails were wide, and the panels narrow.

Base cabinets were not as deep as today's 24" base cabinets. Most were between 20" and 22" but could be as little as 16" to 18" deep.

TYPICAL CRAFTSMAN CABINETS
ADAPTED TO MODERN STANDARD DIMENSIONS

Today's kitchens usually include cabinets and counters on every available wall. Sinks will be built into cabinets, pantries are rarely seen.

Modern dishwashers, ranges, cooktops, and refrigerators are designed to fit standard cabinet dimensions.

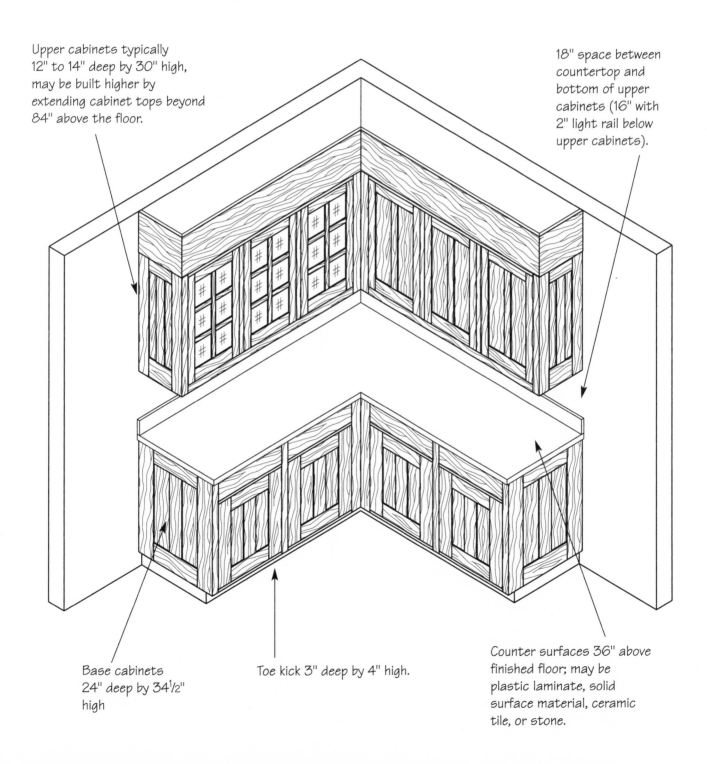

Upper cabinets typically 12" to 14" deep by 30" high, may be built higher by extending cabinet tops beyond 84" above the floor.

18" space between countertop and bottom of upper cabinets (16" with 2" light rail below upper cabinets).

Base cabinets 24" deep by 34 1/2" high

Toe kick 3" deep by 4" high.

Counter surfaces 36" above finished floor; may be plastic laminate, solid surface material, ceramic tile, or stone.

BASE CABINET ANATOMY

Rails at tops of cabinets allow attachment of countertop, and access to inside of cabinet during fabrication and installation.

Plywood cabinet boxes or carcases—several separate boxes may be behind one face frame.

Solid wood face frame with mortise and tenon joints at stiles and rails is attached to cabinet carcase with biscuits or rabbets.

Solid wood drawer fronts—figure should be end-matched across elevation.

Solid wood applied end panel—mortise-and-tenon joints at stiles and rails, panels may be solid wood or veneer in groove in stiles and rails. Attach applied ends to cabinet carcase with screws from inside box, attach to face frame with biscuits or rabbet. Joint should be mitered for first-class work.

Separate base, constructed of solid secondary wood or plywood, makes installation and leveling of cabinets much easier and keeps sheet-good cabinet parts away from floor, which may get wet.

Drawer boxes—solid hardwood with dovetail joints for first class-work. Ball-bearing full-extension slides will take wear and tear of everyday use better than wooden slides.

Doors have solid wood, mortise-and-tenon stiles and rails. Panels may be solid wood or veneered, let into a groove in stiles and rails. Doors should be inset and hung on butt hinges for first-class work.

WALL CABINET ANATOMY

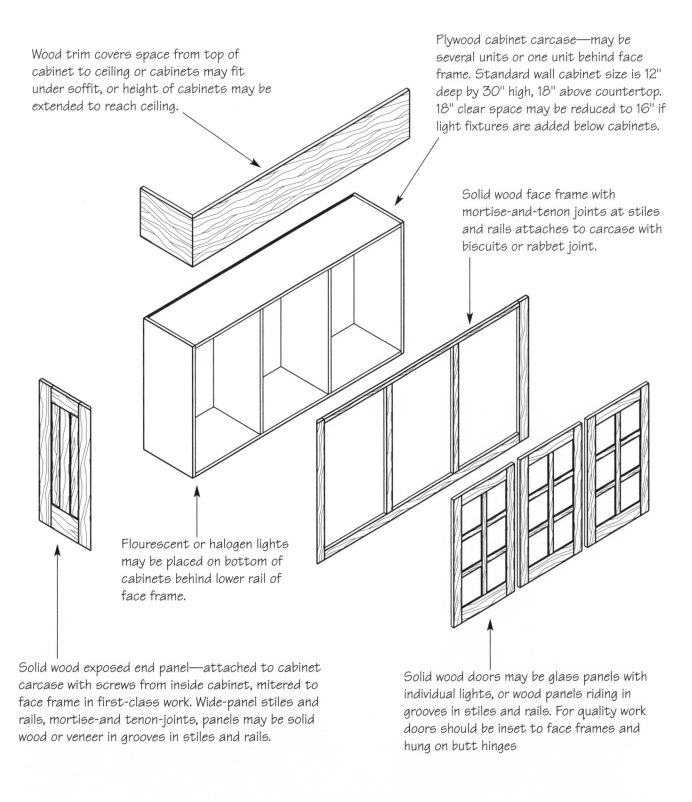

Wood trim covers space from top of cabinet to ceiling or cabinets may fit under soffit, or height of cabinets may be extended to reach ceiling.

Plywood cabinet carcase—may be several units or one unit behind face frame. Standard wall cabinet size is 12" deep by 30" high, 18" above countertop. 18" clear space may be reduced to 16" if light fixtures are added below cabinets.

Solid wood face frame with mortise-and-tenon joints at stiles and rails attaches to carcase with biscuits or rabbet joint.

Flourescent or halogen lights may be placed on bottom of cabinets behind lower rail of face frame.

Solid wood exposed end panel—attached to cabinet carcase with screws from inside cabinet, mitered to face frame in first-class work. Wide-panel stiles and rails, mortise-and-tenon-joints, panels may be solid wood or veneer in grooves in stiles and rails.

Solid wood doors may be glass panels with individual lights, or wood panels riding in grooves in stiles and rails. For quality work doors should be inset to face frames and hung on butt hinges

KITCHEN DRESSER
FROM CRAFTSMAN MAGAZINE HOUSE, OCTOBER 1909

Original kitchen dresser: elevation

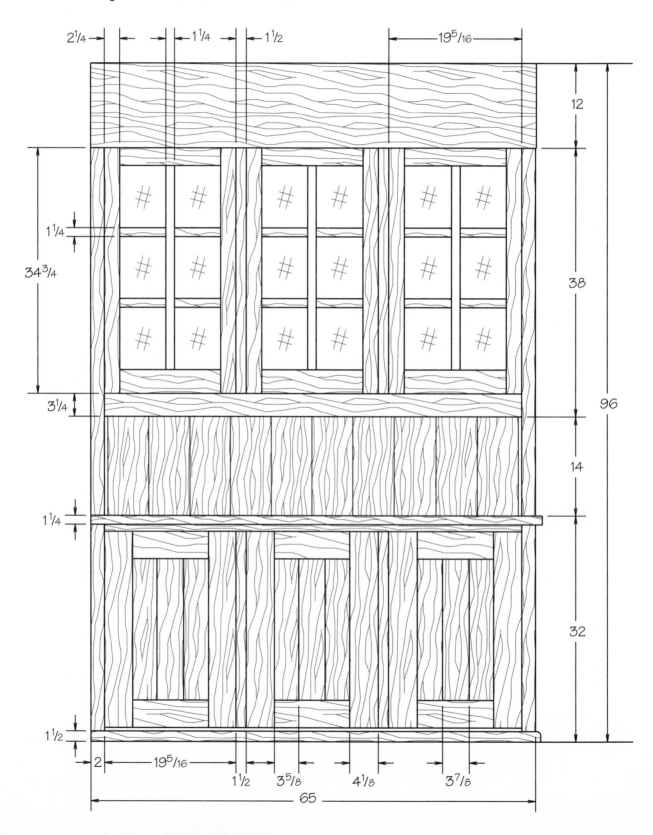

KITCHEN DRESSER (*continued*)
FROM CRAFTSMAN MAGAZINE HOUSE, OCTOBER 1909

Kitchen cabinets adapted to modern standard dimensions: elevation

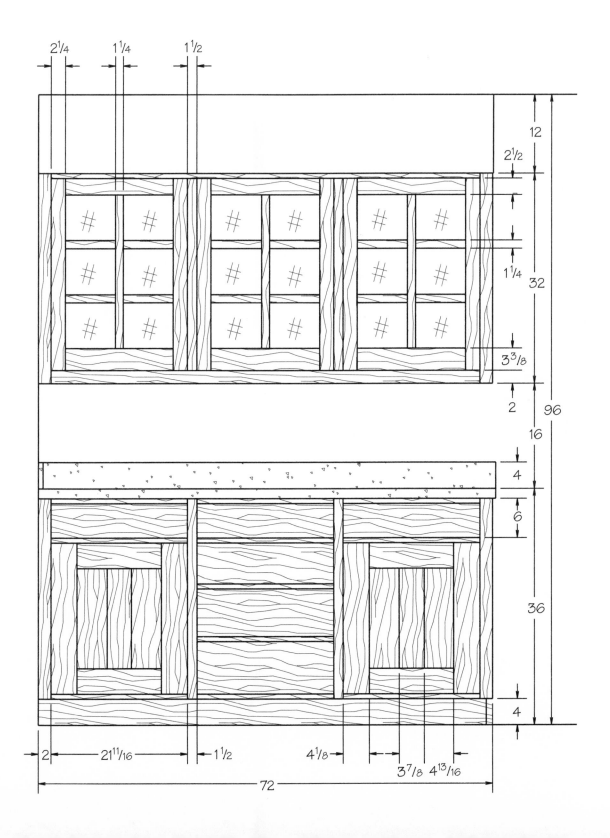

KITCHEN DRESSER (*continued*)
FROM CRAFTSMAN MAGAZINE HOUSE, OCTOBER 1909

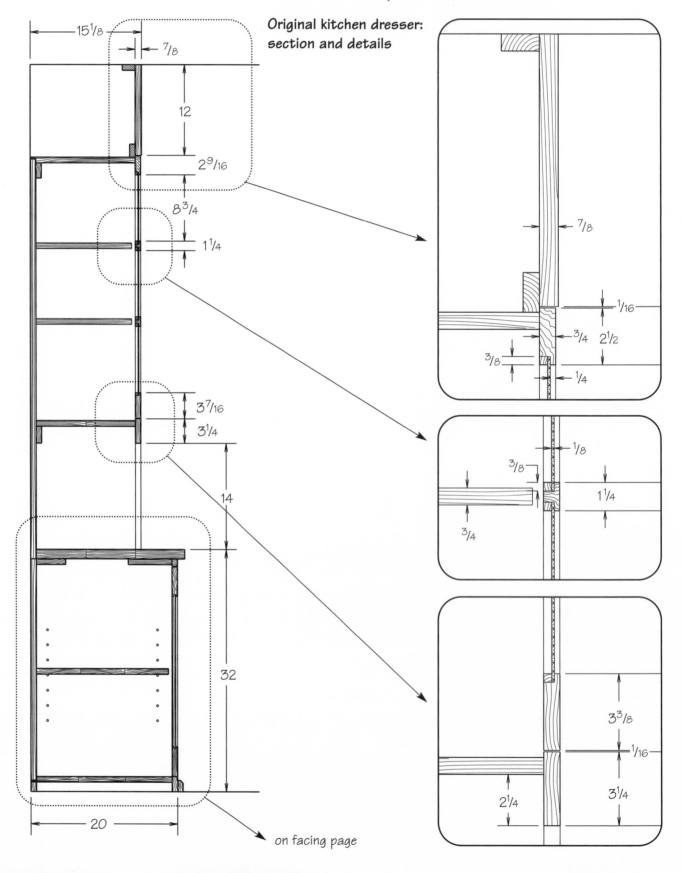

Original kitchen dresser:
section and details

on facing page

KITCHEN DRESSER (*continued*)
FROM CRAFTSMAN MAGAZINE HOUSE, OCTOBER 1909

Original kitchen dresser: section and details of lower cabinet

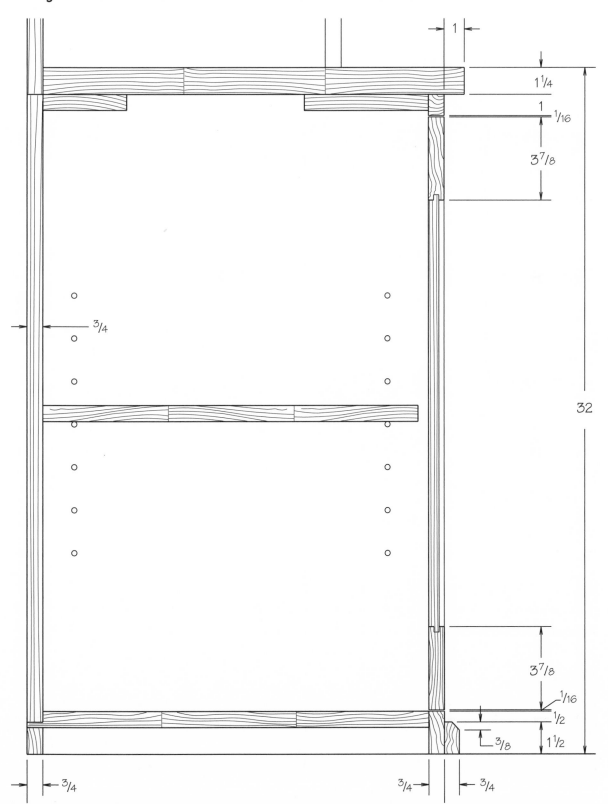

KITCHEN DRESSER (*continued*)
FROM CRAFTSMAN MAGAZINE HOUSE, OCTOBER 1909

Kitchen cabinets adapted to modern standard dimensions: section and upper cabinet details

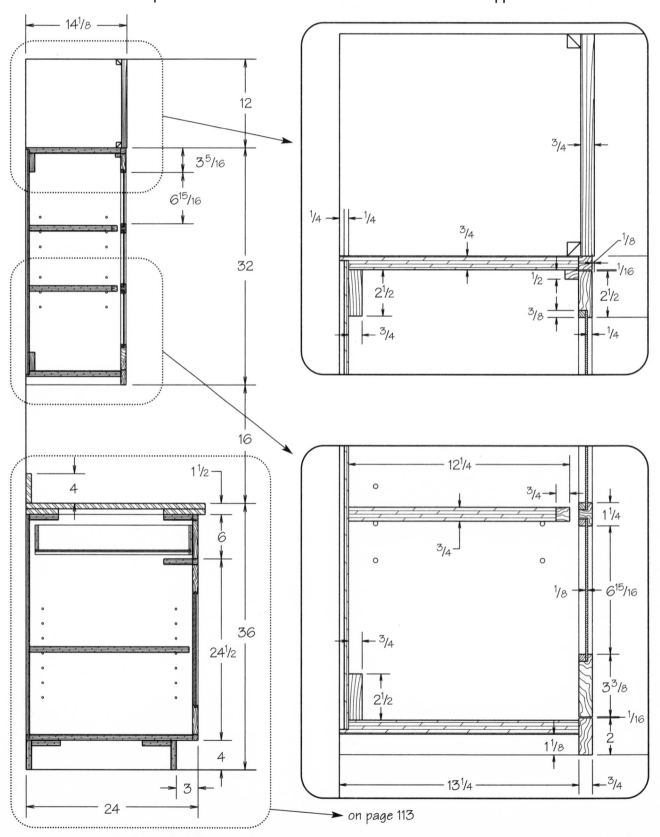

on page 113

KITCHEN DRESSER (*continued*)
FROM CRAFTSMAN MAGAZINE HOUSE, OCTOBER 1909

Kitchen cabinets adapted to modern standard dimensions: base cabinet details

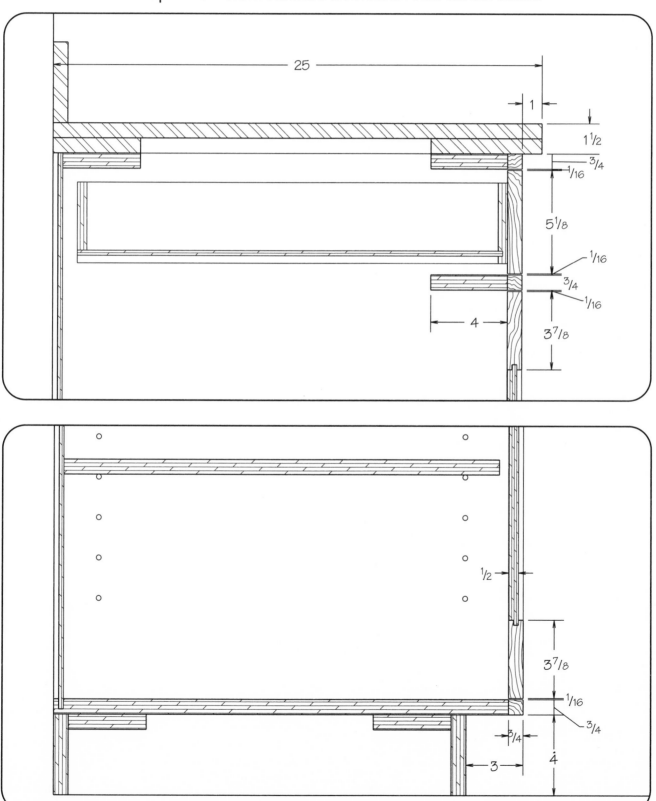

Original Kitchen Cabinet
from Craftsman House, # 14, 1912

Original Kitchen Cabinets: elevation

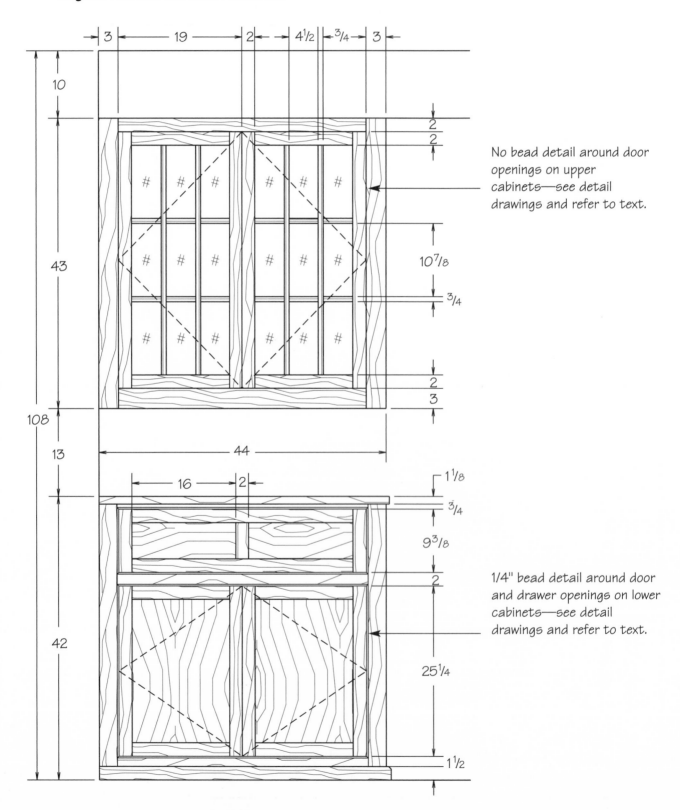

No bead detail around door openings on upper cabinets—see detail drawings and refer to text.

1/4" bead detail around door and drawer openings on lower cabinets—see detail drawings and refer to text.

ORIGINAL KITCHEN CABINET DETAILS FROM CRAFTSMAN HOUSE #14, 1912

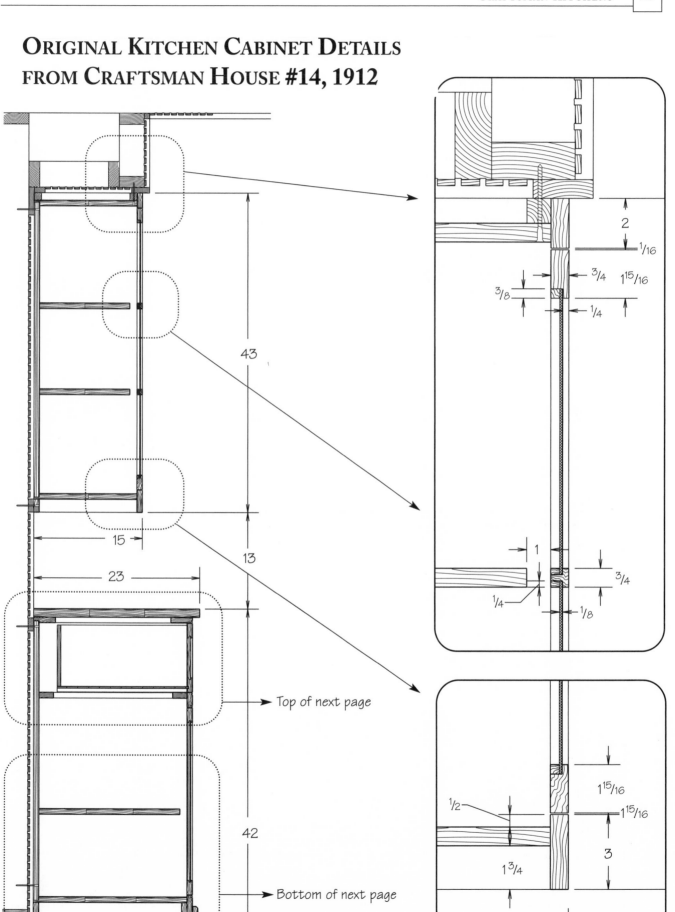

43

15

13

23

42

Top of next page

Bottom of next page

2

1/16

3/4   1 15/16

3/8

1/4

1

3/4

1/4

1/8

1 15/16

1/2

1 15/16

3

1 3/4

Original Kitchen Cabinet Details (*continued*) from Craftsman House #14, 1912

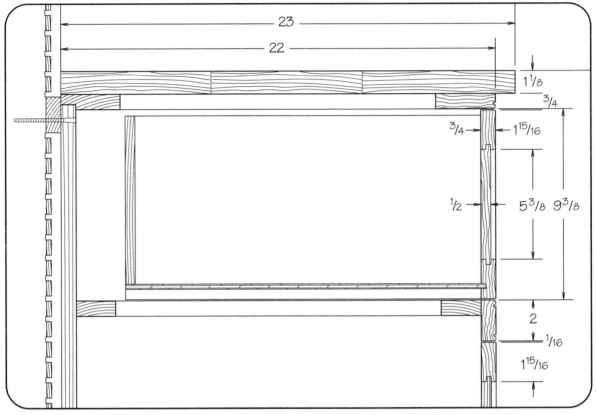

Base Cabinet Details

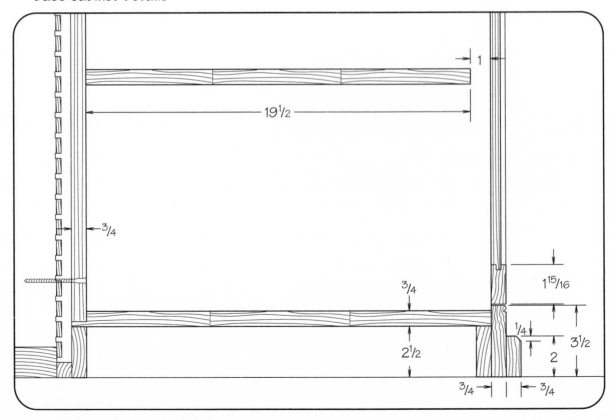

ORIGINAL KITCHEN CABINET DETAILS (*continued*) FROM CRAFTSMAN HOUSE #14, 1912

Full size molding profiles for kitchen cabinets

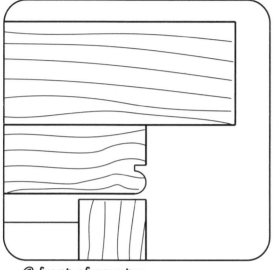

@ front of counter

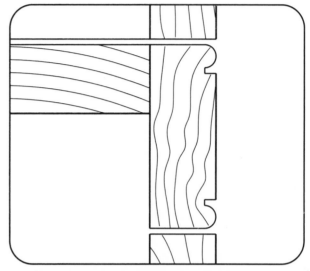

@ rail between drawer and doors

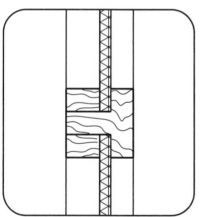

@ mullion and muntin, glass
doors for upper cabinets

@ base- lower cabinets

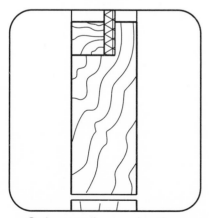

@ door stiles and rails
glass doors for upper cabinets

MODERN KITCHEN CABINET DETAILS FROM CRAFTSMAN HOUSE #14, 1912

In this adaptation of the original designs, the beaded detail between the face frames and the doors is carried to the upper cabinets as well as to the base cabinets. In planning each elevation, try to keep the upper cabinet doors as close to the same size as possible, so that the lights in the glass doors are consistent. The finished width of the doors should be between 12 inches and 18 inches. If there is no soffit, the upper cabinets can be extended in height to the ceiling, or to a band of trim 6 inches to 8 inches wide between the top of the cabinets and the ceiling. In an elevation with appliances and varying cabinet widths, wood paneled doors on the upper cabinets (next page) look better.

Elevation adapted to modern standard dimensions

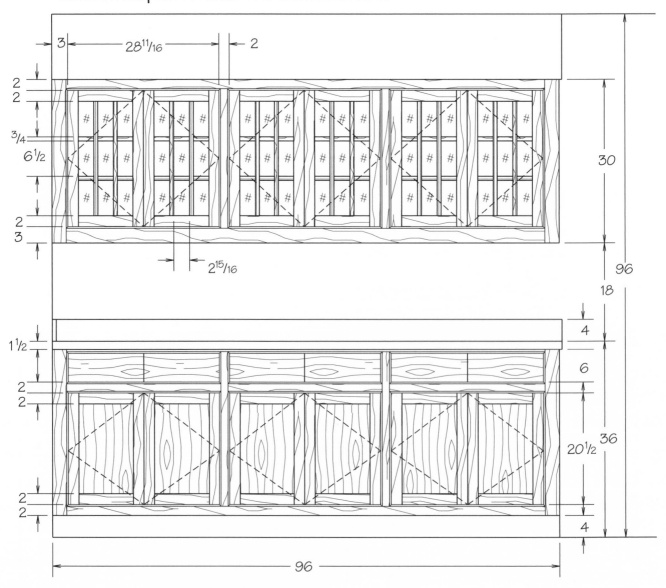

MODERN KITCHEN CABINET DETAILS (*continued*) FROM CRAFTSMAN HOUSE #14, 1912

The drawer fronts in this example are paneled as in the original, taller drawers, but I would choose the plain drawer fronts, as shown on the preceding page. The difference in height makes these appear awkward and too busy. Using one long board far all of the drawer fronts in an elevation allows for the grain to match across the cabinets, and adds an elegant touch to the casework. Exposed ends on both upper and lower cabinets can be a single wide panel, but framed panels similar to the doors will look better.

Alternate door faces and drawer fronts: elevation adapted to modern standard dimensions

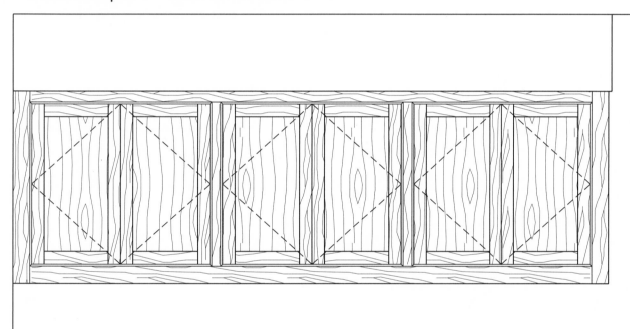

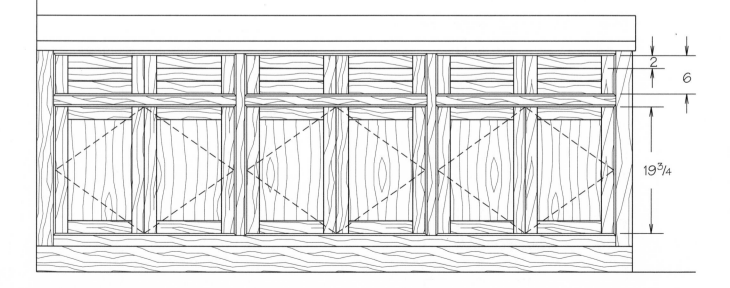

MODERN KITCHEN CABINET DETAILS (*continued*)
FROM CRAFTSMAN HOUSE #14, 1912

Kitchen cabinets adapted to modern standard dimensions

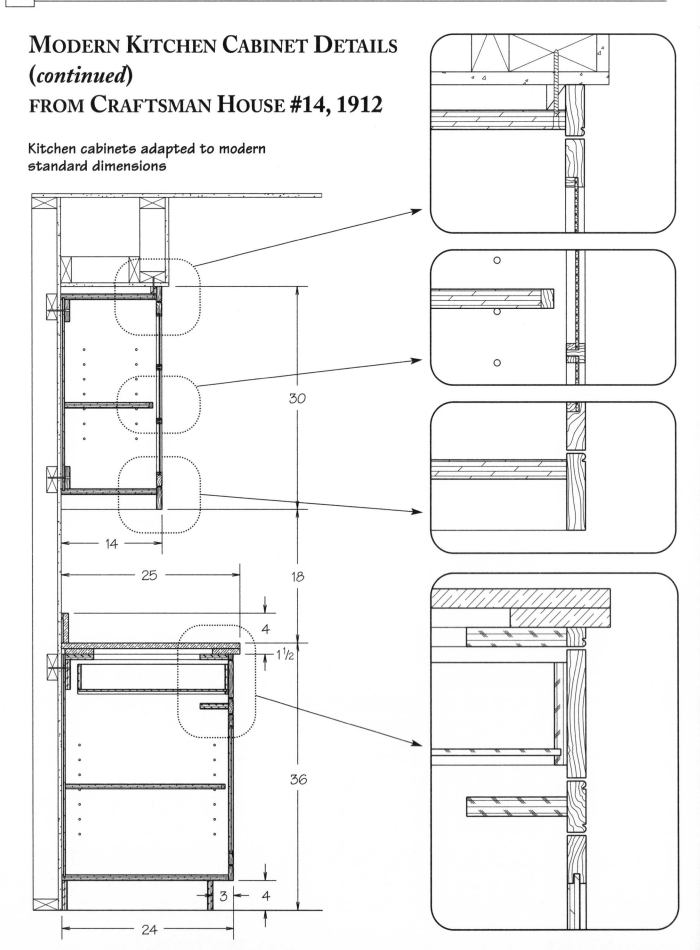

PASS-THROUGH CABINETS
FROM CRAFTSMAN MAGAZINE #108 FEBRUARY 1911

One of the differences between our present-day way of thinking and that of the early 1900s is the way we view cooking and preparing meals, and the relationship of these activities to the rest of the house. Today we tend to design our rooms so that the cook is a part of things—kitchens are often connected directly to family rooms and dining areas. Not so in 1910. At that time the idea was to separate the cooking process from the rest of the house. Many times in the pages of *The Craftsman* keeping odors from cooking away from the dining room and the rest of the house was mentioned as a desirable thing. There were also some sanitary considerations at the time. Dishes for dining were often kept, and washed, separately from dishes used only for cooking. One

of the ways to establish this was with a butler's pantry, a separate room between the kitchen and dining room. Often equipped with its own sink, the butler's pantry was a place to store dishes, glasses, and silverware away from the kitchen.

Another way to keep the kitchen and dining room distinct was with a pass-through cabinet. Appearing much like other kitchen dressers and cabinets, the pass-through was placed within the wall between kitchen and dining room, and featured a sliding door at counter height, allowing serving dishes to go from kitchen to dining room, and dirty dishes to make the return trip, without actually moving from one room to the other.

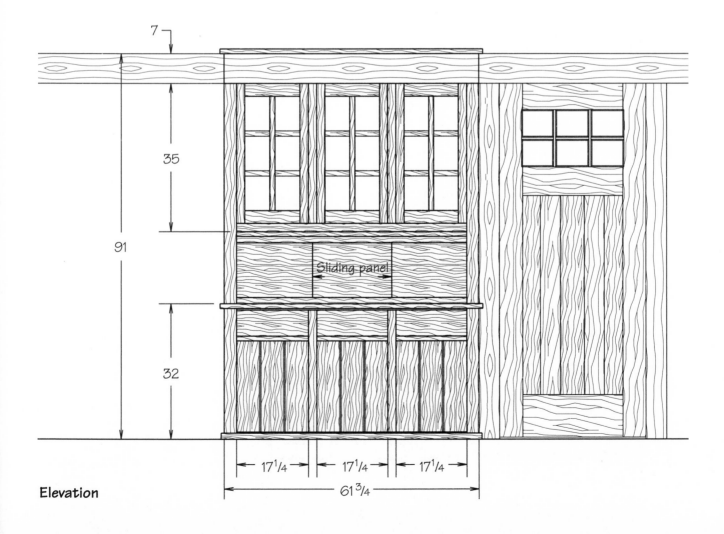

Elevation

PASS-THROUGH CABINETS (*continued*)
FROM CRAFTSMAN MAGAZINE HOUSE #108 FEBRUARY 1911

Pass-through cabinets appeared in *The Craftsman* in both the width shown on the previous page, and in this wider version. Of course, this basic design can be adapted to nearly any width, in units of two, three, or four doors. Generally, this form of cabinet would be between a kitchen and a dining room, or a butler's pantry and a dining room, but in one house it was shown between a kitchen and an enclosed porch listed on the drawings as an "outdoor dining room."

The doors are shown as being constructed of vee-groove planks, but for a more formal look they could also be paneled doors. The drawers above the doors are noted as sliding in both directions, allowing access from both rooms. Originally this would have been done with a simple wooden drawer slide. Accuride makes a ball-bearing slide that operates in both directions, a better choice if reproducing this design today.

The sliding panel was detailed in the original drawings as shown in the section drawings on the following pages. Modern hardware is available for this task in many versions, though the rails above and below the sliding door may need to be modified to accommodate your hardware.

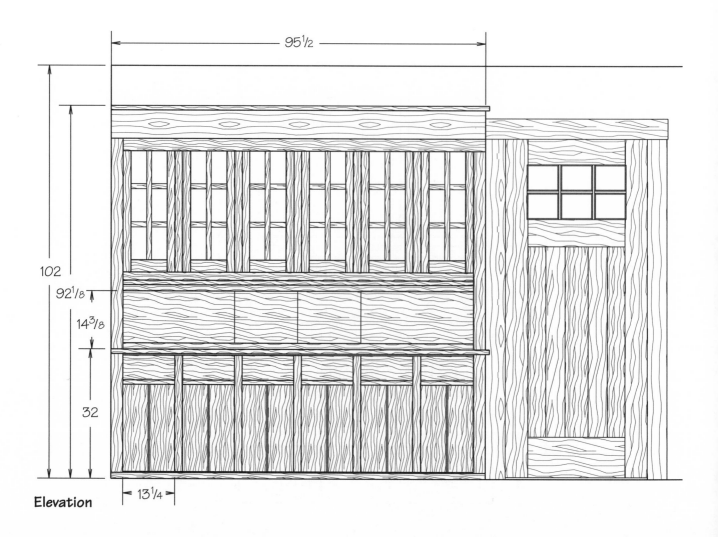

Elevation

PASS-THROUGH CABINET (*continued*)

This section drawing shows the pass-through cabinet centered in the wall between the two rooms. Note that the side of the cabinets return to the walls. On the door side, the casing can be set to meet the cabinet side, but on the opposite side of the cabinet, the finished cabinet side will come tight against the edge of the plaster. The edge of the opening in the wall must be perfectly straight and plumb for this intersection to look acceptable after installation. The opening in the wall for the cabinet should be made a bit larger than the cabinet itself. The cabinet can then be slid in to the opening from one side, and then slid tight to the plaster before anchoring it to the walls, floor, and ceiling. The opening should also be oversized slightly in height, to make it easier to slide the cabinet into place.

I would construct this unit in two pieces, with the countertop screwed from below into the sides of the upper portion. The bottom portion will go in the opening first, and should be leveled perfectly in both width and depth before installing the upper portion.

The vee-groove planked door is shown in plan section below. The individual planks should be sized to equal width, to span the door opening. The ledger across the back should be let in a groove, or dovetailed into the back of the planks. If set in a groove, the ledger should be held in place with screws in oversized holes to allow for wood movement.

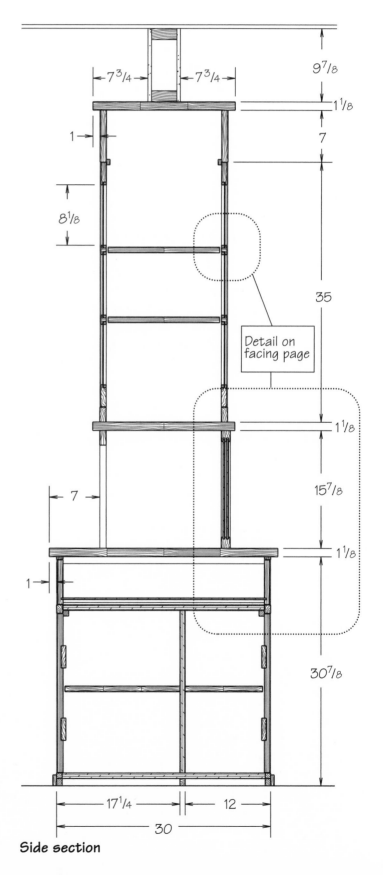

Detail on facing page

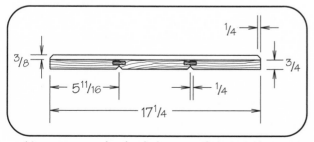

Vee-groove planked doors: plan section

Side section

Pass-Through Cabinet (*continued*)
Sliding Doors

The section at right details the sliding panels. The original drawings showed doors only on the dining room side, but it might be desirable to include another set of sliding doors on the kitchen side. The panel simply slides in grooves in the top and bottom rails. Note that the grooves in the top rail are deeper than those in the bottom rail to permit the panels to enter. Both grooves should also be slightly wider than the panels, and waxed to make the doors easy to slide.

The sliding panels are installed by placing the top edge of the door in the top groove, and raising it until it clears the bottom rail. The door is then dropped into the bottom groove. While this detail is authentic, it can be problematic as the wood panels expand and contract with the change of seasons. These problems can be avoided by using veneered plywood panels and/or modern hardware.

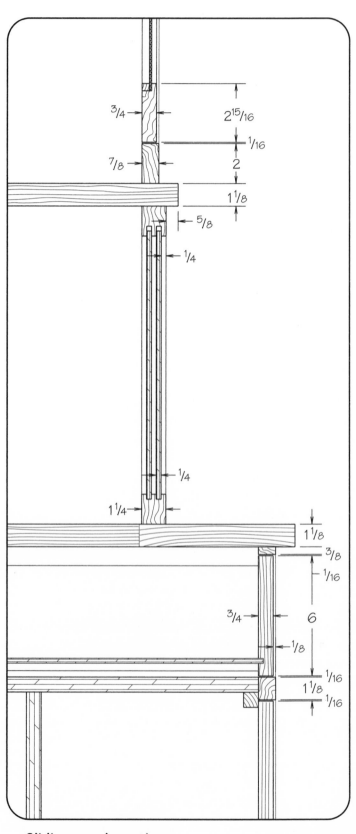

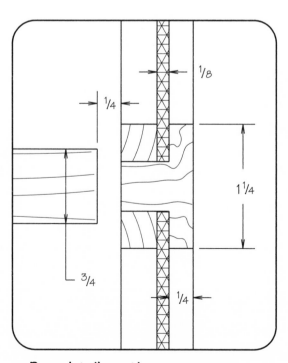

Door detail: section

Sliding panel: section

FRAMELESS CABINETS IN THE CRAFTMAN STYLE: INSET DOORS

European or frameless cabinets are common today, and the following pages show two different approaches to fabrication. In European cabinetry, the face frame is eliminated as a structural element, and the exposed edges of the plywood boxes are edged with veneer or solid wood. I prefer solid-wood edging because it is more durable than veneer, and it adds stiffness. This edge, nominally 3/4 inch by 3/4 inch and normally applied before assembly, can be glued to the front edges of the plywood with simple butt joints.

The example on this page shows the doors and drawer fronts as being inset, inside the edges of the case, and in the same plane as the front edges of the case. The vertical trim pieces at the finished ends, and where two cabinets intersect,

is twice the thickness of the cabinet side. This looks more like the original cabinets and covers the joints between adjacent cabinets and the finished ends. The exploded drawing on page 133 shows how the cabinets are constructed, and how they fit together on installation. I use biscuits to align these field joints, pre-assembling an elevation of cabinets in the shop on a separate base. With inset doors and drawer fronts both the openings and the doors and fronts must be perfectly square and carefully sized. The gaps between the edges of the doors and the cabinets can range from 1/16 inch to 1/8 inch, and should be consistent throughout. The hinges shown will open to 125°, but their mounting plates intrude quite a bit on the interior of the cabinet. Wider-opening hinges (165° to 175°) take even more space.

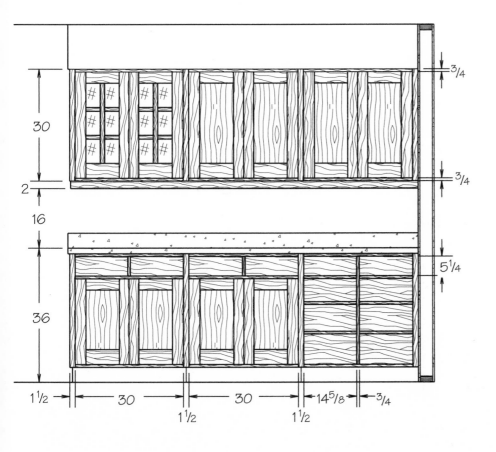

Inset doors: front elevation

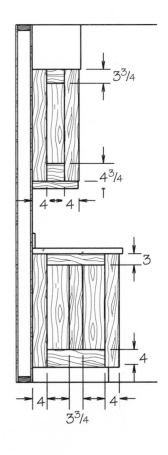

End elevation

FRAMELESS CABINETS: INSET DOORS (*continued*)

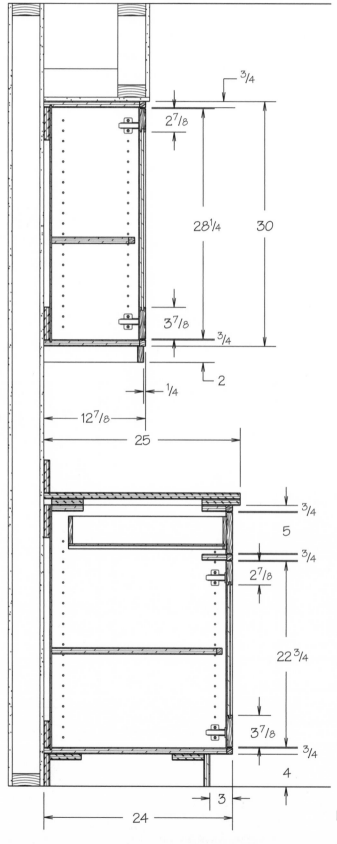

Inset doors: side section

This section view shows construction details for cabinets with inset doors. There are many variations on this type of construction. The backs of both the upper and lower cabinets shown are 1/4-inch thick material set in a groove in the sides and bottoms, with nailers attached on the outside of the back. This makes for a neat appearance inside the cabinet, but it does eat up some interior space. This is not a problem on lower cabinets, but it may be unacceptable for the upper cabinets. When I use this construction, I like to deviate from the standard depth of 12 inches, and make the upper cabinets 14 inches deep.

When the cabinet parts are rabetted for the back, the nailers can be placed inside the cabinet. Some people prefer to use 1/2 inch thick material for the back and eliminate the nailers, but this is not really strong enough to support the weight of the cabinet safely.

The upper cabinets are shown with a 2-inch rail across the bottom, for the purpose of concealing lights on the bottoms of the cabinets. This is shown as being added to the standard 30-inch height of the cabinets, reducing the distance between the top of the counter and the bottom of the cabinet to 16 inches. If the standard distance of 18 inches is needed for appliances, the entire cabinet and soffit can simply be 2 inches higher. If the soffit is not used, the upper cabinets can be increased in height right up to the ceiling.

FRAMELESS UPPER CABINETS:
INSET DOORS AND DRAWER FRONTS

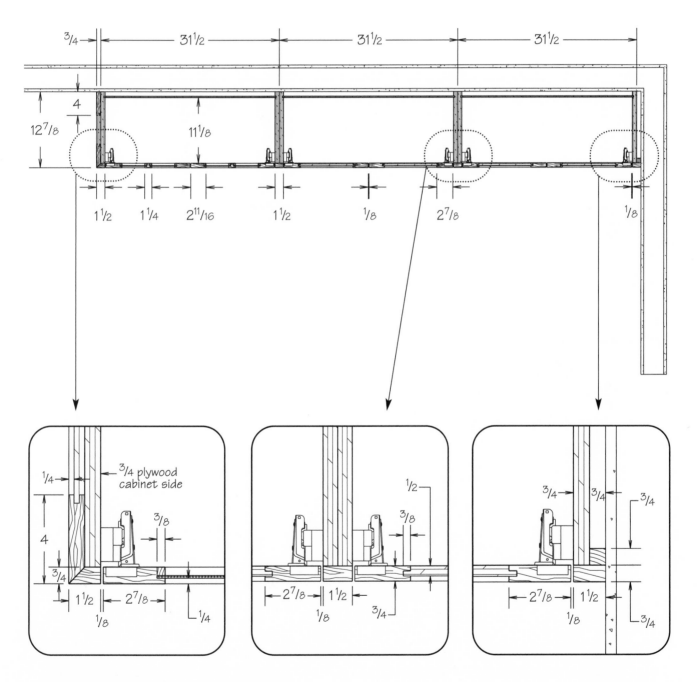

Upper cabinet details: plan section

FRAMELESS BASE CABINETS:
INSET DOORS AND DRAWER FRONTS

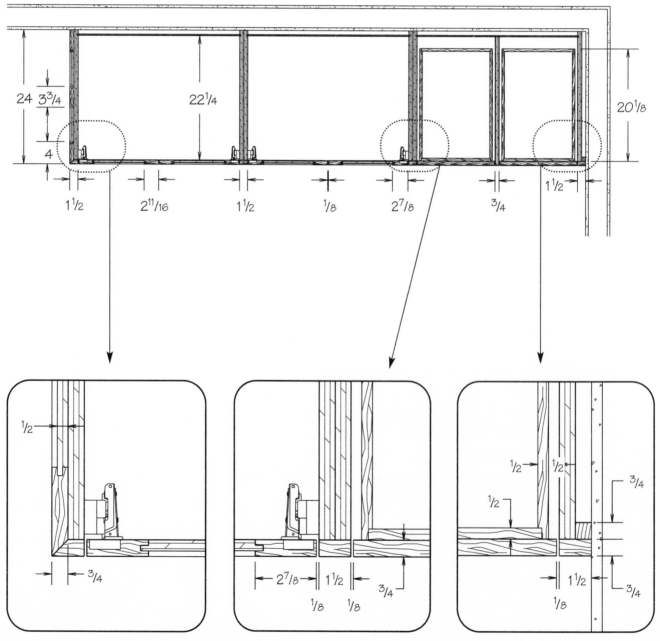

Base cabinet details: plan section

FRAMELESS CABINETS: OVERLAY DOORS

Another way to deal with the doors and drawer fronts of European cabinets is to have them overlay the front edges of the boxes, as shown in this elevation. I would still extend the finished ends past the doors, so that the edge of the door isn't seen from the end. The end panels can be attached to the cabinets with screws from the inside of the cabinet. At the opposite end of the elevation, a filler strip between the cabinet and the wall is shown in the detail on page 132. This strip can be scribed to the wall, and then attached to the cabinet in the same way that the finished side is attached. Where the top of the upper cabinet meets the lower edge of the soffit, a filler strip may also be used, or a simple crown or

cornice molding may be applied. The appearance of this option is not as true to the period as the others presented, but it does simplify construction and installation.

With the doors overlaying the cabinet sides, the concealed hinges don't intrude quite so much into the cabinet interior, but this still is an issue, particularly with wide-opening 165°-175° hinges. The doors and drawer fronts must be made precisely for the finished appearance to be acceptable. Since the edges of the cabinets are all behind the doors and drawer fronts, they are not as susceptible to wear as with inset doors, making veneer acceptable for the cabinet edges.

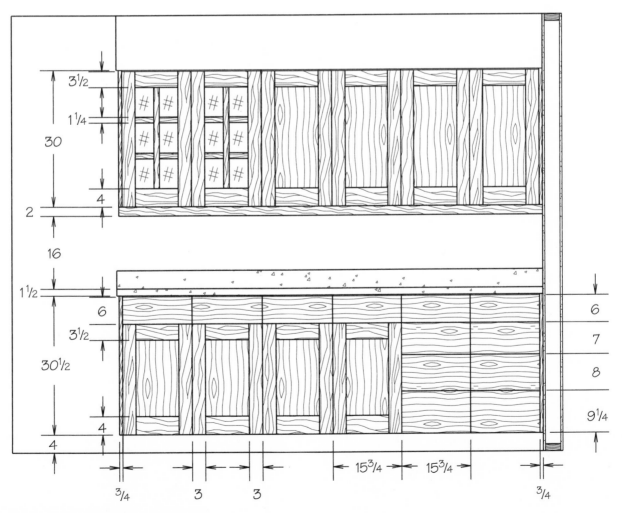

Overlay doors: front elevation

Frameless Cabinets: Overlay Doors (*continued*)

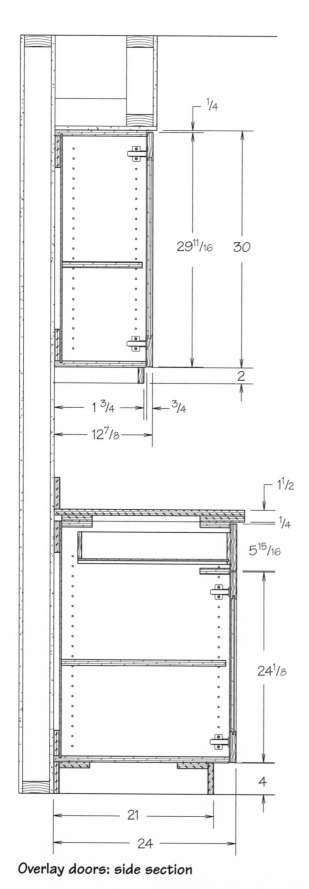

Overlay doors: side section

The biggest difference between the inset door cabinets and the overlay door cabinets is in the depth of the cabinets, with the overlay door cabinets being smaller than the inset. The inset door cabinets should finish at 24 inches deep. Overlay door cabinets are usually made at $23\frac{1}{8}$ inches, so that when completed, the face of the door is 24 inches from the back of the cabinet. This is assuming a $\frac{3}{4}$ inch thick door, with the hinges mounted to leave a $\frac{1}{8}$ inch gap between the front of the cabinet and the back of the door.

The holes for the shelf pins are shown as 5mm in diameter, on 32mm centers, which is standard for frameless cabinet construction. This allows one set of bored holes to be used for shelf support pins, hinges, and drawer slides. While this is desirable when boring equipment is available, it is probably better for the home cabinetmaker to deal with the shelf pins and hardware as separate entities, without boring all the holes the 32mm system would dictate. 5mm shelf pins seem a bit small to me, I would use $\frac{1}{4}$ inch diameter holes, and only drill six or seven on $1\frac{1}{4}$ inch or $1\frac{1}{2}$ inch centers measured from the center of the shelf space. Jigs are available to locate the holes for mounting the hinge plates, or they can be quickly made to locate the holes in from the cabinet edge, up from the bottom, and down from the top.

FRAMELESS UPPER CABINETS:
OVERLAY DOORS AND DRAWER FRONTS

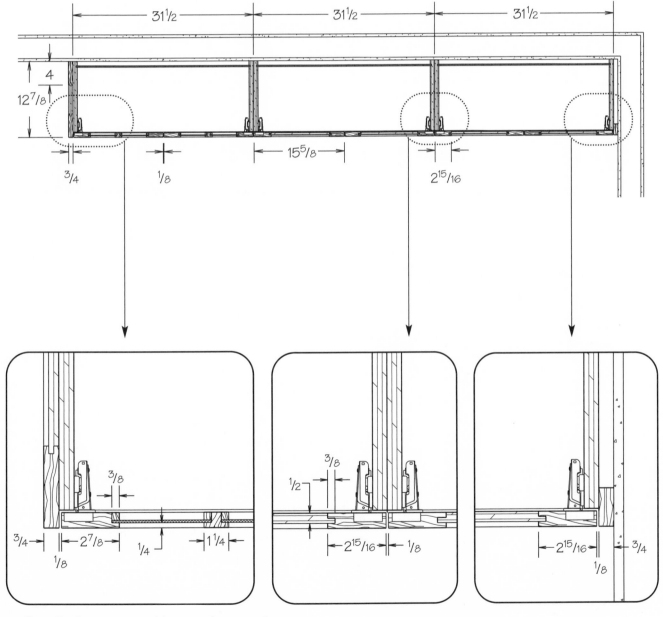

Details for upper cabinets: plan section

Frameless Base Cabinets:
Overlay Doors and Drawer Fronts

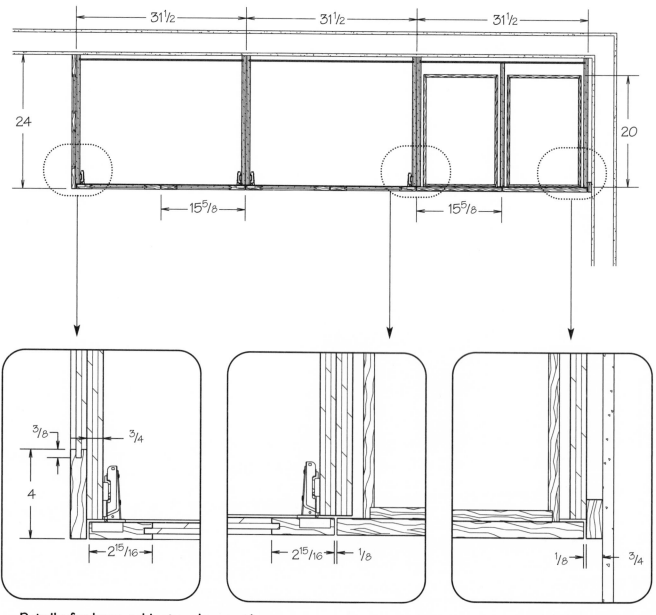

Details for base cabinets: plan section

FRAMELESS CABINETS: BASE INSTALLATION

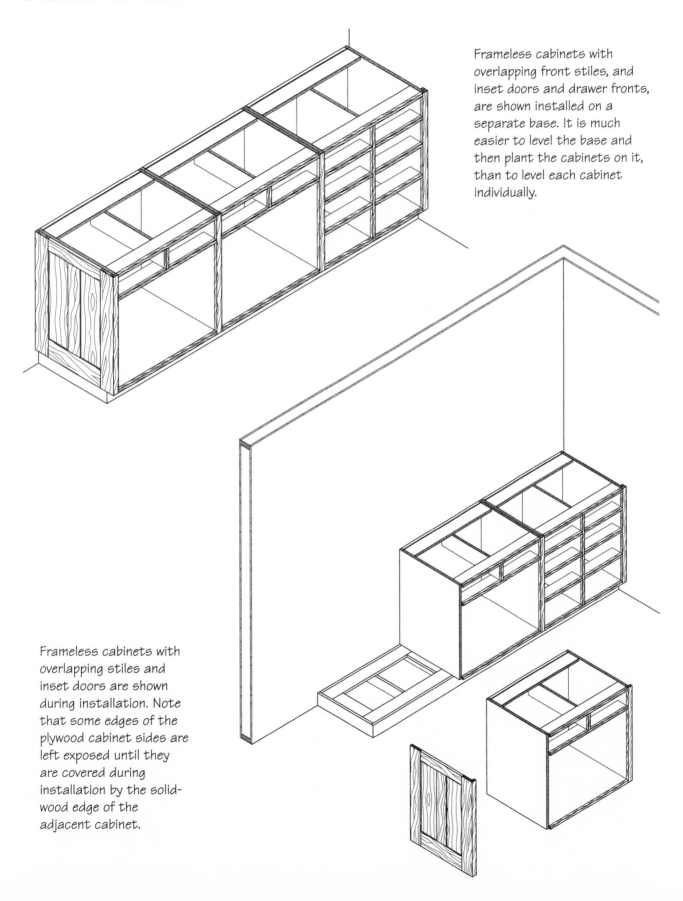

Frameless cabinets with overlapping front stiles, and inset doors and drawer fronts, are shown installed on a separate base. It is much easier to level the base and then plant the cabinets on it, than to level each cabinet individually.

Frameless cabinets with overlapping stiles and inset doors are shown during installation. Note that some edges of the plywood cabinet sides are left exposed until they are covered during installation by the solid-wood edge of the adjacent cabinet.

CABINET VARIATIONS

Here are some examples of different door and finished end panels that would be in keeping with the Craftsman style. These are shown as upper cabinets, but they can easily be adapted to lowers.

The two drawings at right show typical frame-and-panel construction. The panels can be of solid wood or veneered plywood. Plywood panels can be either $1/4$ inch or $1/2$ inch thick, but because of the poor quality and inconsistent thickness of $1/4$-inch plywood, I would use $1/2$ inch, and mill a tongue on the edge.

The drawing at lower left shows the finished end and doors constructed of solid tongue-and-groove planks. I would construct the case from plywood, then screw the boards for the end panels to the side of the cabinet from the inside. These end boards should not be glued to the plywood cabinet sides, and the holes for the screws should be elongated to allow for wood movement.

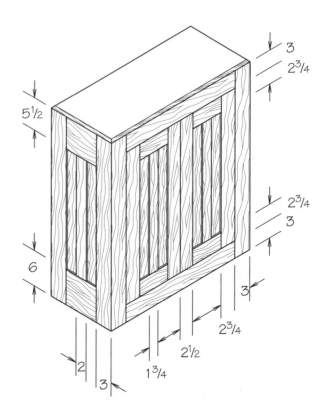

Frame with solid-wood panels

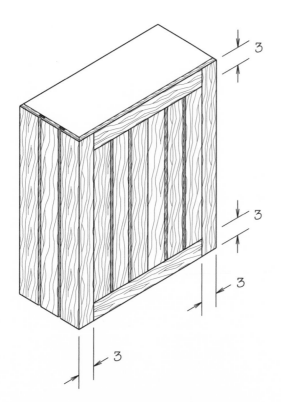

Solid-wood tongue-and-groove doors

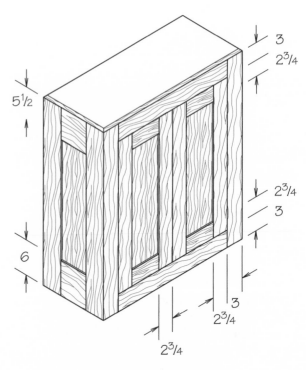

Frame with plywood panels

CABINET VARIATIONS (*continued*): GLASS DOORS

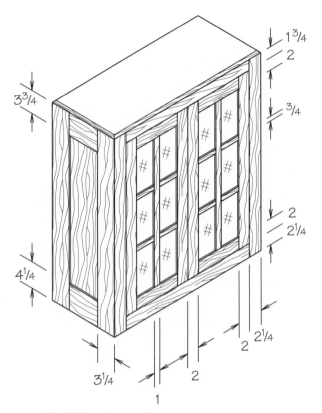

Six-light glass door

Here are two common types of upper cabinets with glass doors. Details for assembling the doors and glass are similar to the construction used in free-standing bookcases and china cabinets. Traditionally, each light would be an individual piece of glass, the muntins and mullions would be half-lapped to one another and tenoned into the stiles and rails. It is also possible to assemble the muntins and mullions from $1/4$ inch thick material, fasten that as a unit to the stiles and rails, and back it with a single piece of glass. I would go with tradition, because the thickness of the material doesn't really allow for adequate joinery, and the traditional door is much stronger.

The corbel shown below was often used at the end of an elevation of upper cabinets, particularly where the cabinets break for a sink or a window. A $3/4$ inch wide by $3/4$ inch deep groove can be run in the back edge of the corbel, allowing it to be fastened to the wall by means of a cleat secured at the proper place on the wall. This technique allows the corbel to be invisibly mounted with construction adhesive and pins through the sides into the cleat.

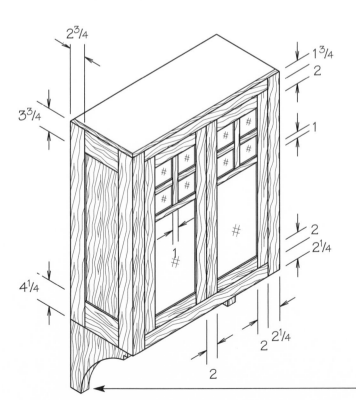

Five-light glass door

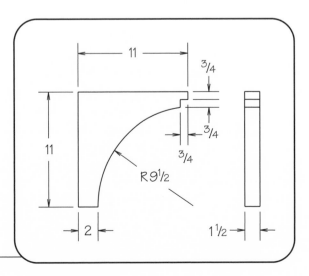

Corbel detail

KITCHEN NOOK

If space allows, every house should have a nook—a delightful little space off the kitchen for breakfast or lunch, a place for the kids to do homework while dinner is being prepared, the ideal spot for coffee and conversation. This illustration from *The Craftsman* is a typical example. The actual dimensions will vary, of course, depending on the available space. The drawings on the following pages give some parameters.

The tabletop should be a smooth surface, either solid-wood planks glued together, or edged plywood. If the top is glued up, the individual boards may be held together with a dovetailed cleat below the surface, as shown in detail three on page 138, or they may be splined together, or simply butt-joined. The table is fastened to the wall by screws through the cleat shown below the top. The holes for the screws at the outer ends of the cleats should actually be slots, if the top is solid wood, to allow for seasonal movement. Do the same at the opposite end, where the support is fastened to the top in a similar manner.

The wainscot helps to define the space and adds coziness. Windows are always nice to include in a nook, adding light and fresh air. In the original house where this example is from, the window does not actually lead to the outside, but to a closet in an adjacent bedroom. Details for the casement window will be found on page 96.

KITCHEN NOOK (*continued*)

The wainscot is made of vee-grooved boards; more details on fabricating, laying out, and installing the wainscot may be found in the section on paneling and wall treatments, page 55. Nooks often were entirely painted, but could also receive a clear finish. A decorative groove might also be added to the top surface of the cap molding at the top of the wainscot.

The tabletop and benches should be finished on all surfaces, and it is much easier to do this before they are installed. The paneling and trim should also be finished before the table and benches are attached to the walls. Since they are fastened through the cleats from below, the fasteners will all be hidden, and the finish won't need to be touched up after installation.

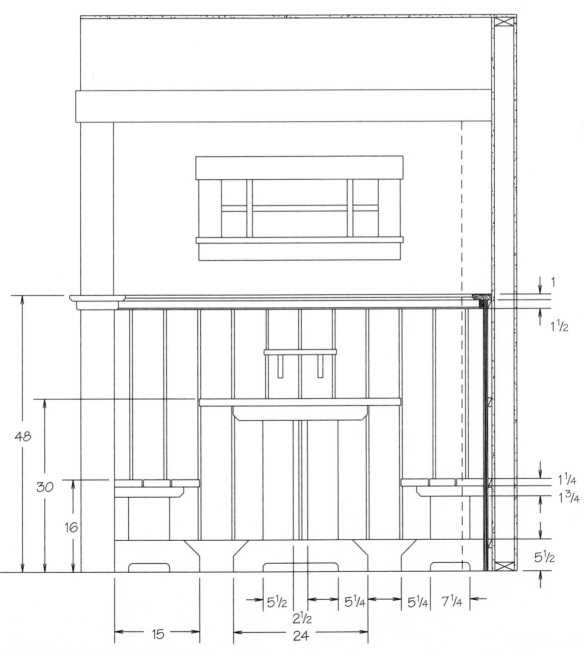

Kitchen nook: elevation

KITCHEN NOOK (*continued*)

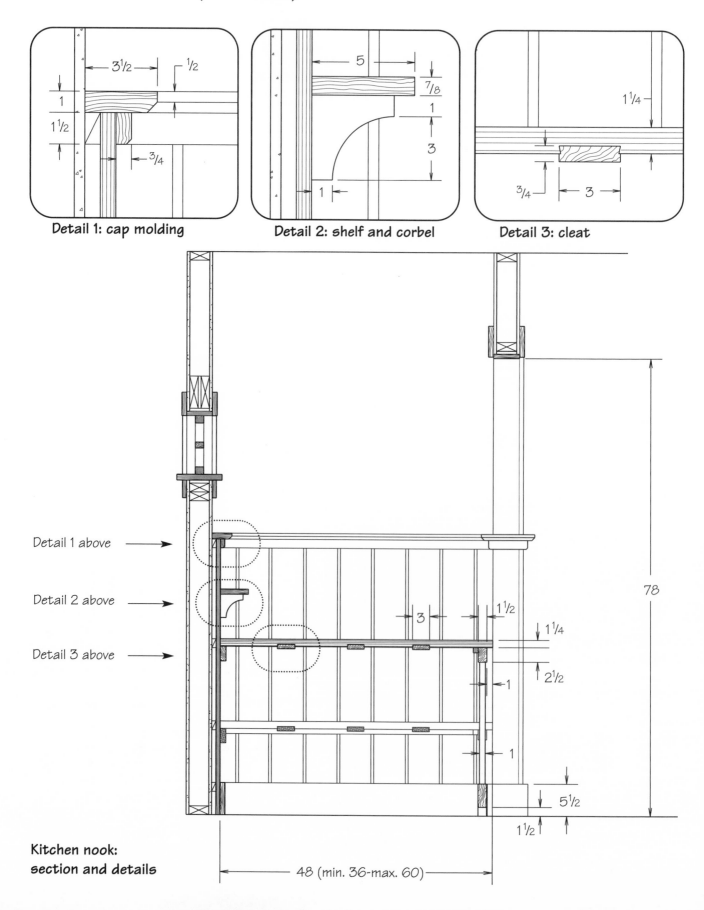

Detail 1: cap molding

Detail 2: shelf and corbel

Detail 3: cleat

Detail 1 above →

Detail 2 above →

Detail 3 above →

**Kitchen nook:
section and details**

KITCHEN NOOK (*continued*)

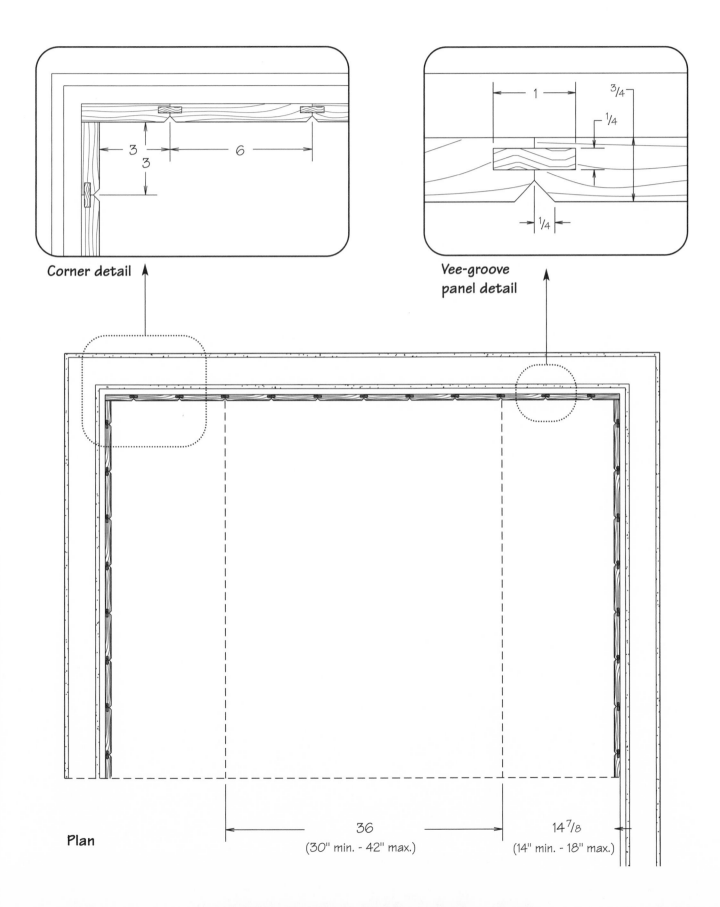

Corner detail

Vee-groove
panel detail

Plan

36
(30" min. - 42" max.)

14 7/8
(14" min. - 18" max.)

BUILT-IN CABINETS

In October 1909, *The Craftsman* published an article titled "Country Houses for All Year Use" with the illustration shown above of one end of the living room. The living room was centrally located in the house, and covered the entire depth of the structure from front to back. It is perhaps the best example of a Craftsman room, in that it not only displays all the architectural and design elements, but also evokes the positive feelings that Stickley tried to infuse in his designs. As the magazine article put it, "The object has been to bring as much of the outdoor feeling as possible into the house, and to this end especial attention has been given to the windows, of which there are a great many."

The opposite end of this room, at the front of the house featured a long window seat between two built in bookcases. This elevation was also largely of glass, with casement windows above the bookcases and a large window above the seat. One of the long walls contained a massive stone fireplace at its center, and the vertical vee-groove paneling, stopping short of the ceiling, was carried throughout the room. Along with the abundance of wood in this room comes an abundance of light, via the French doors and many windows.

One of Gustav Stickley's true gifts, along with his impeccable sense of proportion, was his ability to define a space while keeping it as an essential part of the whole design. This dining area is as much a part of the pergola-covered porch and garden on the other side of the French doors, as it is an integral part of the room on this side. The built-in casework provides continuity between the furniture and the walls, while the wood paneling and built-in furniture tie the whole design together.

CHINA CABINET

As can be seen from this elevation, symmetry and order are key elements in the success of this design. Glass is present everywhere, yet it is discretely organized by the surrounding wood. The wood is present on nearly every surface of the room, but it does not become overwhelming due to the abundance of light streaming through the windows. And the entire design works to make the house a part of its surroundings. The original design was one of the first houses actually constructed by Stickley, and was located on a hillside in what was then rural New Jersey.

The vertical-plank paneling runs around the perimeter of the room, and is used as the back of the cabinets, a common method of the time. The two mirror-image cabinets can be completely fabricated in the workshop, and installed as units. All of the finishing should be left until the cabinets are in place, and care should be taken that all of the material is similar in figure and color.

A close-up elevation of one of the cabinets is shown on the next page, and that, along with sections on the following pages, give the relevant details for construction. The doors, drawer fronts, and frame elements should all be made of solid wood, but it makes sense to use veneered plywood for the shelves and partitions.

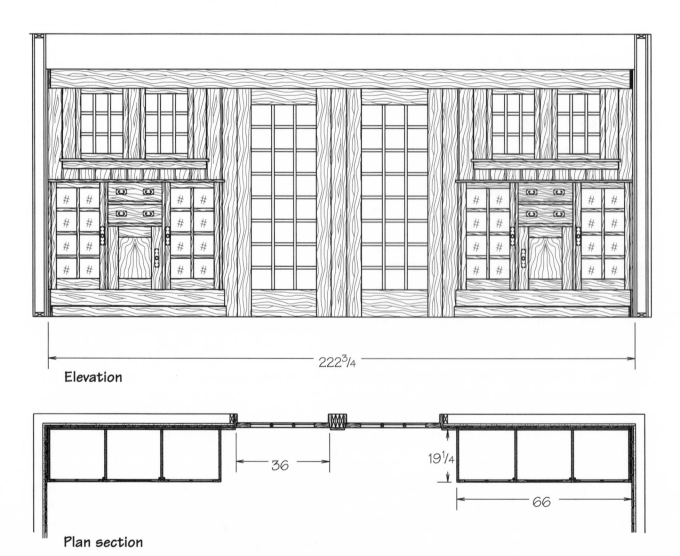

Elevation

222³/₄

Plan section

36   19¹/₄   66

CHINA CABINET (*continued*)

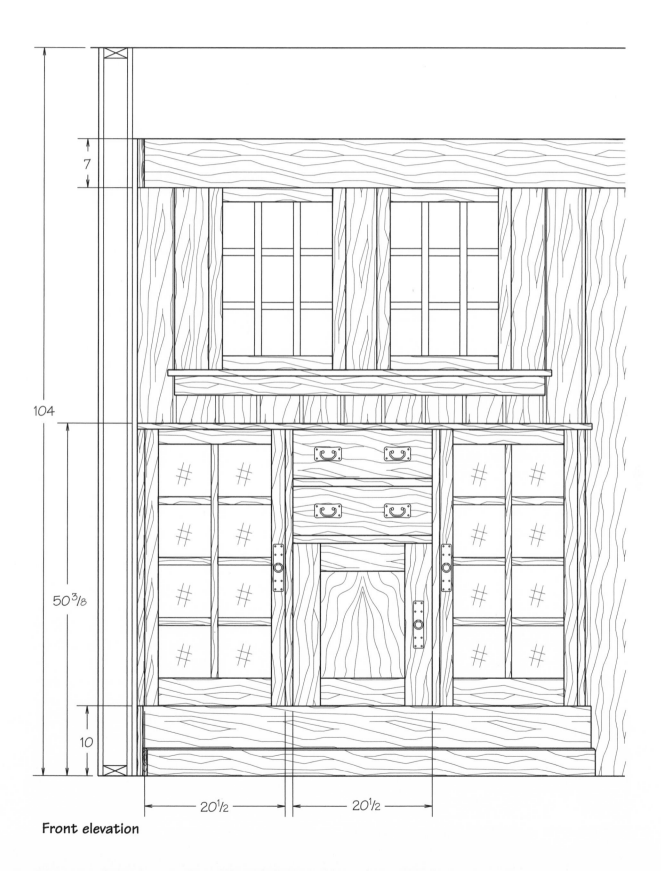

Front elevation

CHINA CABINET *Continued)*

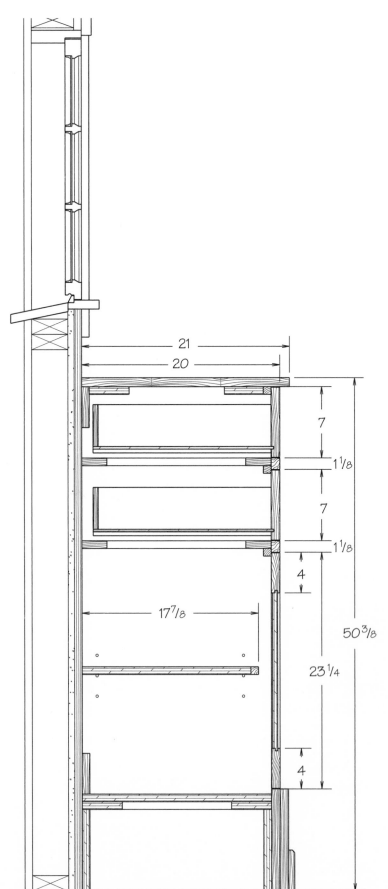

Middle unit: side section through glass doors

This section view is of the middle of the cabinet, with the two drawers and the wood paneled door. Since the room paneling forms the back of the cabinet, stout nailers are placed between the uprights of the cabinets to provide a firm means of attaching the cabinet to the wall. Rails are also placed horizontally at the front and back at the top of the cabinet, so that the cabinet top may be fastened to the cabinet as the last step, after the carcass has been secured to the wall. A separate base is also shown, which should be leveled and fastened to the floor and wall before the cabinet is put in to place. Web frames are shown below each drawer, and the drawers may be placed on modern ball bearing slides, or the sides of the drawers may be extended to ride on the web frames, with some wooden runners attached to keep the drawers aligned.

The door panel may be veneered plywood as shown, or may be fabricated from solid wood. In either case, the wood for these panels should be selected carefully for grain and figure, as they will become a focal point for these cabinets. The dimensions in this drawing show the sizes of the openings for the doors and drawers, the actual parts will need to be fit to the openings, with the desired gaps. I prefer seeing these gaps as small and consistent as possible, no more than $1/16$ inch. Many makers prefer larger gaps, especially if the cabinet is made during a dry season. Even if the gaps are made larger, they should be of a consistent size all the way around the perimeter.

CHINA CABINET (*continued*)

The outer units of the cabinets each have a single glass paned door, as shown here and in an exploded view on page 146. Doors such as this are an exercise in precision and fussiness, and it is extremely important that wood used be at equilibrium with its environment before fabrication begins. If the small pieces need to be milled from larger stock, and the moisture content is not known, it would be a good idea to mill the parts $\frac{1}{4}$ inch to $\frac{1}{2}$ inch over-size, and to wait a week or two before reducing these parts to their finished size and fabricating the joints. The addition of the glass will make the doors heavy, so each and every joint must be made with this in mind. The glass is held in place with thin strips of wood, mitered at the corners and secured with brads driven carefully into the doorframes. Resist the temptation to make the mullions and muntins as a thin applied frame over a single large sheet of glass. In this case, it will prove to be more time consuming to do shoddy work, and the results will be disappointing. The quality of this design deserves to be rendered with quality workmanship.

The shelves are shown in line with the mullions on the doors, but they are also shown as being adjustable. The shelves could be made fixed at these points, but that wouldn't leave enough room for items such as stemware. The third shelf will probably not be used in most situations.

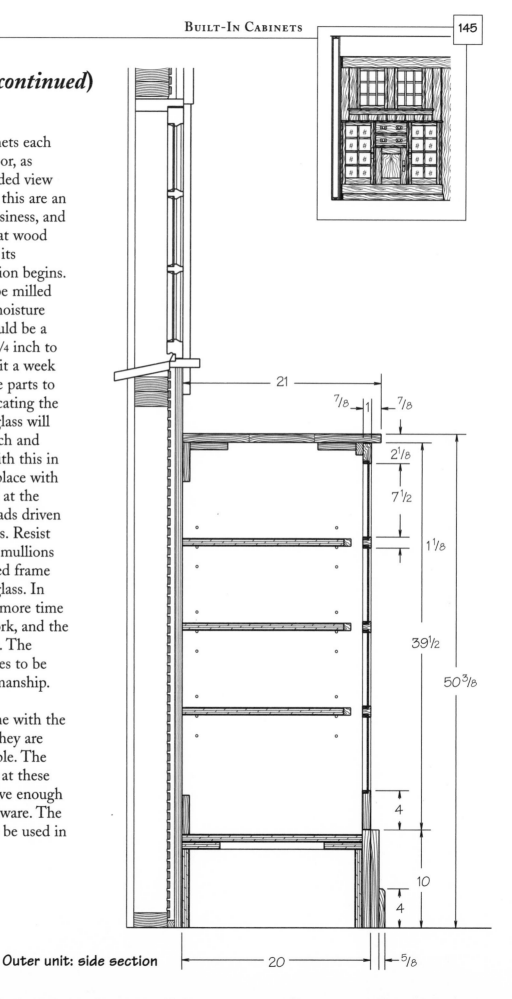

Outer unit: side section

CHINA CABINET (*continued*)

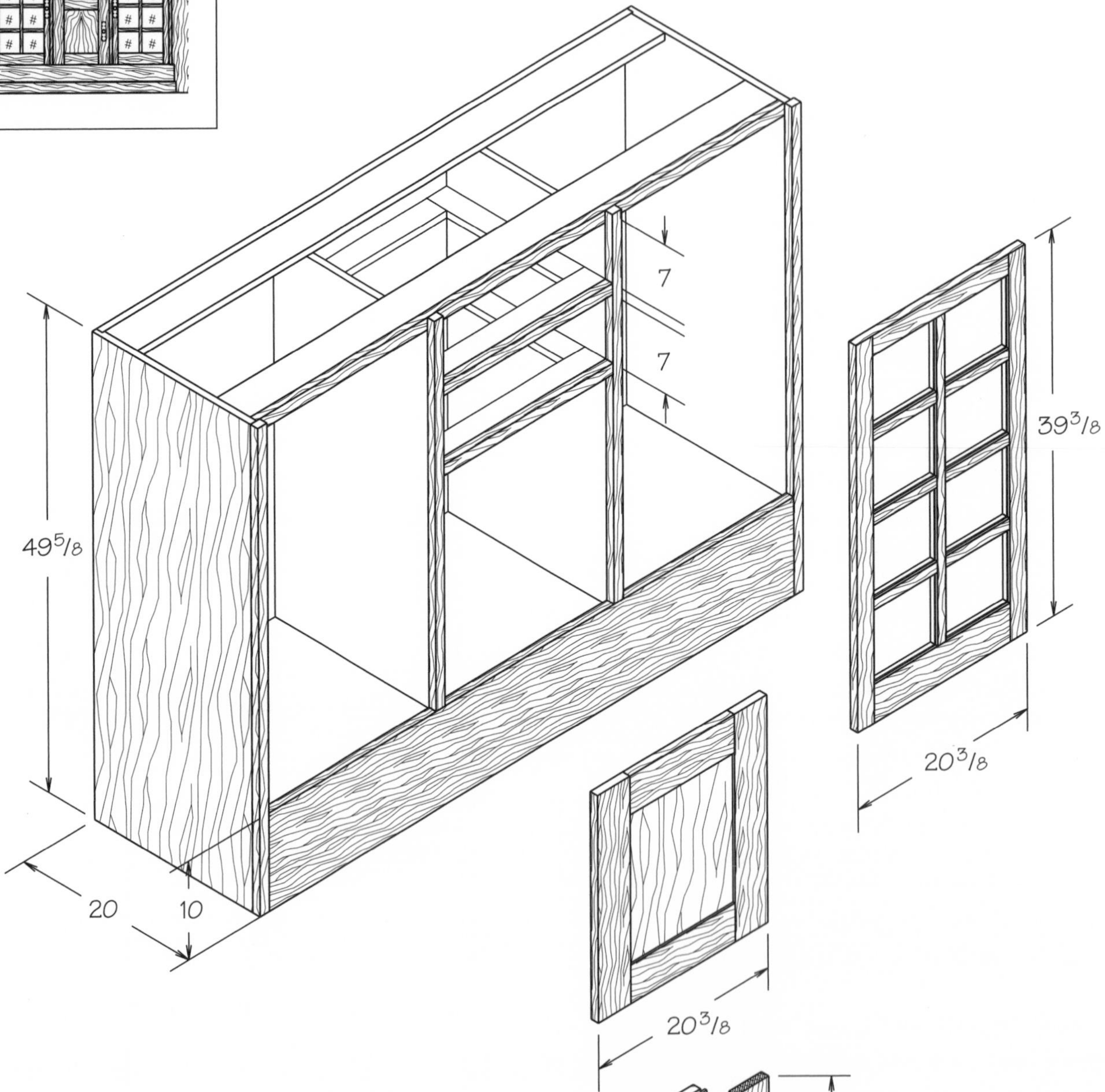

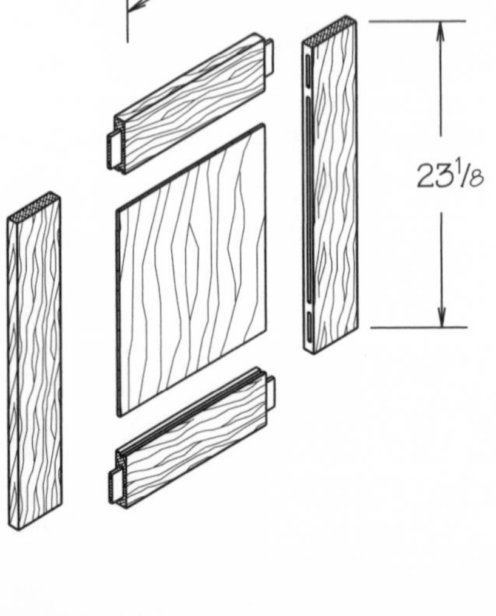

49⁵/₈

20

10

7

7

39³/₈

20³/₈

20³/₈

23¹/₈

China cabinet: exploded view

CHINA CABINET (*continued*)

The stiles and rails are mortise-and-tenon construction, and may be pegged after assembly. I believe that such pegs should only be used to reinforce a tightly assembled joint, and not drilled with one part off-center to force the joint together. The mullions and muntins are half-lapped to each other, and mortised-and-tenoned to the stiles and rails.

The back side of each of the pieces requires a rabbet for the glass and the glass stop, and it should be noted that the rabbets on the two stiles stop at the juncture with the rails. These rabbets could instead be run the complete length of the pieces, but then the tenons on the ends of the rails would need to be haunched. Either method will work—it is a matter of personal preference as to where to do the extra work.

The tenons on the ends of the mullions and are shown as haunched so that the back of the piece comes flush with the edge of the rabbet, not the edge of the stile or rail. The best way to become an excellent woodworker is with practice, and making these doors will give you the opportunity for plenty of that.

Time spent in carefully laying out this work will be well rewarded when it comes to cutting and fitting the glass and the glass stop. If all of the openings are square and of a consistent size, then this will be an exercise in repetitive work. If the openings are not consistent, it will be an exercise in frustration.

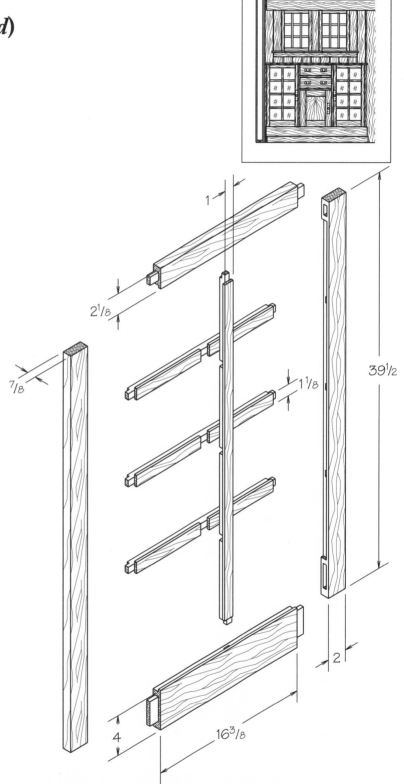

Joinery details for the glass cabinet doors.

China Cabinet (*continued*)

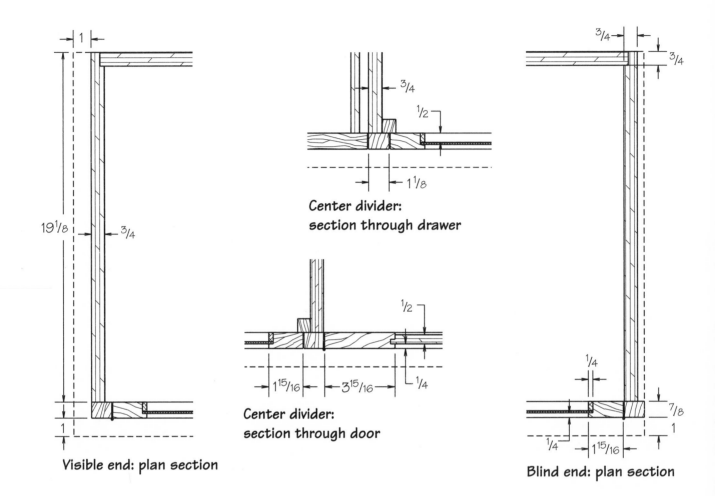

Center divider:
section through drawer

Center divider:
section through door

Visible end: plan section

Blind end: plan section

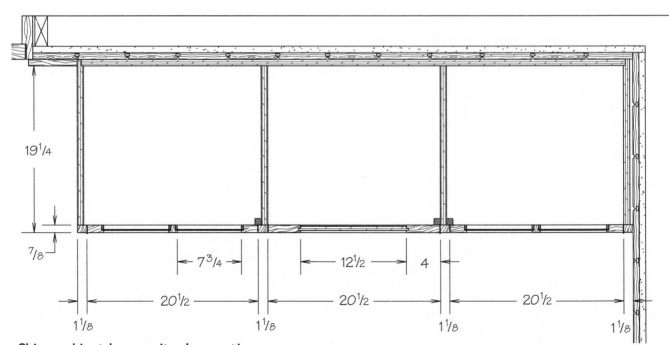

China cabinet base unit: plan section

SIDEBOARD

The long, low sideboard is the the other common form of built-in furniture for the dining room, shown here placed between panels below ceiling beams. These pieces were also placed wall-to-wall in smaller rooms. This unit, at 8 feet in width, is of an average size, but sideboards were also seen in larger versions, up to 12 feet.

If you want to build a larger piece, the width should be gained by adding in additional drawer units, or doors, keeping the width of each unit about 2 feet. Heights can also vary, but should not stray too far from a standard 36 inch counter. This piece was designed to fit two rows of 8 inch

tiles between the top of the sideboard and the window. All of the woodwork was specified to be oak, with the hardware of hammered copper.

The paneled divider, at 5 feet high, creates a transition between interior areas, and *The Craftsman* magazine suggested that "this adds to the apparent size of the room, and the open spaces permit the introduction of well chosen flowering plants, an old copper vessel, or an attractive piece of pottery, any one of which would add an attractive color note."

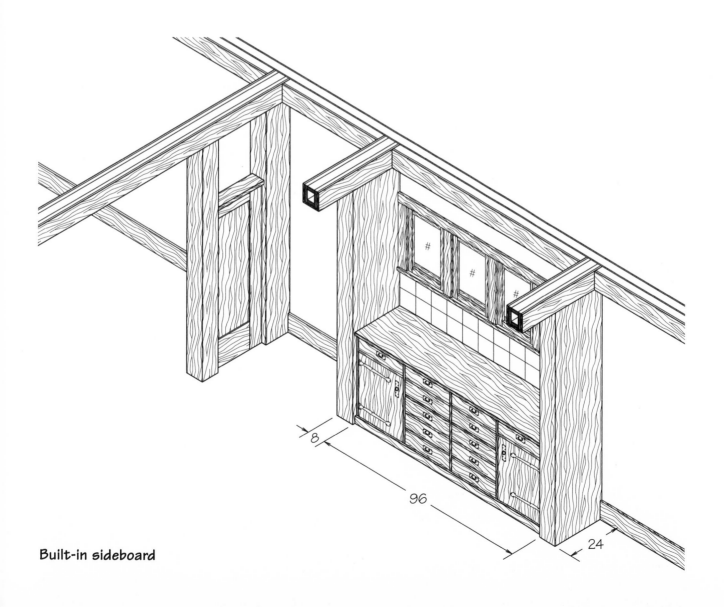

Built-in sideboard

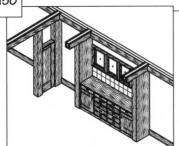

SIDEBOARD (*continued*)

The detail at right shows the construction of the end panels, which are ³/4 inch thick veneered plywood at the sides, solid wood at the front, supported by blocking of 2x material. These panels must be carefully fit to the floor and wall, and the top must be level, to make a neat transition at the beam. Note that the baseboard only occurs at the walls, and not around the cabinet, panels, or columns. Practically speaking this is quite difficult to achieve, for the bottom edges of all these pieces must be scribed to the floor. While *The Craftsman* drawings rarely showed a shoe molding, authentic examples, including Stickley's own home in New Jersey, included it.

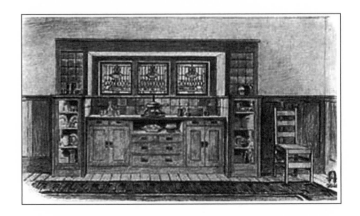

The cabinet itself can be built as a single piece, and units like this were often seen with the lower rail of the cabinet, below the doors and drawers, at the same height as the baseboard. This looks nice, but comes with the loss of some storage space. The visual difference is more noticeable in architectural drawings than it is in real life.

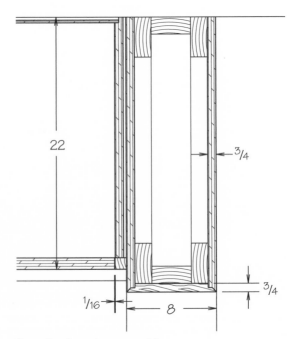

Detail of end assembly

SIDEBOARD (*continued*)

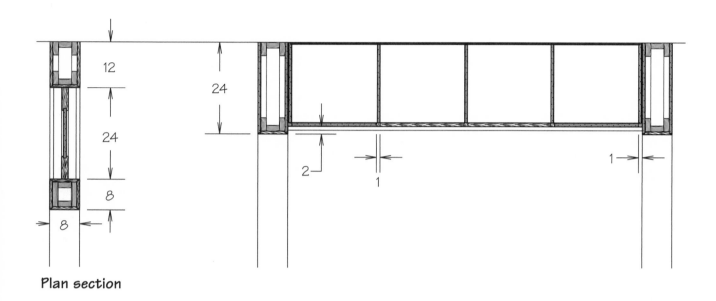

Plan section

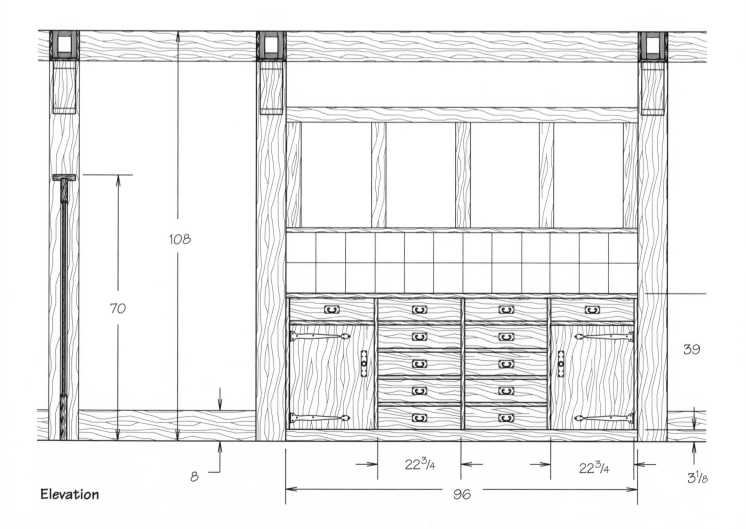

Elevation

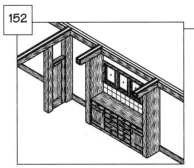

Sideboard (*continued*)

The construction of the drawer portion of the cabinet is shown here, with some variation from the china cabinet on pages 142-148. This represents more contemporary construction, and is simpler. The web frames have been replaced by rails between the drawers, with modern drawer slides. These will tie the front of the cabinet together, while saving a good deal of material and labor. The cabinet back is shown as ¼ inch thick plywood, set in a rabbet in the cabinet sides and bottom. The vertical dividers between the sections of the cabinet are ½ inch narrower than the ends, with the back overlaying the back edges of these

entirely. This thin back needs to be securely attached with screws into the back edges of the sides and dividers. A fillet of hot glue around the perimeter of the back will strengthen and secure it. The top is designed to be installed after the cabinet is in place. This facilitates the attachment of the drawer hardware, and the installation of the cabinet, since it is possible to reach through the open top of the case. The top is fastened with screws through the cabinet rails from below. If the top is made of solid wood as shown, the screw holes through the rails should be enlarged to allow the wood to move. A veneered plywood top, with a solid front edge, could be used instead.

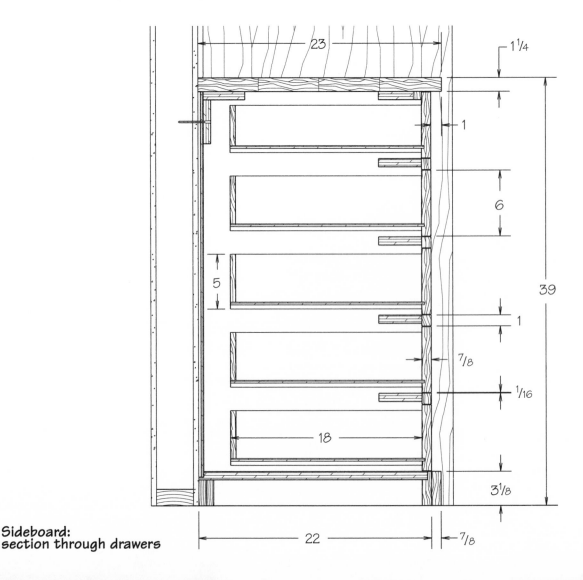

Sideboard:
section through drawers

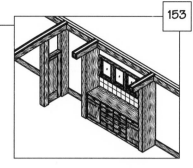

SIDEBOARD (*continued*)

This section is through the door unit of the cabinet. The doors are shown as a single panel, and should be made of a veneered panel, rather than of solid-wood. A solid-wood panel of this size is likely to cause problems due to wood movement, particularly if made of oak. The doors could be replaced by frame-and-panel doors. The drawer fronts can be either solid wood or veneer. Although we like to think of the good old days when everything was made from solid wood, many Stickley pieces were specified as being veneered. It also makes sense to fabricate the adjacent column walls with veneered plywood instead of solid wood.

Installations of pieces like this can lead to a lot of "chicken or egg" arguments about what to do first. There isn't an easy way out. The columns need to align with the beams overhead, and be set plumb. The distance between the columns will also be fixed, so the cabinet must be accurately and squarely made, and set in place plumb and level. I suggest the sequence of installing one column, then the cabinet, and then the other column, to avoid having to shove the cabinet into the opening between the two columns.

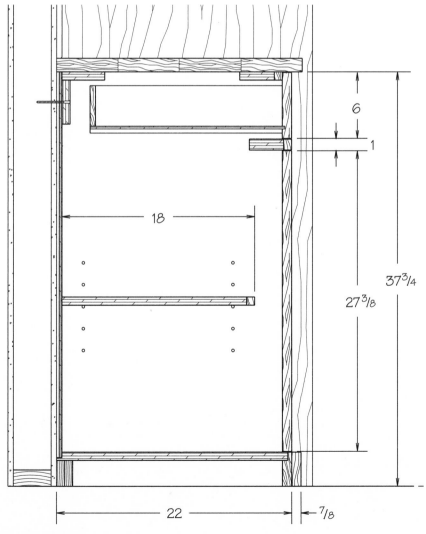

Sideboard: section through doors

Room Dividing Panels

Here is a situation where there is no margin for error, as all the many elements must fit tight to the floor, the wall, and each other, and no molding is indicated to cover any gaps. The parts of the columns should be made a little longer than necessary, and wider where they join the walls, with the corner joints milled in their edges. This way each piece may be scribed to the floor and wall, and when all of the parts are fitted, the entire column may be glued together in place. This is the reason behind the rabbeted miter joints at the column corners—they can be brought together without the tendency of a simple miter to slide apart.

The panel in between the two columns also can be assembled a bit long, so that it may be scribed to the floor. If a gap should be left at the floor, a simple shoe molding could be added. I would consider it historically accurate to do so, although the work would be a lot more impressive if all the pieces were to end neatly at the floor, as shown.

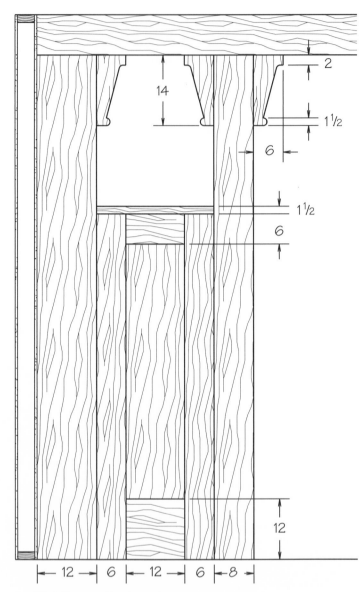

Dividing wall: elevation

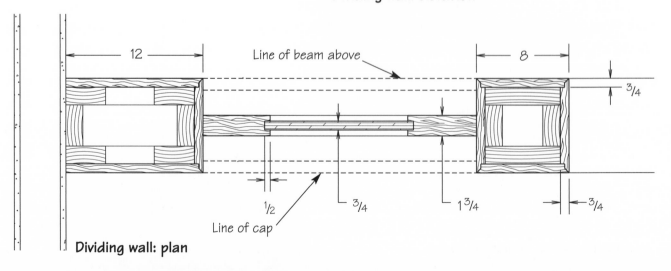

Dividing wall: plan

ROOM DIVIDING PANELS (*continued*)

The panel for the room divider is a piece of $^3/4$ inch thick veneered plywood, centered in a groove in the $1^3/4$ inch thick stiles and rails. The groove in the bottom of the bottom rail fits over a $^3/4$ inch square cleat. On installation the panel is raised above the cleat, then dropped over it. Some construction adhesive plus a few discretely placed nails or trim-head screws will hold it in place. Screws can be run at an angle through the top rails in to the columns to secure the top of the panels before the cap is put in place.

The thick corbel will likely need to be laminated. Four pieces of $1^1/2$ inch thick stock, if cut from the same length of board and kept in order, should allow the grain on the exposed edges to match nicely. Grooves in the back and top of the corbels allow them to be attached to the column and beam in the same way the panel fastens to the floor.

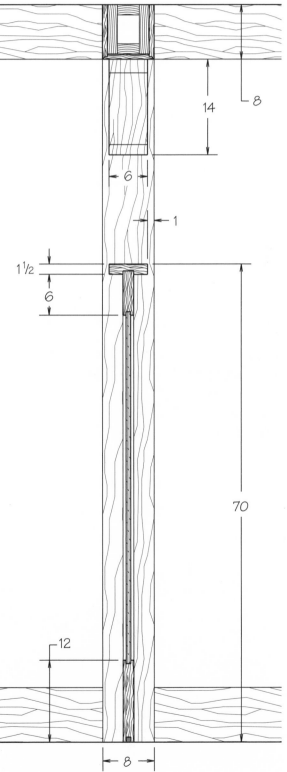

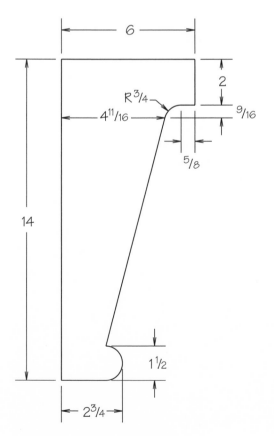

Corbel detail: elevation

Panel detail: side section

China Cabinet of 1912

This built-in china cabinet from 1912 is a form that is familiar to us. Similar pieces were seen many times in *The Craftsman* and varying in width from around 4 feet to this example at a little over 10 feet. What is unusual about this example is the width of the stiles and rails on the cabinet doors, considerably thinner than usually seen, and closer to "standard" sizes of today.

The ears on the countertop make it difficult to build and install as shown, because it would have to be assembled and installed in one piece.

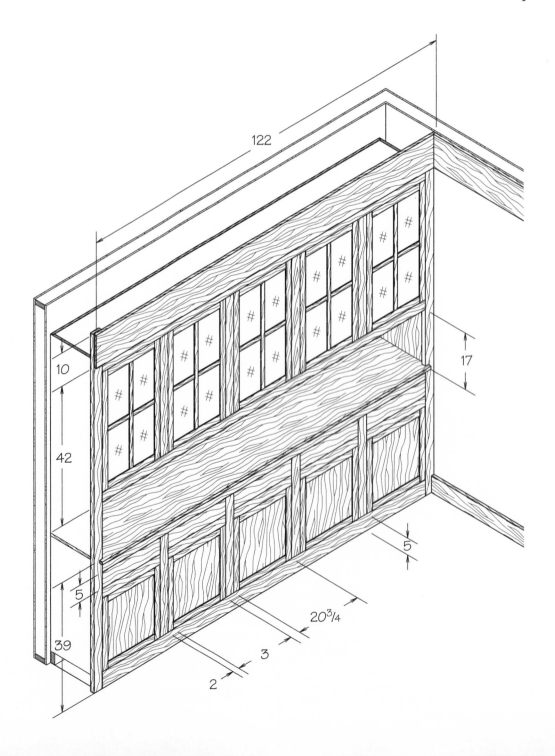

CHINA CABINET OF 1912 (*continued*)

In this example, the design has been modified so that the bottom cabinet, countertop, and upper cabinet are three distinct pieces, which simplifies construction and installation. If there is not enough depth to build this piece flush with the wall, one or both ends can be finished, and it can either be built into a corner, or built as a free-standing piece. Widths in between the two extremes shown can be made, keeping the same general proportions and adding a section or two to the width. Cabinets of this style were often seen in a butler's pantry, a small room between the kitchen and dining room used for the storage of dinnerware. If desired, a bank of drawers could be substituted for one or more of the cabinet doors.

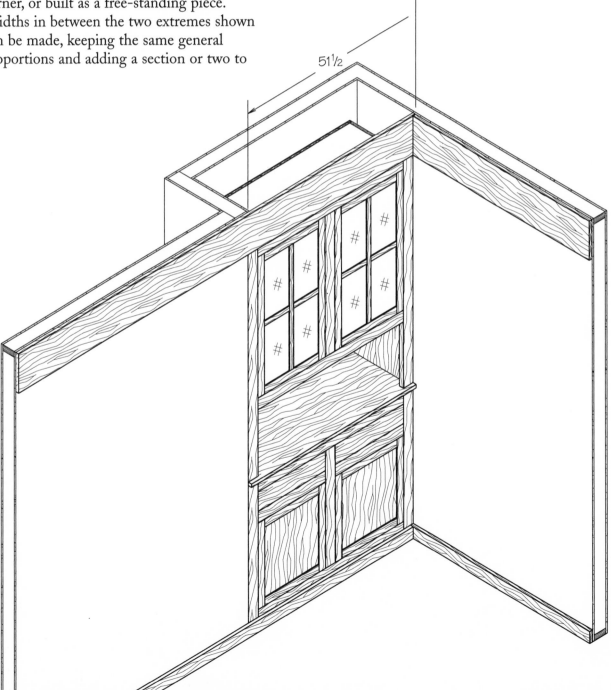

CHINA CABINET OF 1912 (*continued*)

If this piece is intended to be placed in a room with an 8-foot ceiling, it can be adapted by slightly reducing the width of the trim across the top, and the width of the cabinet rails. The depth could also be adjusted—anywhere between 14 inches and 24 inches deep would prove to be useful.

The elevation shows the countertop as wood, but it could also be of a material such as stone or solid surface material, keeping in mind that such a choice would require extending the top all the way to the walls, and building the cabinets as upper and lower units. It is theoretically possible to slide a top into place between notches cut in the two outer stiles, but practically it would be quite difficult, and there would be only one chance to get it right.

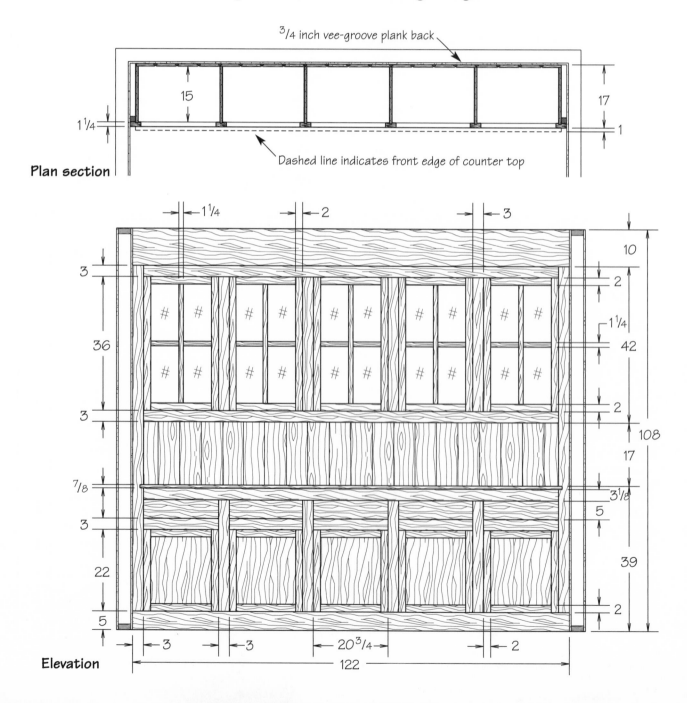

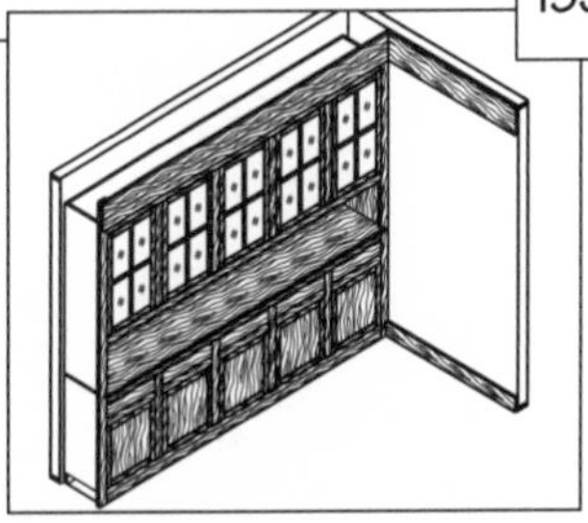

CHINA CABINET OF 1912 (*continued*)

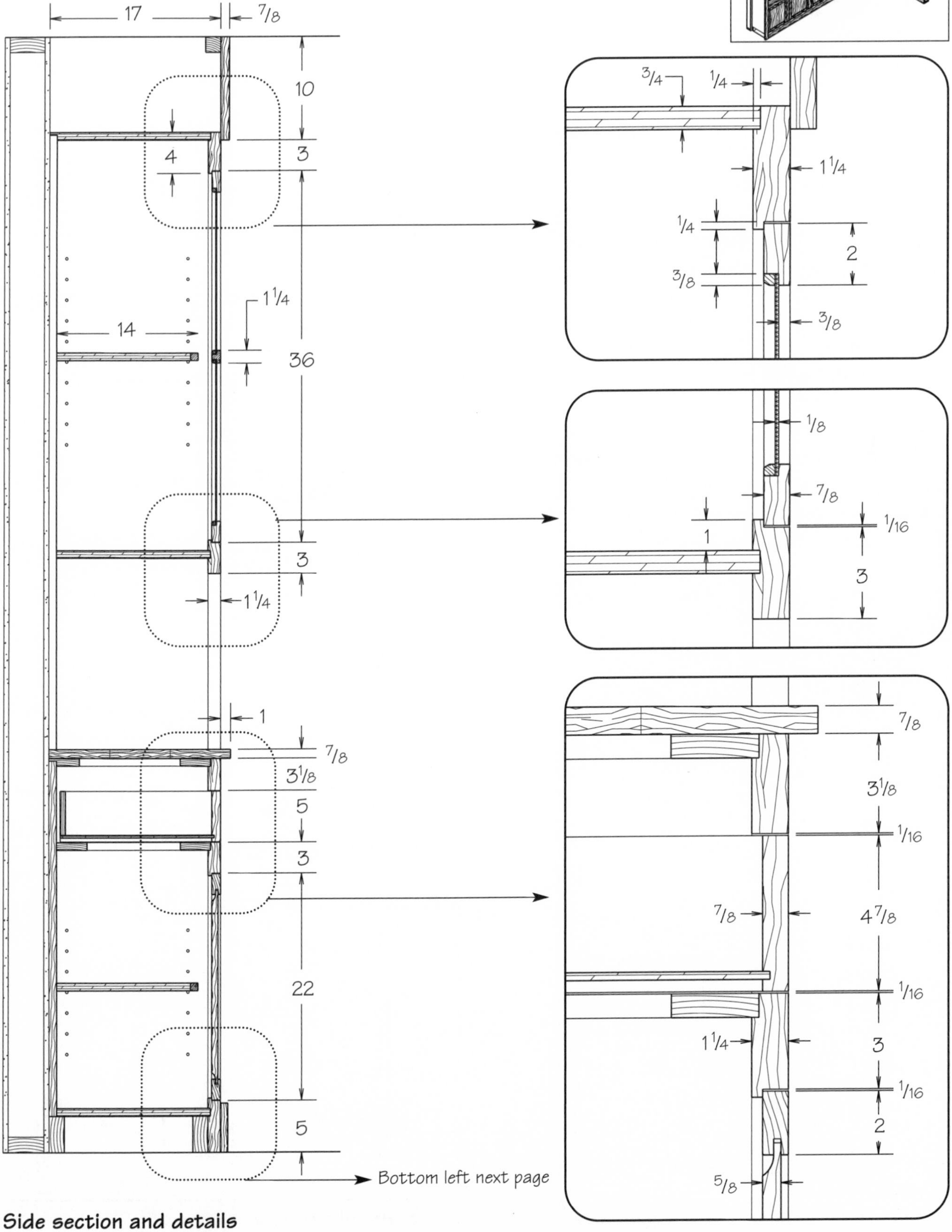

Side section and details

Bottom left next page

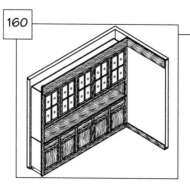

CHINA CABINET OF 1912 (*continued*)

The architectural drawings detailed the face frames as shown, 1¼ inch thick with a rabbet around the edge for the doors. Given the spans covered by the face frame, especially in the wider version of this cabinet, the extra strength of the thick stock makes sense and the rabbet will help keep dust out. The back of the entire cabinet was shown as tongue-and-groove planks running vertically. These could be replaced with a plywood back, but there would need to be a seam in the plywood somewhere.

The drawer boxes are shown in this drawing as being flush with the drawer fronts, which would have been the construction method of the day, the drawers being guided by either narrow wood runners at the sides, or a sliding-dovetail runner below.

Detail at floor: side section

From previous page

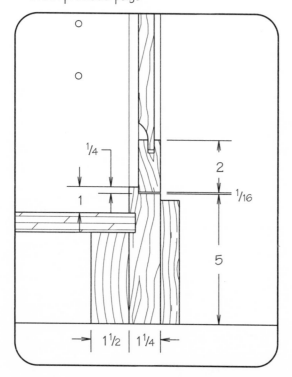

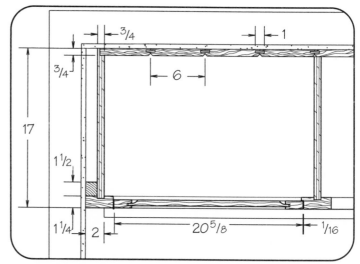

Upper unit: plan section

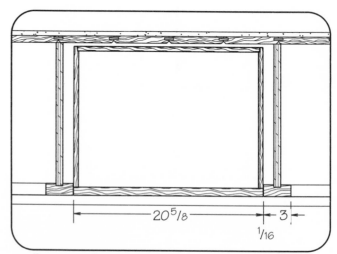

Drawer: plan section

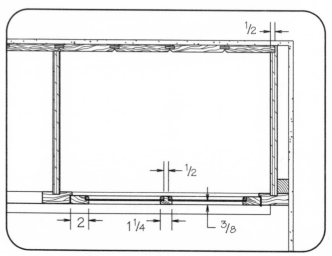

Lower unit: plan section

TALL CHINA CABINET

Here we see the basic form of the china cabinet, with the door stiles and rails widened to the dimension seen in other Craftsman built-ins. The upper doors have also been brought down to the line of the countertop. Structurally the details are the same as in the examples on the preceding pages. A bullet catch, or some other form of catch, should be added to keep the bottom of the glass doors closed. I favor this version, both because it looks more in keeping with the style, and because the doors, particularly the glass doors on the upper portion, will be considerably stronger.

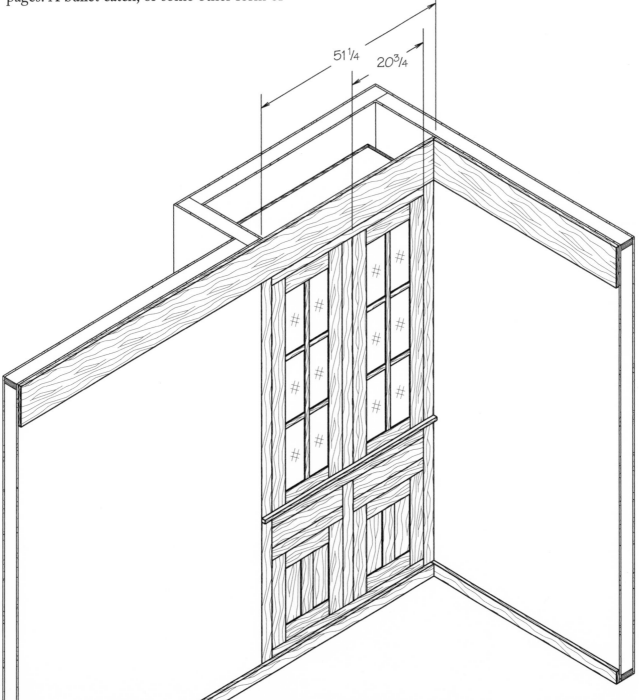

TALL CHINA CABINET (*continued*)

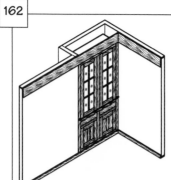

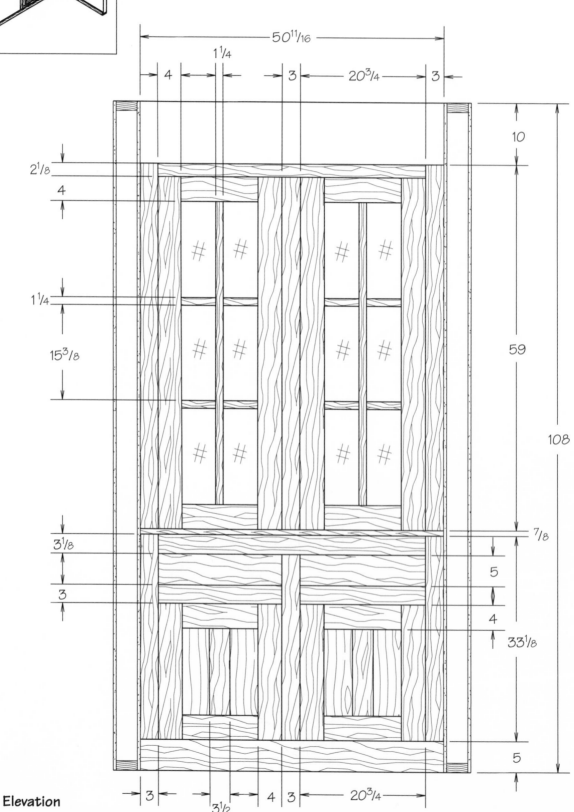

Elevation

TALL CHINA CABINET (*continued*)

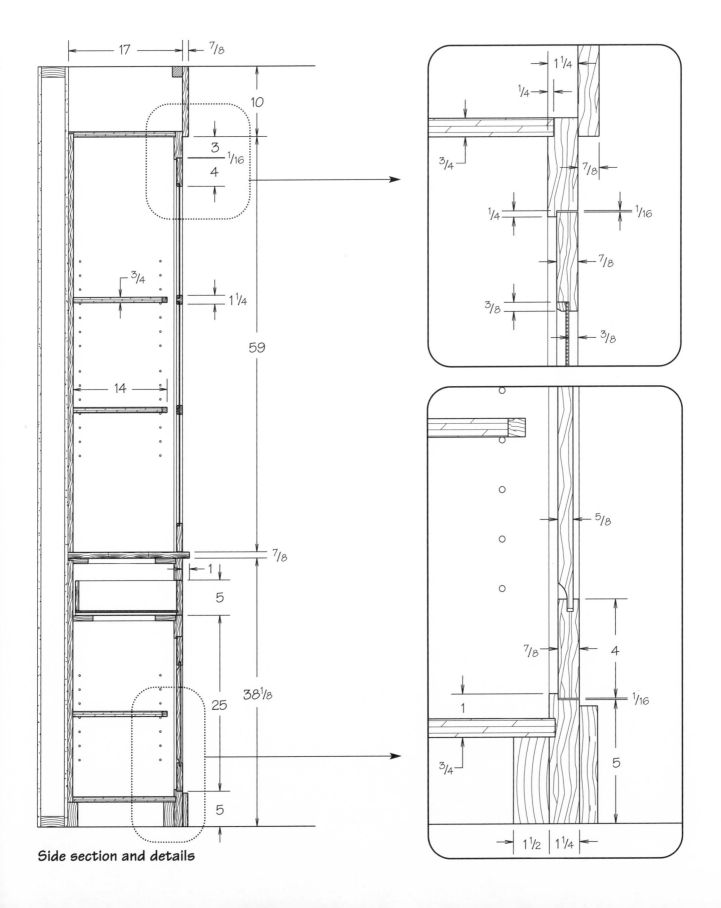

Side section and details

BOOKCASE

No Craftsman home would be complete without built-in bookcases somewhere. Most often seen in the living room, bookcases could also be found in studies, libraries, halls, bedrooms, and as a divider between two rooms. The first two drawings show bookcases built out from the walls, but they were also often built in to the walls, as seen in the examples on page 169 and page 174. Bookcases could stand alone, or be part of other built-ins, such as at fireplaces where mantels, bookcases and seats all flow together to define a space.

Bookcases were almost always integrated with the rest of the trim in the room, with the tall baseboard continuing around or across the case, and the top of the case continuous with the chair rail. Most were 5 feet high, although those that served to divide rooms were generally a foot lower. This height allows the top of the bookcase to serve as a display shelf, dividing the room into wide horizontal bands.

Construction is straightforward, and while the originals were usually made entirely of solid wood, veneered plywood is a reasonable choice for today's builder. When rooms were paneled, the cabinet was made without a back, and in rooms without paneling, beadboard was most often used for the back. The sides of the case should extend beyond the back about 1/4 inch to allow for scribing to the wall. The top should be connected to the carcass with figure-eight table irons, and attaching it last, after the case has been fastened to the wall, makes installation easier and neater.

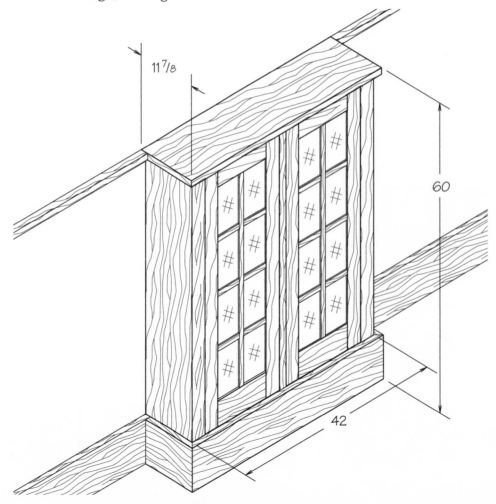

BOOKCASE (*continued*)

Because the cabinet itself is so simple, visual interest comes from the selection of wood, careful construction, and the variation of lines and shadows due to the differing thicknesses of pieces used. Note the setback of the doors from the face frame, the step where the bottom of the cabinet meets the baseboard, and the overhang of the top. All of these elements combine to make an elegant cabinet.

The shelves are shown aligned with the muntins of the glass doors, but it would be more practical to make them adjustable by means of pins in holes bored in the case sides. This is the method that was usually detailed in original drawings. At the time, there were a variety of other devices to make shelves adjustable. Wooden brackets, either saw-toothed or radiused, were fastened inside the case to fit the ends of the shelves, which needed to be cut to match the brackets. While clever, these methods are a lot of extra work, and tend to detract from the simple appearance of the case.

Handles for the doors were similar to that used in Stickley's furniture, hand-hammered copper with a ring bail. Reproductions of this hardware are available, but are not inexpensive. Simple wood knobs can also be used. Brass bullet catches work well for holding the doors closed, a lock and escutcheon may also be used.

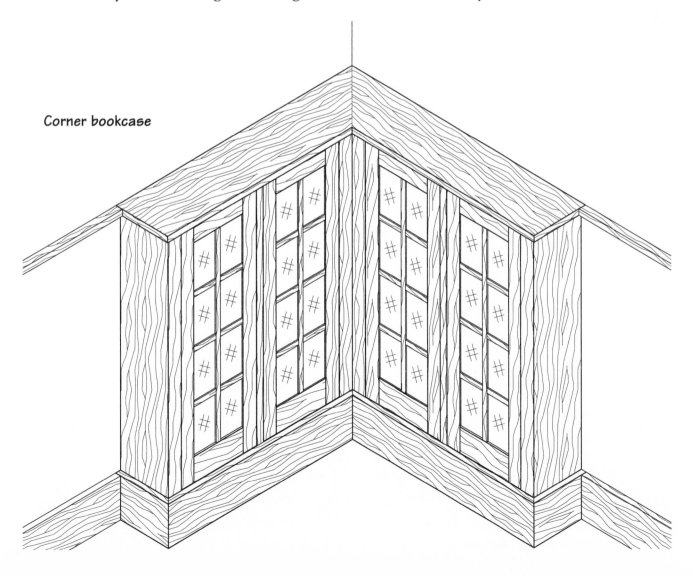

Corner bookcase

BOOKCASE (*continued*)

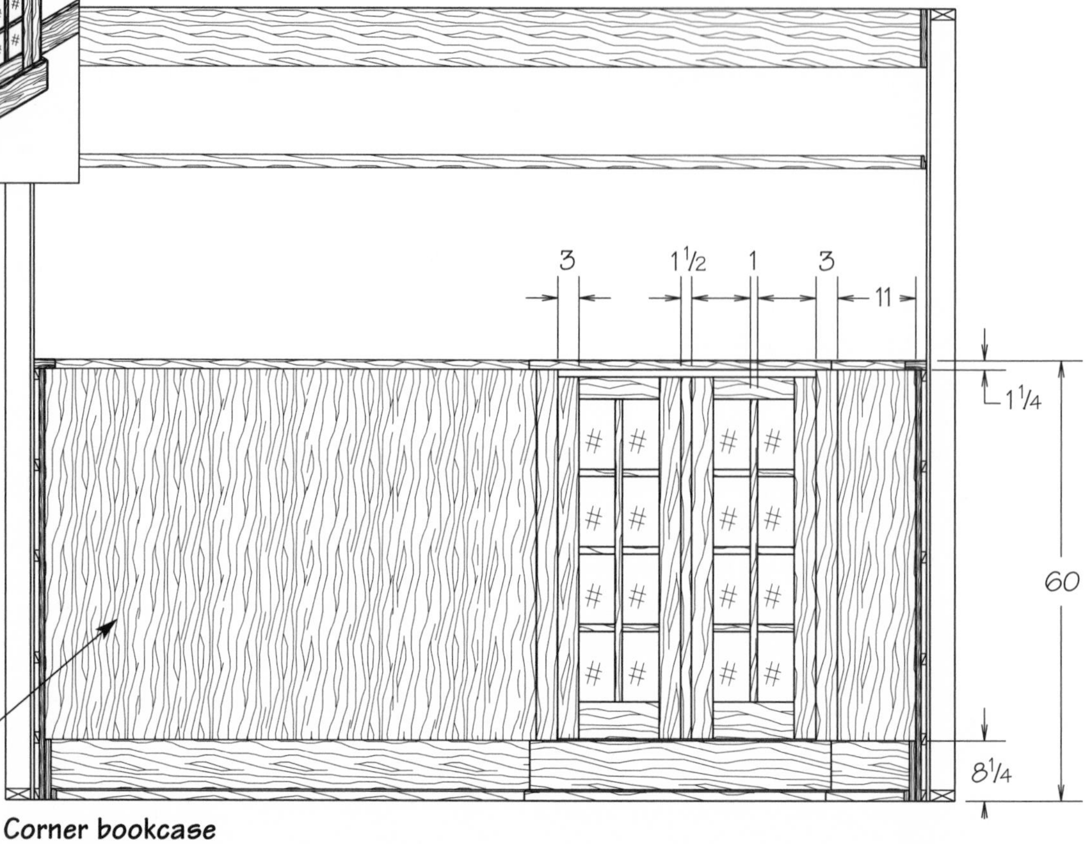

3   1½   1   3   11

1¼

60

8¼

Corner bookcase

Vee-groove
paneling

44

17¼   5⅛   1

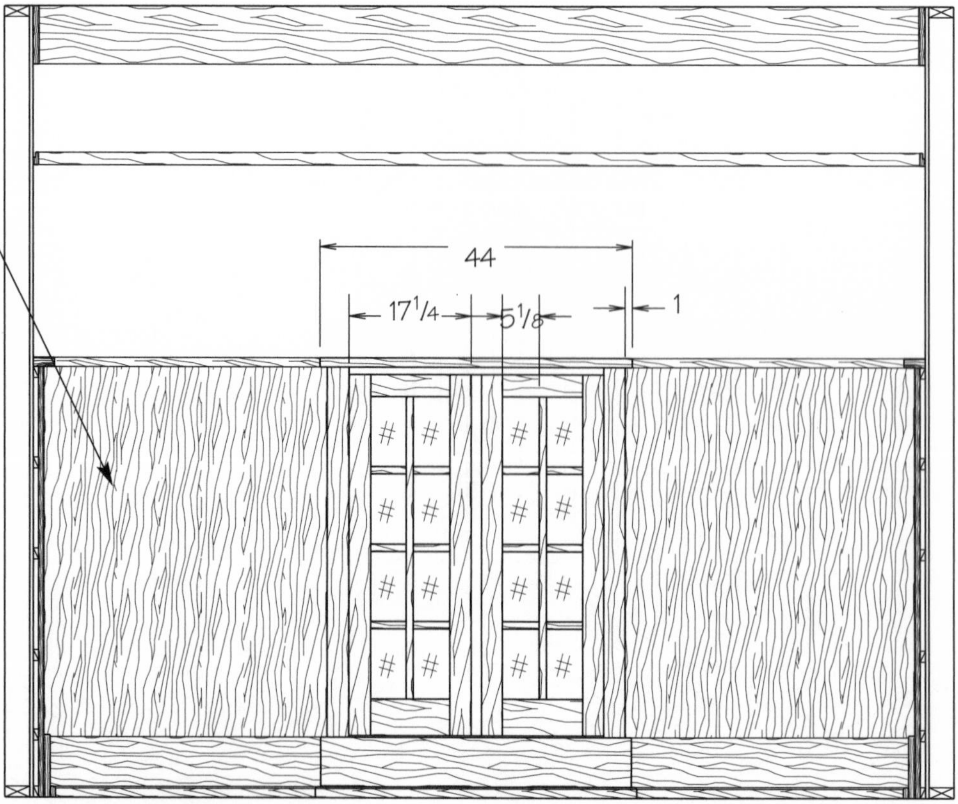

Centered bookcase

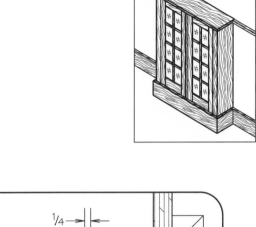

BOOKCASE (*continued*)

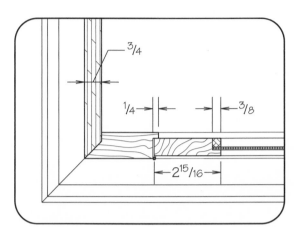

**Detail 1:
outside
corner**

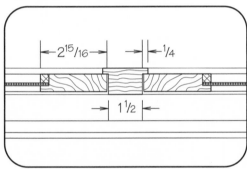

Detail 2: meeting stile

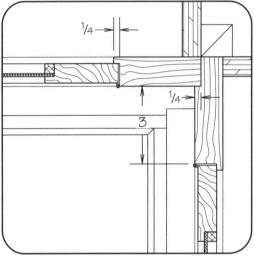

Detail 3: inside corner

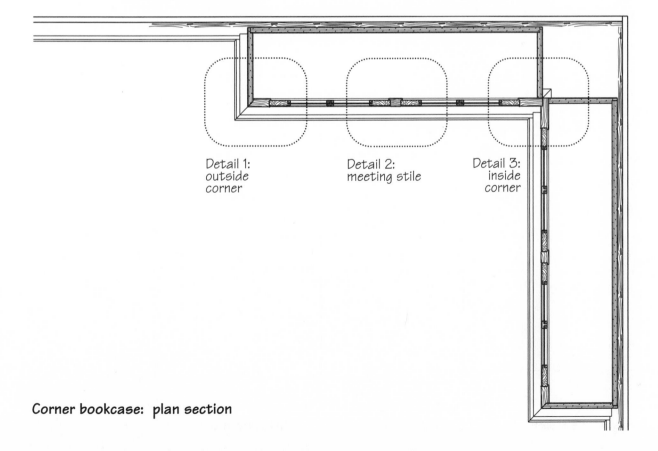

Corner bookcase: plan section

Detail 1:
outside
corner

Detail 2:
meeting stile

Detail 3:
inside
corner

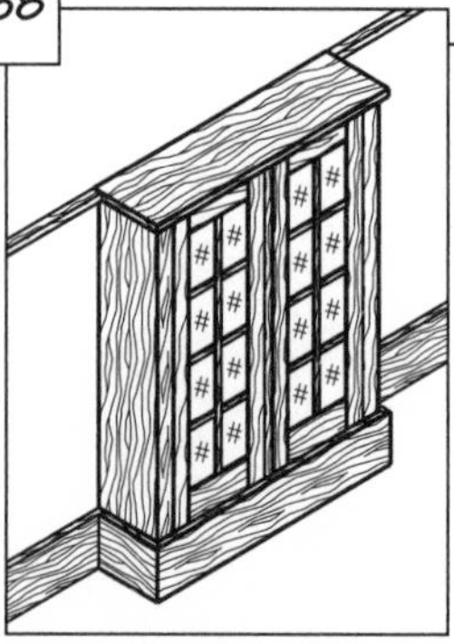

BOOKCASE (continued)

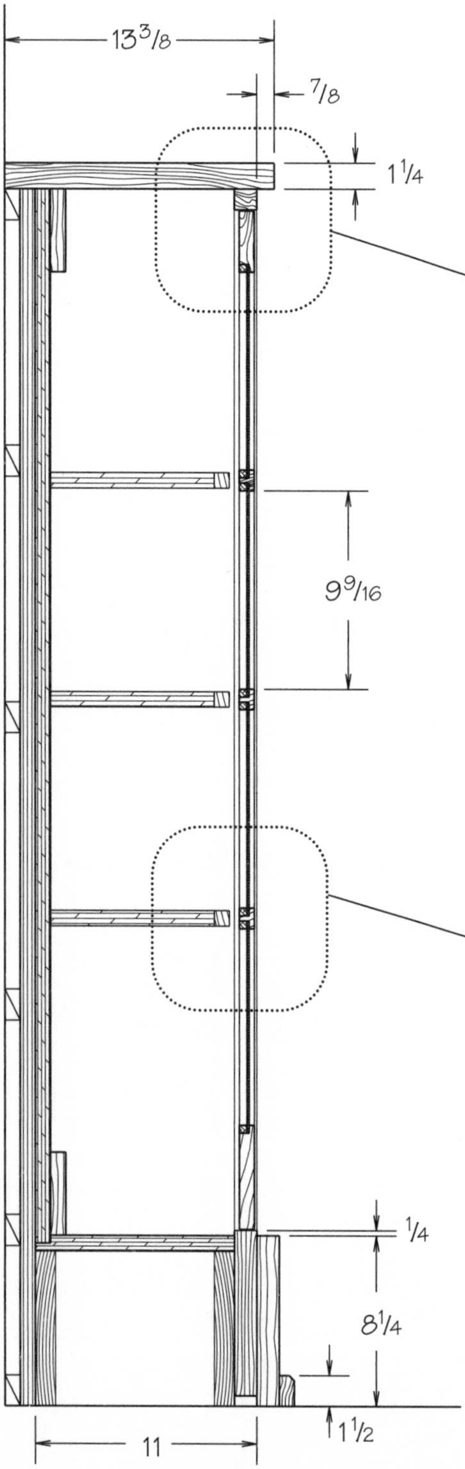

13³/₈

7/8

1¹/₄

9⁹/₁₆

¹/₄

8¹/₄

1¹/₂

11

Bookcase: section

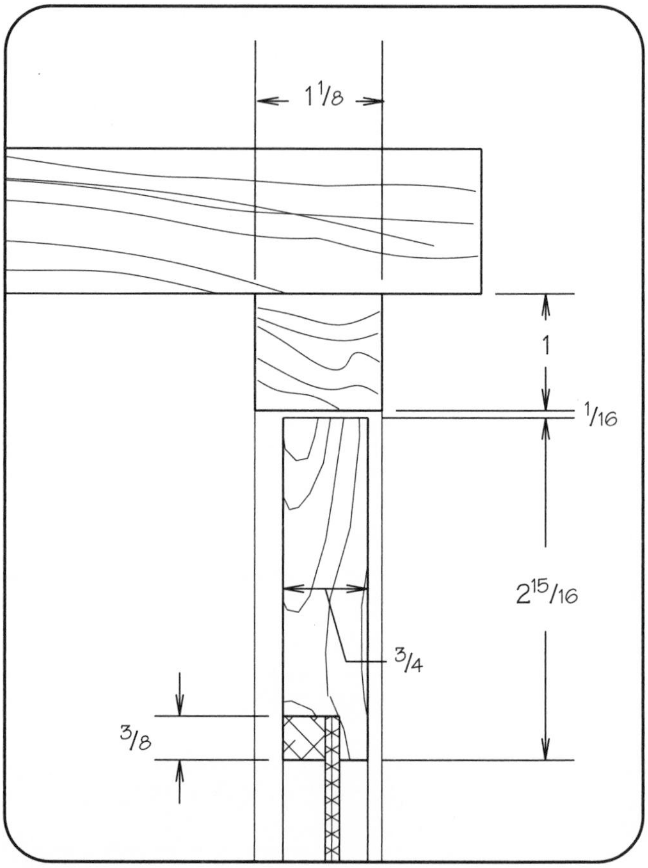

1¹/₈

1

¹/₁₆

2¹⁵/₁₆

³/₄

³/₈

Top detail

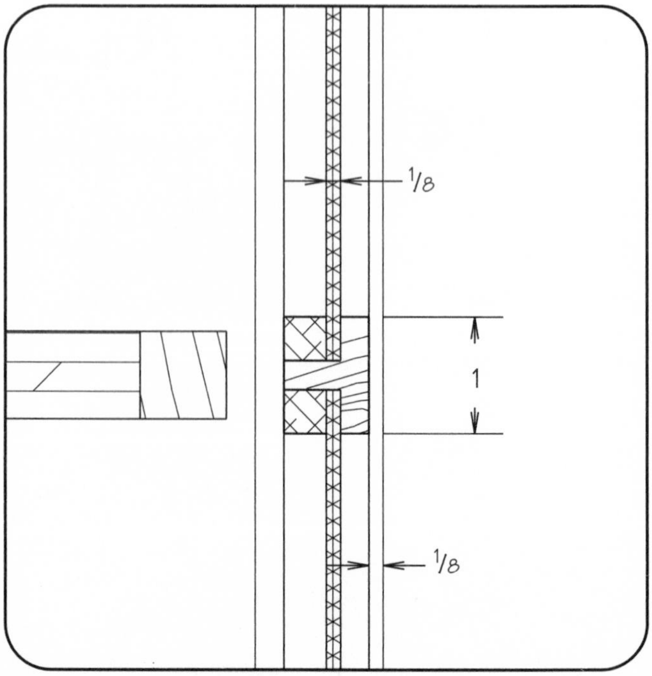

¹/₈

1

¹/₈

Shelf and muntin

BUILT-IN BOOKCASE

Bookcases were often built into walls, and integrated with paneling and other trim elements. This example appeared in the living room of a house featured in *The Craftsman* in June of 1905. The wall and the rough opening for the cabinet must be carefully framed, since the baseboard, chair rail, and vertical stiles are all part of the finished cabinet. The cabinet carcase should be slightly smaller than the opening, and a separate base for it should be constructed and installed level in the opening before the cabinet is set in place. Both the adjacent walls and the cabinet need to be plumb, since the cabinet doors are hinged from the stiles on the walls. Make sure the plaster or drywall surface next to the cabinet is straight, as any deviation would show

as a gap at the back edge of the cabinet stile.

Once the cabinet is in place, the horizontal trim elements—the chair rail and baseboard—can be installed using the top and bottom of the hinge stiles on the cabinets as a benchmark and continuing around the room. The section drawings on page 171 show the construction of the cabinet, with the stiles and bottom rails attached to the cabinet box. Note that the top of the cabinet box sits slightly above the top of the doors and stiles. The chair rail is put in place after the cabinet has been secured. The chair rail is shown as the same thickness as the cabinet stiles, but it could be made $1/8$ inch or $1/4$ inch thicker to create a shadow line.

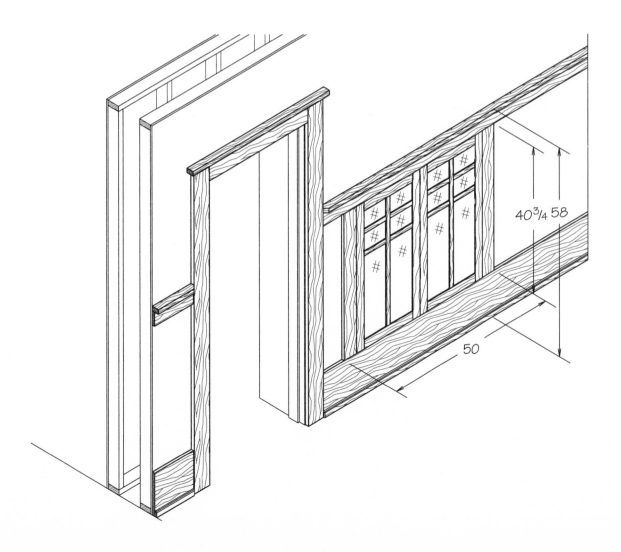

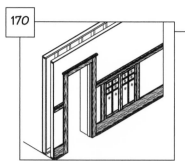

BUILT-IN BOOKCASE (*continued*)

The elevation shows the use of horizontal lines to tie the various elements of the room together. Note that the chair rail and baseboard pick up the lines from the rails on the door, and that the doors of the cabinet are similar in size to the panel of the door. The vertical stiles can also be repeated at regular intervals around the room, to create a paneled effect.

Because there is no vertical divider behind the cabinet doors, the shelves are shown with a $^7/_8$ inch by $1^1/_8$ inch solid wood edge at the front of the shelves, to prevent the front of the shelves from sagging. If the shelves are made fixed, the top shelf should line up with the cross-bar on the door. This cabinet could be made any width, depending on the available space, though the size shown represents a maximum width both for the doors and for the span of the shelves. The cabinet can certainly be made narrower, but I wouldn't go much beyond the point where the small glass lights become square. The depth of the cabinet will depend on the depth of the space between the two walls. Many bookcases are deeper than necessary. The interior depth of the cabinet could be as small as 9 inches, and it would fit most books.

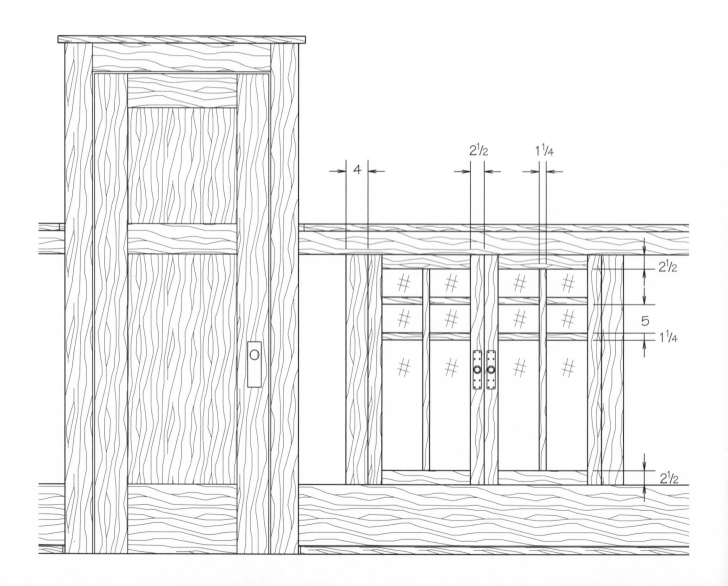

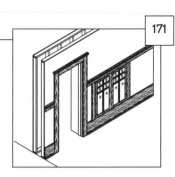

BUILT-IN BOOKCASE (*continued*)

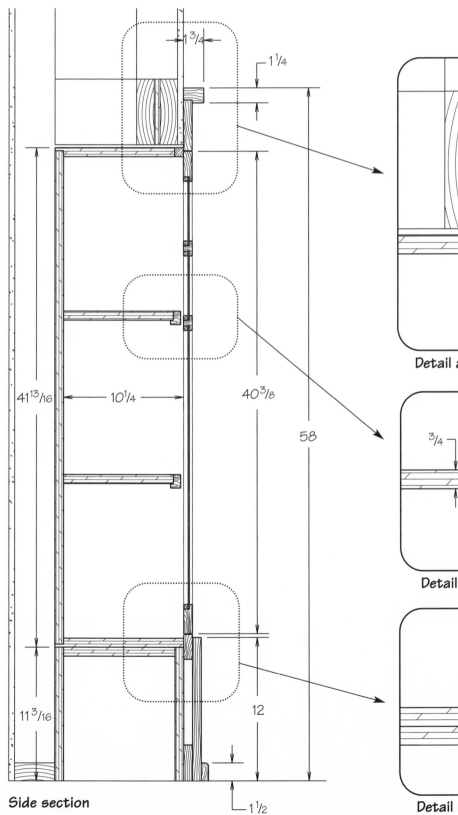

Side section

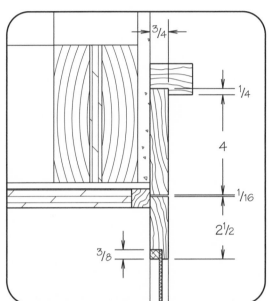

Detail at chair rail

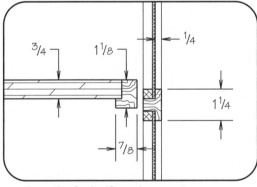

Detail of shelf and muntin

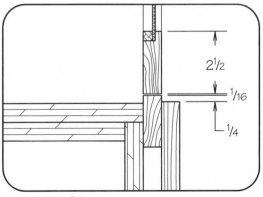

Detail of base

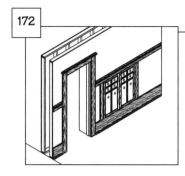

BUILT-IN BOOKCASE (*continued*)

The sections show typical construction details. The top of the doors will stop against the top of the cabinet, but either a bullet catch or some other form of stop should be used at the bottom of the doors. If a lock is desired, then an elbow catch or library catch should be used at the bottom of the doors.

The back of the cabinet is shown as a single piece of $^3/_4$ inch-thick plywood rabbeted into the cabinet sides, top and bottom. A thinner back could be used, but in that case horizontal rails should be added to provide a secure method of attaching the cabinet to the wall.

The interior of the cabinet can be finished before installation. The exposed surfaces of the doors, and the stiles and rails, should be finished with the rest of the trim in the room to ensure that they all match for color and sheen.

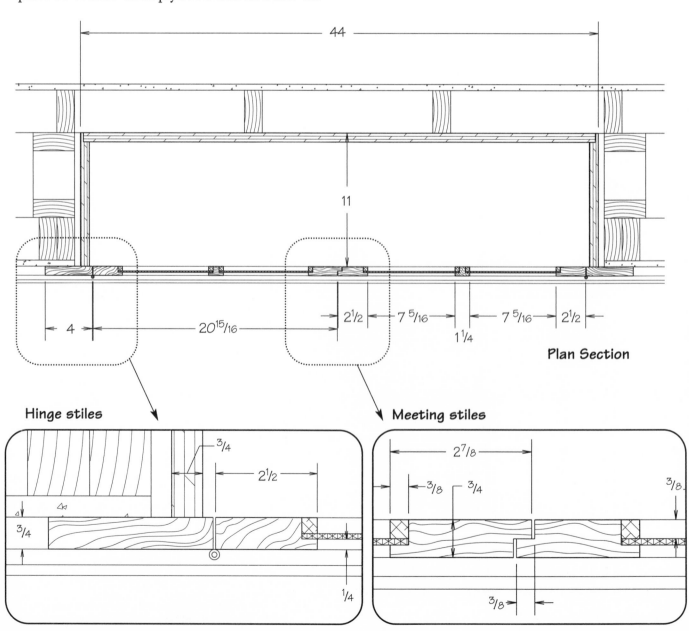

Plan Section

Hinge stiles

Meeting stiles

PANELED ROOM WITH BOOKCASES

In the living room of *The Craftsman* house from June 1905 is another elevation of bookcases, in this case wide and integrated into wood paneling that continues around the perimeter of the room. Basically, this is a pair of cabinets similar to those already seen on the previous pages. The cabinet doors are hinged from what is actually a stile in the paneling, and the center stile between the two cabinets bridges the fronts of both. The cabinet boxes could be assembled as a single unit, but it would be so large and heavy that it would be quite difficult to move and install.

The importance of framing of the opening in the wall, and the condition of the wall, cannot be stressed enough. If the walls are not in a flat plane, the paneling could be mounted on ledger strips instead of directly on the wall, as shown in the section view on page 168. The ledger strips can be shimmed to a flat plane. This option will, however, affect the width of the chair rail and the door casing. The panel elements can be assembled as units of stiles, bottom rail and panels. The units will be much easier to apply to the wall surface than assembling the panels during installation.

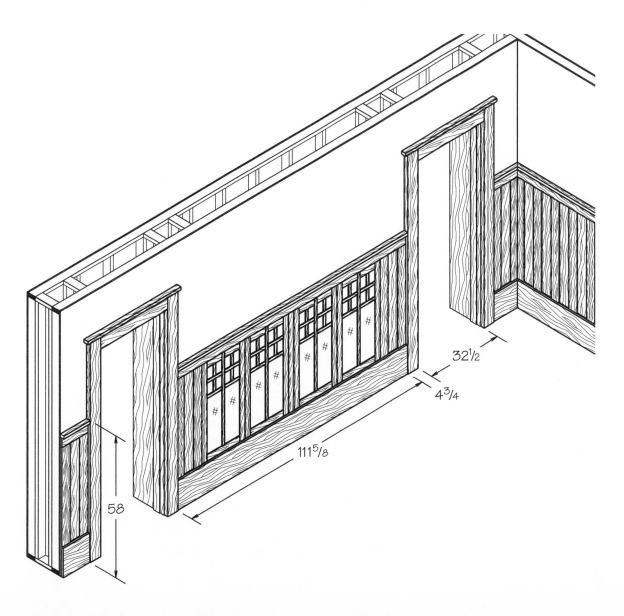

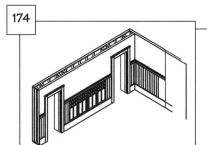

PANELED ROOM WITH BOOKCASES (*continued*)

Closer views of this plan and elevation are shown on the next page. The continuity of the horizontal lines, as the eye moves from door to bookcase to panels around the room has a significant effect on the way the room feels. This is both pleasing to the eye and calming to the mind. Adjustments in size will likely be needed to fit a particular room, but these horizontal lines should not be broken up or stepped in height.

Also, notice the extensions of the door jambs, shown in detail on page 176. The rabbet on the back of the jamb on the extension side will keep the joint neat should the extensions shrink in size. The sequence of installation for this room would begin with setting of the passage doors, then the installation of the cabinet boxes. The panels would then be installed, followed by the baseboard and chair rail.

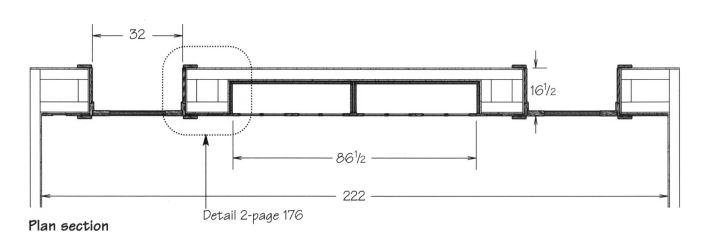

Plan section

Detail 2-page 176

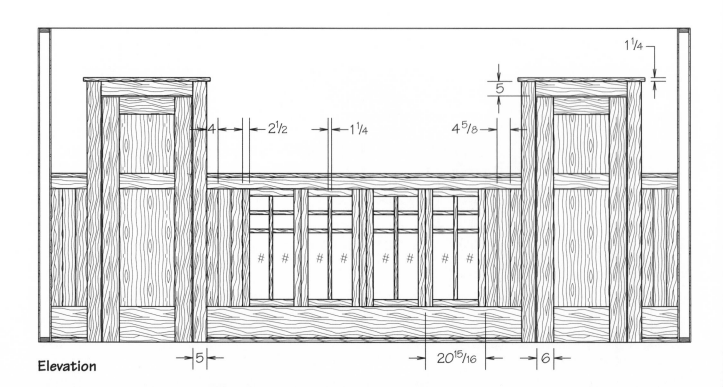

Elevation

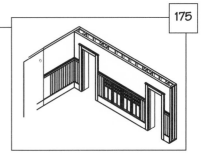

PANELED ROOM WITH BOOKCASES (*continued*)

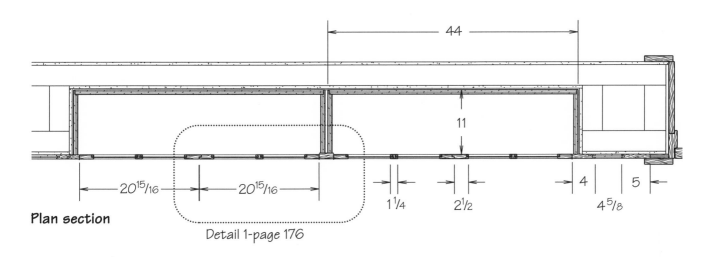

44

11

Plan section

20¹⁵/₁₆   20¹⁵/₁₆   4   5

1¹/₄   2¹/₂   4⁵/₈

Detail 1-page 176

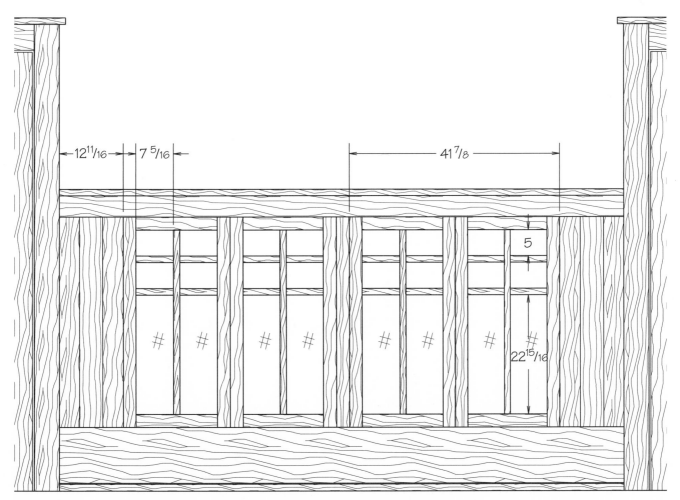

12¹¹/₁₆   7⁵/₁₆   41⁷/₈

5

#   #   #   #   #   #   #   #

22¹⁵/₁₆

Elevation

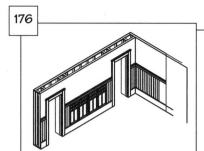

PANELED ROOM WITH BOOKCASES (*continued*)

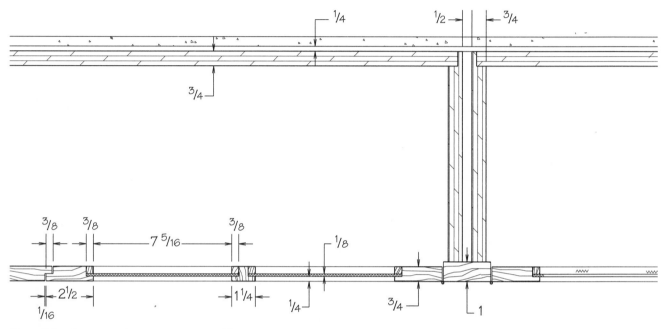

Detail 1: plan section at center stile

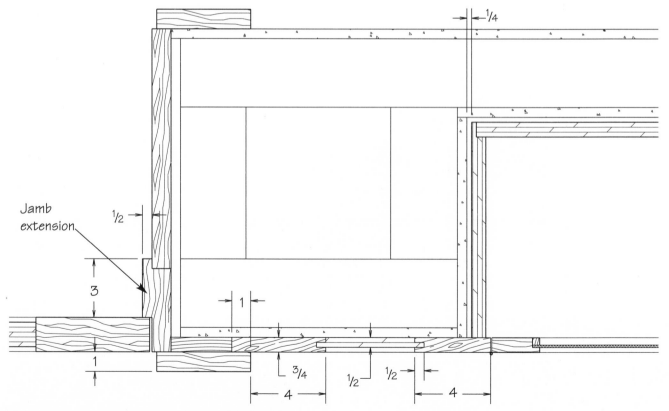

Detail 2: plan section of panel and door jamb

Paneled Room with Bookcases (*continued*)

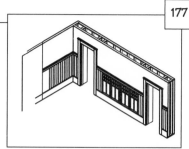

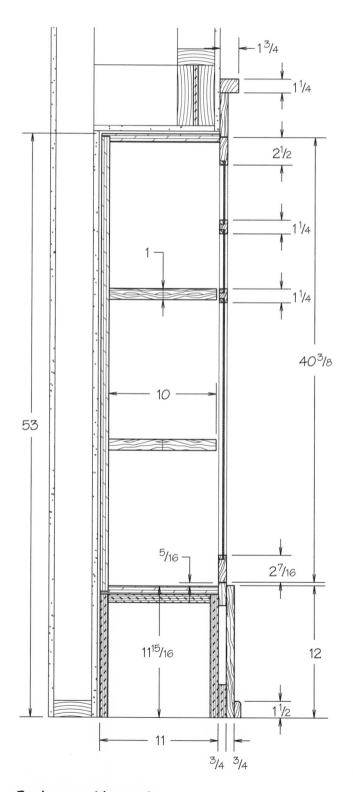

Bookcase: side section

Dimensions: 1³/₄, 1¹/₄, 2¹/₂, 1¹/₄, 1, 1¹/₄, 40³/₈, 10, 53, 5/₁₆, 2⁷/₁₆, 11¹⁵/₁₆, 12, 1¹/₂, 11, 3/₄, 3/₄

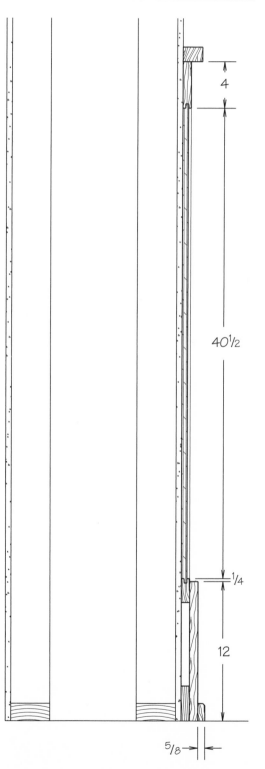

Wall paneling: side section

Dimensions: 4, 40¹/₂, 1/₄, 12, 5/₈

BEDROOM &
BATHROOM

BEDROOM: CLOSETS AND STORAGE

Many period bedrooms lack closet space, particularly when judged by today's standards. Without encroaching too much into the space of the room, these cabinets add both closet space, plus an attractive and inviting window seat. This simple bit of casework can transform a drab room in an older home, or give a wonderful period feel to a bedroom in a newer home. The door panels are full-length mirrors, a detail seen in many period rooms. The soffit adds intimacy to the seat area, and the trim at the upper and lower edges of the soffit can continue around the room with the lower rail also serving as door head-casings. Paint was the preferred finish for bedrooms of the period, although this installation could also be a light, natural wood finish. This seat and closet combination has been planned for a room 12 feet wide, but it could easily be made wider or narrower. The closet doors, at 28 inches, are close to the maximum practical width, though they could be stretched to 32 inches wide. The seat is detailed with storage beneath, for extra bed linens or out-of-season clothing. Cedar lining in this area would be a nice addition.

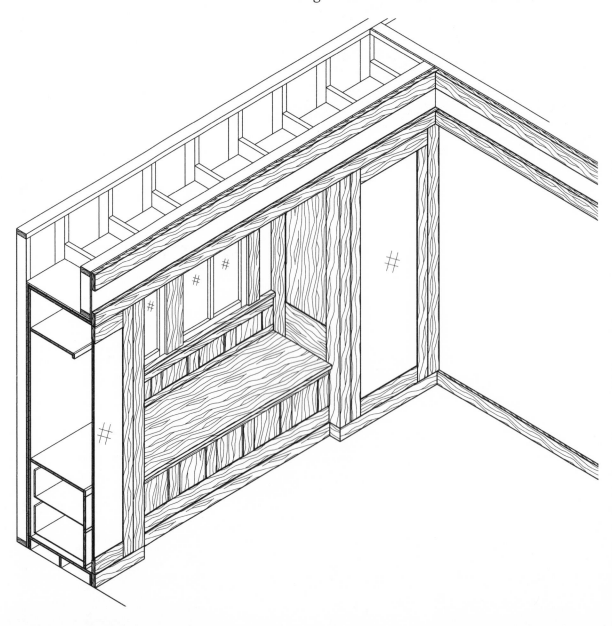

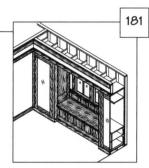

BEDROOM: WINDOW TRIM

The elevation view shows the window trim, with the head casing and window stool extending across the opening between the two closets. This echoes the strong horizontal lines of the soffit trim above. The horizontal line of the bottom door rails also carries across the front of the seat. The strength of these lines makes the room appear spacious and unified

Construction is simple, the important points being to ensure that the two exposed end panels of the closets are parallel, and that the face of the closets and the soffit are all in the same plane.

The section view at right shows web frames of 2x material supporting the seat at the ends and in the center. The following section and plan details show the condition of the seat where the lid is hinged to access the storage below.

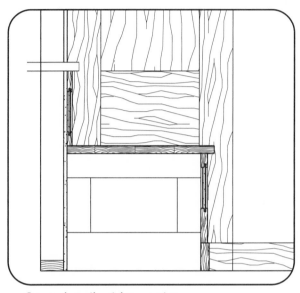

Seat detail: side section

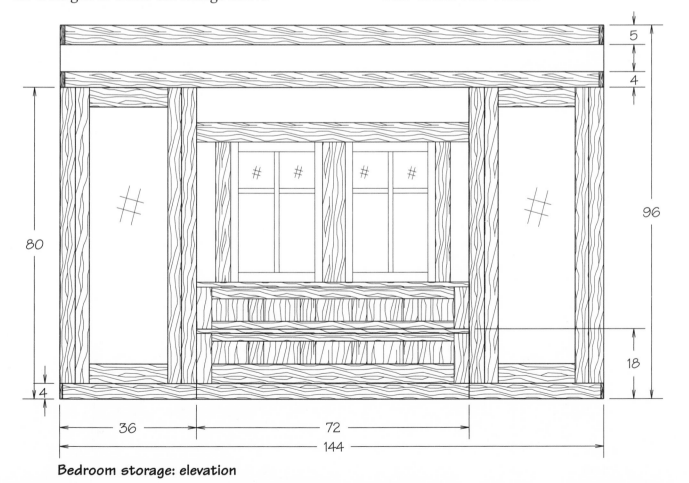

Bedroom storage: elevation

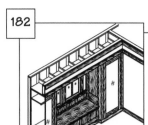

BEDROOM CLOSET: END-PANELS

The end-panels of the closets are shown as frame-and-panel construction. The closet units should be set in place in the room before the seats. The stile at the back of the closet end-panel should continue down the same length as the front stile. A bottom rail-and-panel could also be included, although it will be hidden behind the seat. The front rail of the panel also extends beyond the soffit, so that the face of the cabinet is flush with the face of the soffit trim.

The section view at lower left shows the interior of the seat in the area used for storage. The hinge rail is placed so that the seat will lean against the wall when open, but it would also be prudent to include stays to prevent the lid from accidentally closing.

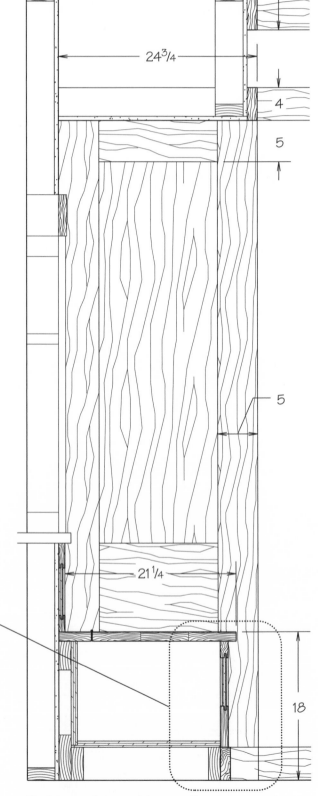

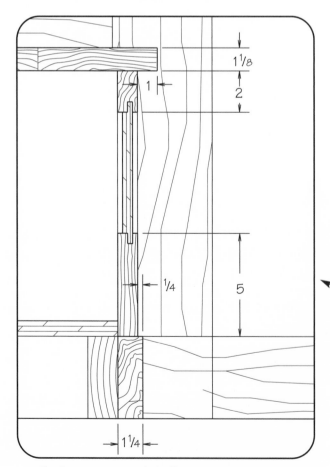

Bedroom seat: detail

Bedroom Seat: side section

BEDROOM CLOSET (*continued*)

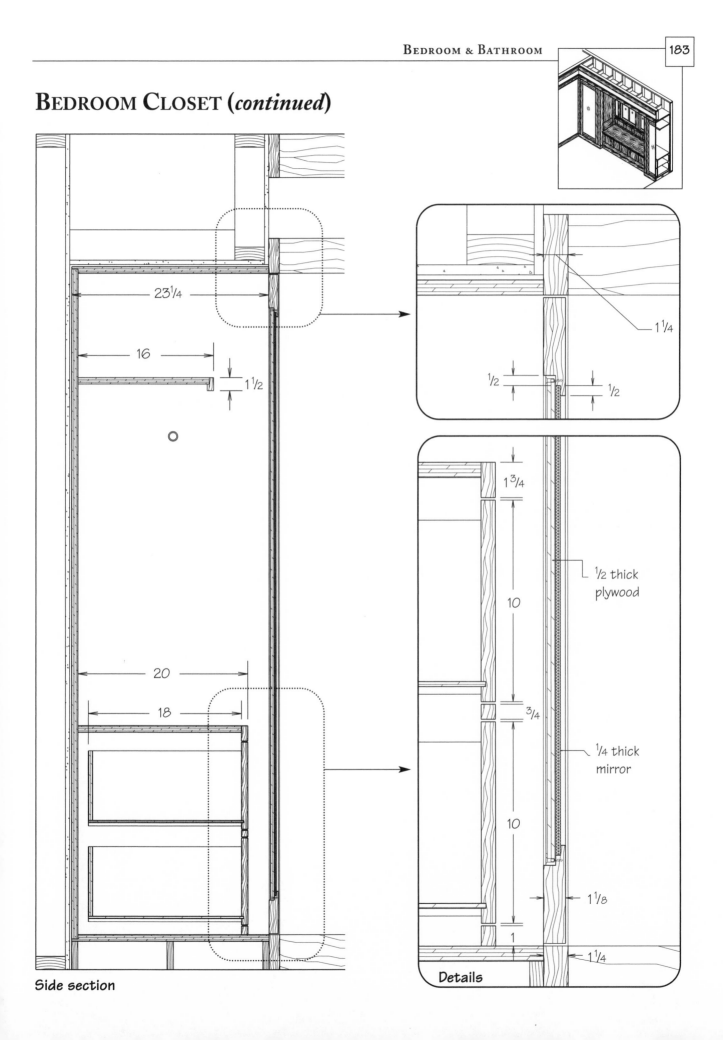

23¹/₄

16

1¹/₂

20

18

1¹/₄

¹/₂   ¹/₂

1³/₄

10

³/₄

¹/₂ thick
plywood

¹/₄ thick
mirror

10

1¹/₈

1

1¹/₄

Side section

Details

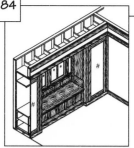

BEDROOM CLOSET (*continued*)

The vertical section on the preceding page, and the plan sections on this page, show the construction of the closet units. Particular attention should be paid to the construction of the closet doors, since they will be about the size of a passage door, and the mirror will add to their weight. Three sturdy hinges should be used for each door, with the cabinet solidly attached to the walls of the room.

A stud should be present within the wall to attach the cabinet at the hinge stile. The door stiles and rails should be mortised-and-tenoned together; the detail shows the 1/2 inch thick plywood back set into a rabbet in the back of the door to hold the mirror in place. This plywood piece will stiffen the door, and if held in with screws only, will allow for replacing the mirror whenever that becomes necessary.

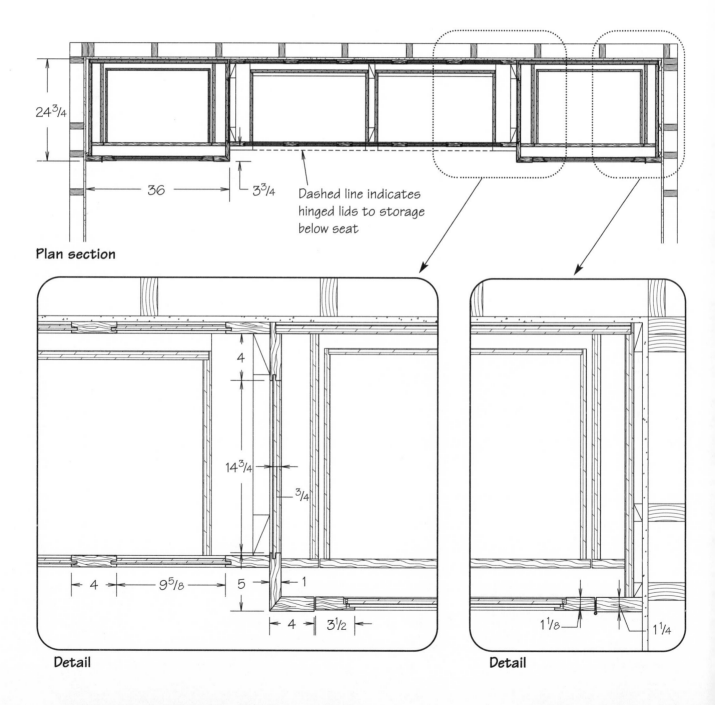

Plan section

Dashed line indicates hinged lids to storage below seat

Detail

Detail

BATHROOM: MEDICINE CABINETS

Bathrooms of the early Twentieth Century were purely functional rooms, not the design statements that we know today. The few times they were mentioned in *The Craftsman* was in the context of keeping them sanitary and what was new in fixtures. This medicine cabinet is typical of the period, and will help to create a period look. The box part of the cabinet sits behind the face frame and attaches through the sides to the framed opening in the wall. The shelves would normally be of glass, and the cabinet can be made deeper if the wall allows for it. The detail at right shows the molding at the top of the cabinet, also a common treatment for door head-trim.

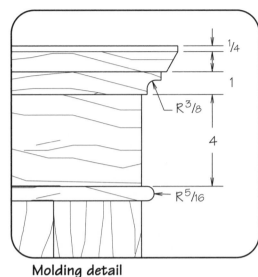

Molding detail

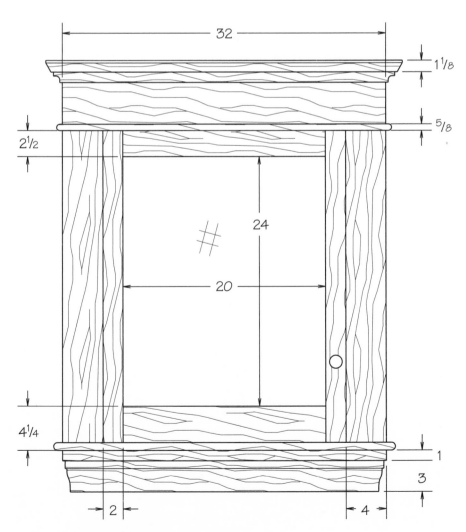

Medicine cabinet elevation

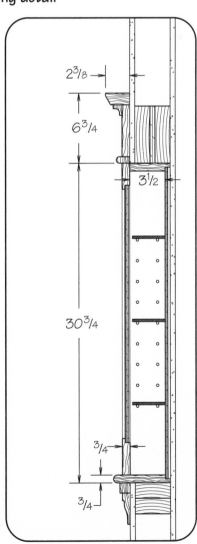

Side section

BATHROOM: HIS-AND-HERS CABINETS

During the Craftsman period sink cabinets were not in favor because the enclosed plumbing was not regarded as sanitary, and wall-hung or pedestal sinks were the norm. These two cabinets, flanking the pedestal sink, provide plenty of storage space and would likely have been painted, as would all of the bathroom woodwork. The medicine cabinet is the one shown on the previous page. If you decide to build the sink into a vanity cabinet, it can be modeled after the examples for kitchen cabinets, but built to a 32 inch or 34 inch height. It should convey the period look, even if it is not quite proper.

Molding detail

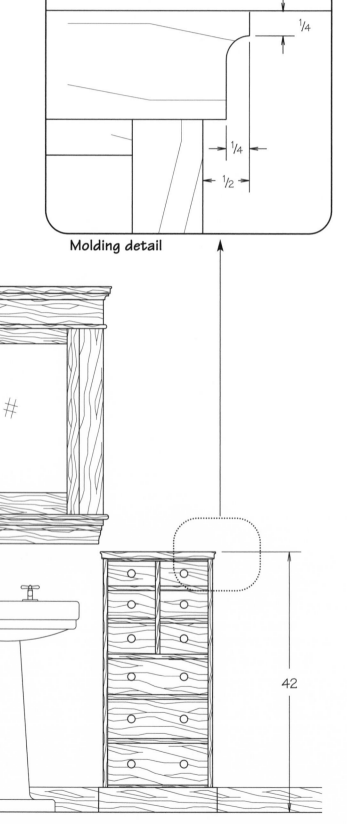

Elevation

BATHROOM: HIS-AND-HER CABINETS (*continued*)

The large detail at right shows the profile for the molding at the bottom of the medicine cabinet. Though more curved than other moldings, it was common for the period, and also used for window casing. Note in the elevation that the ends of this trim are mitered and return to the wall. In many ways, Craftsman design stopped at the bathroom door, and the typical Craftsman bathroom looked like any other of the era.

These cabinets are simple to construct, and would be a good exercise in drawer making and fitting. The horizontal divider supports the bottom edge of a vertical divider between the two banks of narrow drawers. If the cabinets are to be painted, the case and the drawer fronts can all be made out of a paint-grade plywood, such as birch. The only solid wood necessary would be the trim around the edges of the top, and perhaps some simple wooden knobs. If a wood finish is desired, then the cabinet rails, front edges of the cabinet sides, and drawer fronts should all be of solid wood.

Before you begin work, consider what type of hardware to use for drawer slides. Most modern slides take up ½ inch on each side of the drawer, so if they are used these narrow drawers will become even narrower. Concealed bottom-mount slides, or wooden slides, wouldn't use so much space.

The baseboard should run continuously around the room, and the molding at the top of the cabinets can also be run around the room like a chair rail. If wainscot is included, it and the cabinets should end at the same height above the floor.

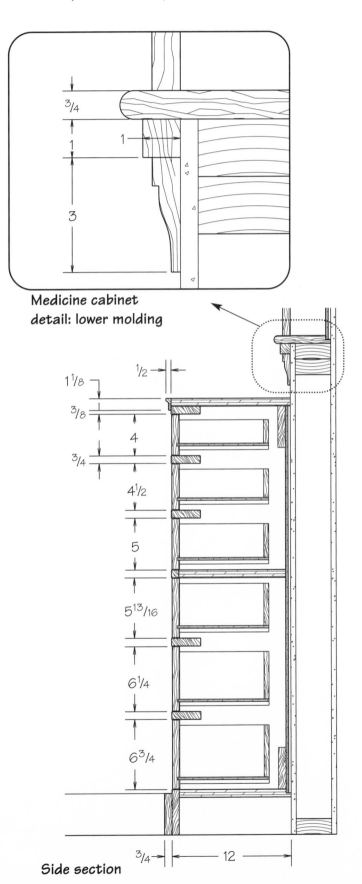

Medicine cabinet
detail: lower molding

Side section

BATHROOM CABINET

If there is not enough space for the his-and-hers cabinets shown on page 186, this cabinet would be a nice alternative. It can be placed below the medicine cabinet as shown, or it can stand alone. As with the smaller cabinets, it is simple to construct. It can of course be made narrower or wider to suit its surroundings, but the lower drawers will not work well if made much wider, and the upper drawers can become practically useless if made much narrower.

The detail at right shows the same molding profile that trims the top of the smaller cabinets, here used as a cornice molding combined with a cove molding. All of the moldings and trim in the bathroom should be smaller than molding profiles for larger rooms.

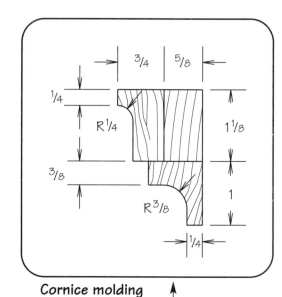

Cornice molding

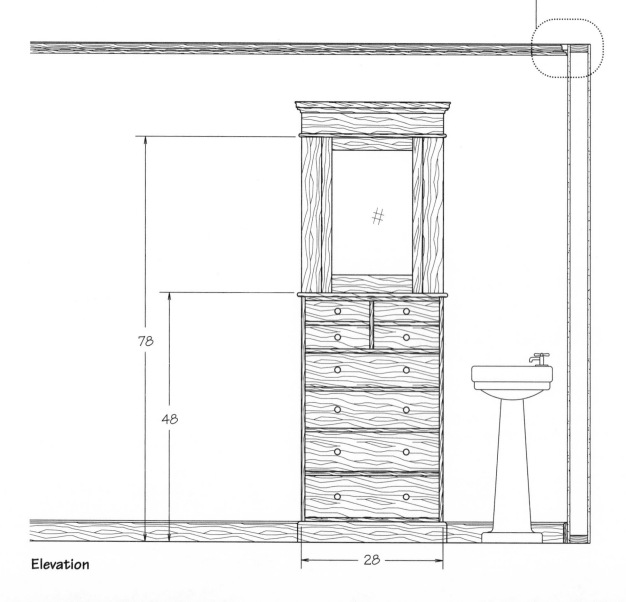

Elevation

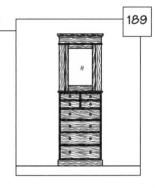

BATHROOM CABINET (*continued*)

The drawer fronts should all be set back about $1/16$ inch behind the front edges of the cabinet sides and rails. This makes the otherwise plain cabinet visually more interesting. The visible edges should all be broken, just slightly rounded or chamfered. "Slightly" should not be taken as an excuse to do sloppy work, because the setbacks and gaps around the drawer fronts need to be consistent, and the drawer fronts need to be flat.

This cabinet is designed to take up minimal floor space, and its shallow depth was common for the period. If space is available, however, a few more inches of depth would make the drawers much more useful.

Since the bottom of the cabinet is wrapped by the baseboard, the case can be built slightly short of the distance between the floor and the bottom of the medicine cabinet, then shimmed up to fit before it is fastened to the wall.

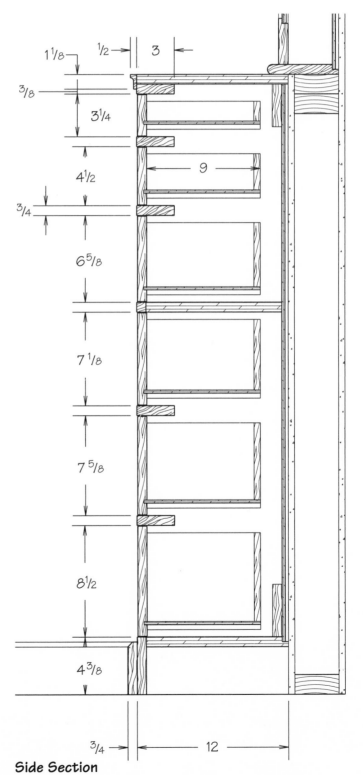

Side Section

FIREPLACE, MANTEL & STAIRWAY

FIREPLACE SURROUND

Ceramic tile was frequently used to face the fireplace in a Craftsman home, sometimes banded with wood trim as shown here, but often accented with wrought iron or hammered copper bands. The soffit above the seats helps to define the fireplace as a distinct area within the room. The paneling helps to unify the design of the room by carrying the horizontal lines at the top of the doors and bottoms of the windows around the room. It also serves to delineate the separate elements by carrying the vertical lines of the window casing down across the structure of the seats. The face of the soffit, and the area above

the door head, would be plain plaster, perhaps decorated with a stencilled or painted motif.

The panels are of a basic stile-and-rail form, with the vertical stiles used as casing at the door and window openings. Except at the door locations, the panels are fabricated as an upper section, with individual boards applied to the face of the wall, and lower section. In many old houses the casement windows adjacent to the fireplace have been covered over, and if restoring an older home it would be worth investigating to see if windows, or their remnants, are present.

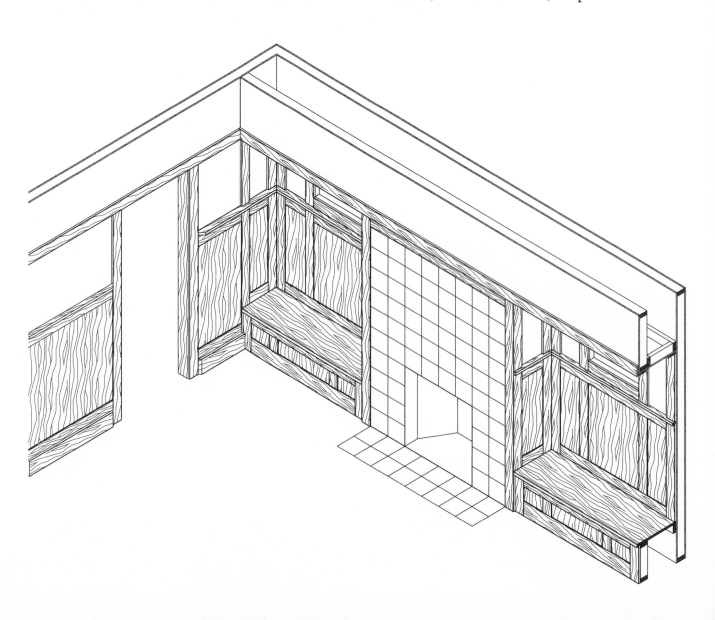

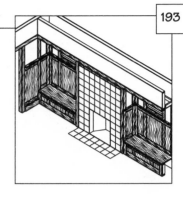

FIREPLACE SURROUND (*continued*)

Tight areas like this need to be carefully planned, with the final appearance kept in mind during layout and framing. Window and door openings will often be centered in rough walls without considering the final thickness of wall paneling. The result will either be the loss of symmetry, or the expensive moving of already installed elements. The wood panels could be carried up above the rail at the bottom of the windows, or to the ceiling. If casement windows are not used,

the panels at the seat should be divided equally.

Little nooks like this can be used almost anywhere in the home, and if placed below a lower window, the height of the panels at the back of the seat should be reduced to be in line with the sill. The soffit establishes the seat as its own distinct area.

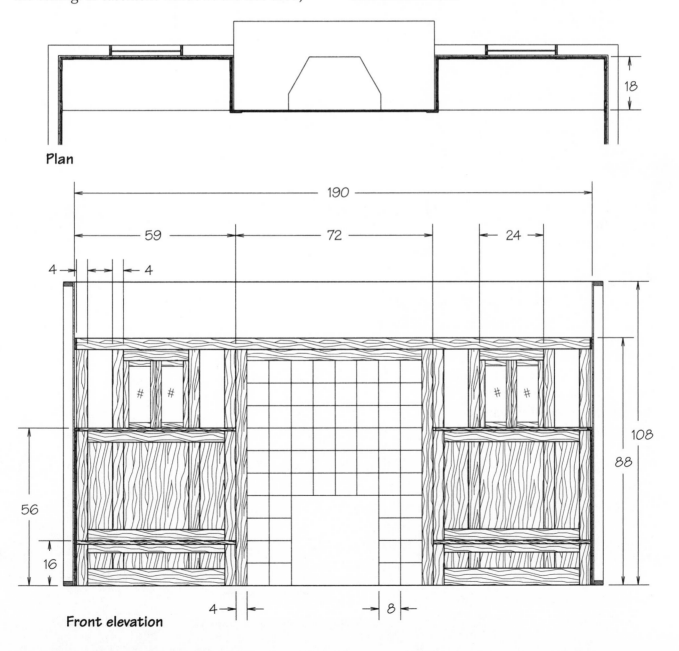

Plan

Front elevation

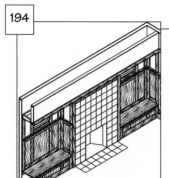

FIREPLACE SURROUND (*continued*)

Construction of the seat and panel is the same as already detailed, with the seat itself being made of solid wood. Care must be taken so that the wood will be able to expand and contract with changes in humidity. In no case should it be glued down to the framework below, but it should be fastened from underneath with screws. The holes for the screws in the framework at the front should either be enlarged to form slots, or should be oversized, with a large washer between the screw head and the wood. After the seat is in place the front panel below the seat can be installed. A bead of construction adhesive can be used on the rails, and a few small nails will hold the panel until the adhesive sets.

Alternately, the front panel can be installed first, attached to the framing with screws from the backside. Figure-8 tabletop fasteners, or metal mending plates with slotted holes, can be secured to the top rail. The front edge of the seat may then be attached to the front panel with screws from below.

The seat could be made from ³/₄ inch thick plywood, with a 1¹/₄ inch solid-wood edge. In this case, the framing would simply be made ¹/₂ inch higher than shown in the drawing. The plywood seat could be glued down to the framing, because wood movement would no longer be a consideration.

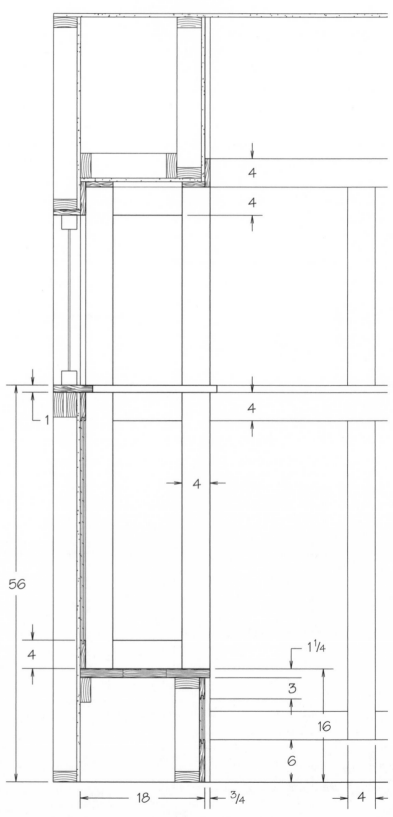

Seat and window: side section

FIREPLACE NOOK

This design is well suited for one end of a room, with the fireplace nook set off by a pair of columns with an overhead beam, and by the curved end-panels on the seats. The overhead beam has been omitted from this three-dimensional view so that the panels can be seen. The beam's location is detailed on the plan view on the next page. The panels below the chair rail and below the seats are plywood, as is the seat,

which has a solid wood front edge. A groove in the bottom and back of the end panels can be anchored by sliding over ³/₄ by ³/₄ inch cleats attached to the floor and wall.

This arrangement is cozy because the fire can be readily seen, and felt, from the seats. It doesn't, however, leave much room for freestanding furniture in front of the fireplace.

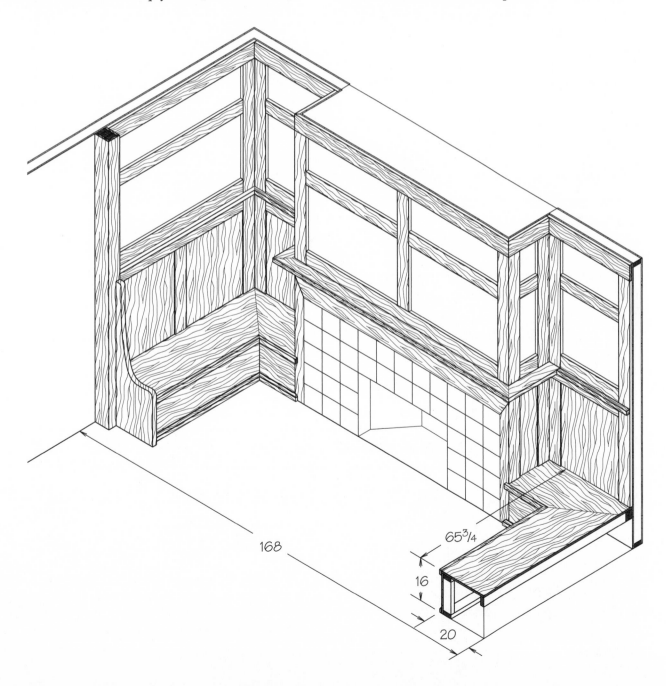

168

65³/₄

16

20

FIREPLACE NOOK (*continued*)

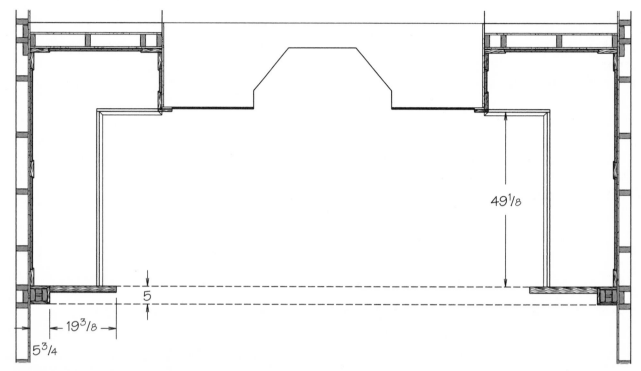

49¹/₈

5

19³/₈

5³/₄

Plan section above seats

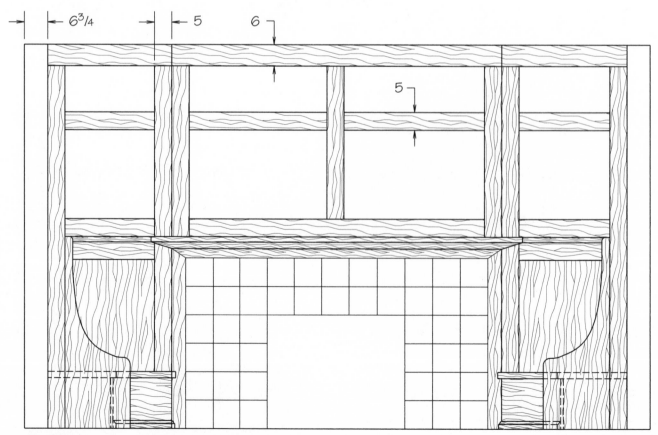

6³/₄   5   6

5

Elevation

FIREPLACE NOOK (*continued*)

Mantels of wood were not featured in *The Craftsman* as often as other materials such as brick, stone, or concrete. If the mantel is intended for display of a clock or other objet d'art, it easily could be made a few inches deeper.

The panels represent an economical approach to construction of the seats. Stile and rail construction, or vee-groove vertical boards, would have a nicer appearance. The horizontal plywood would likely be acceptable because it would be difficult to see these panels in an actual installation. If the seats were visible head-on from across the room, the characteristic figure of veneered plywood would be much more noticeable.

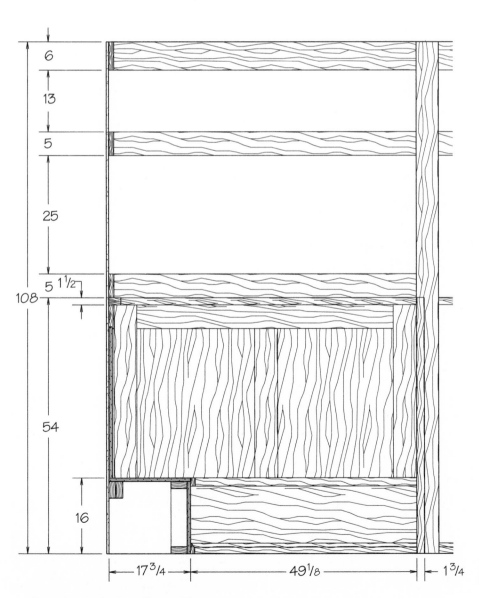

Seat and chair rail: section

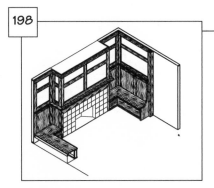

FIREPLACE NOOK (*Continued*)
DETAILS: BUILT-IN SEAT

End panels at fireplace nooks are one of the few details in Craftsman homes that were typically curved, serving to define the space without creating a barrier. If possible, I would make the seat a few inches deeper, and several inches longer, so that one could stretch out and nap before the fire. The front edge of the seat could be extended for an upholstered pad. What an excellent place to sit and while away a winter's evening!

The panels on the walls are shown as $3/4$ inch thick, with the $1\frac{1}{8}$ inch stiles and rails rabbeted to fit over the plywood. The panels can be attached to the walls with construction adhesive, or with screws around the outer edges that are concealed by the applied stiles and rails. The chair rail is shown with a groove along the back, which fits over a cleat attached to the walls. The chair rail can be screwed to the cleat, with the screws hidden by the wide rail above. This method can also be used to secure the end-panel to the floor and to the column.

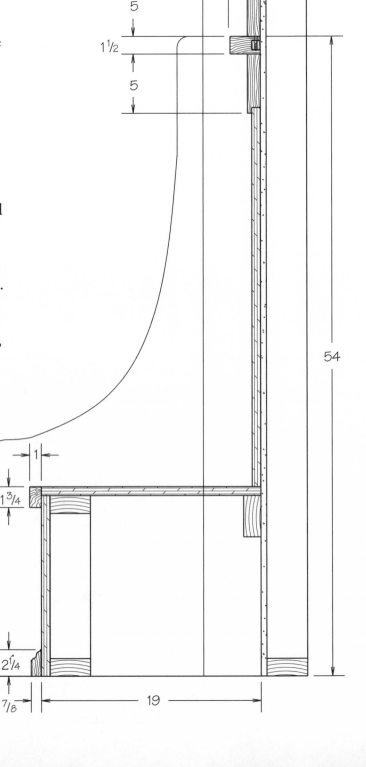

Side section

FIREPLACE NOOK WITH ANGLED SEAT-BACK

This fireplace nook was illustrated in an article in *The Craftsman* about a house constructed from cement, but the drawings show conventionally framed walls. Gustav Stickley began his working life as apprentice to his stonemason father, and attributed his love of working with wood to his early experience with stone. Stone, preferably locally quarried or gathered from the site, was a prominent feature in many of his homes. Combined with the vertical vee-groove planks of the panels and seats, it provides a more rustic look than those done in brick or tile. This seat would be quite comfortable due to its angled back. The small casement windows above the seat contribute

to making this a delightful spot all year long.

Note on the plan view, page 200, how the columns sit on the corners, traversed by an overhead beam. The two low walls at the ends of the seats are framed as stud walls, with the cap serving as a convenient armrest for the end of the seat. The panels below the seat lean back, serving the practical purpose of providing foot-room while sitting, and the visual purpose of echoing the angle of the seat backs. This detail was also shown on other built-in seats without backs, such as those below windows or adjacent to stairs, and vee-groove material was typically used.

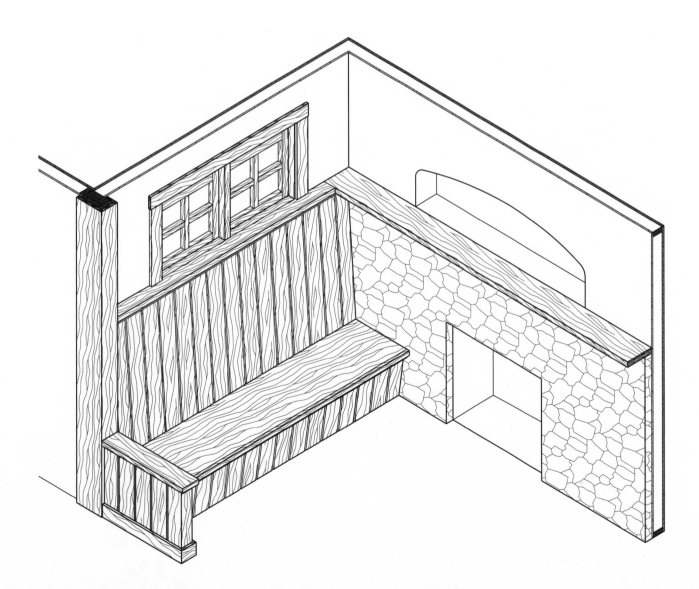

FIREPLACE NOOK WITH ANGLED SEAT-BACK (*Continued*)

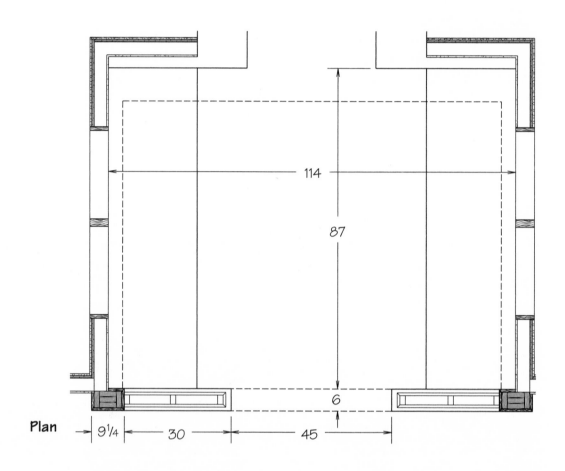

Plan

Side section

FIREPLACE NOOK WITH ANGLED SEAT-BACK (*Continued*)

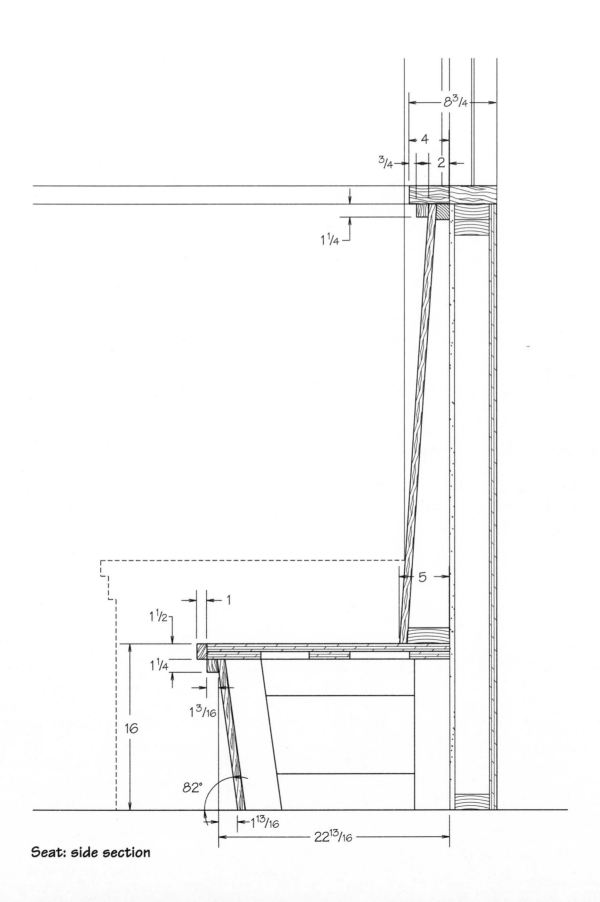

Seat: side section

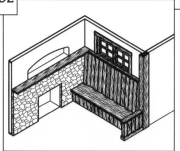

FIREPLACE NOOK
WITH ANGLED SEAT-BACK (*continued*)

The section view on the preceding page, and the detail at right, show a different method of supporting the seat. Instead of a cleat running lengthwise at the back of the seat, and a low stud wall supporting the front, frames as assembled as shown and placed on 16 inch to 24 inch centers, attached to the floor and walls. Both details were shown in the original magazine and architectural drawings, and in some cases the only supports for the seats were shown as 2 x 2 cleats at the wall, floor, and between the seat and front panels. Arguments could be made for any of these methods, although the last is nowhere near as sturdy as the first two. I prefer the cleat-and-stud-wall method, especially with tongue-and-groove planks, as it provides a continuous surface for attaching the planks. If the panels are of rail and stile construction, the second method will save some time and material.

The columns are also shown solidly constructed, and should be well made, even if they are not structural. Someday, someone will come along and attach something very heavy. Build with that person in mind. The blocking inside the column should also be $1/4$ inch to $1/2$ inch smaller in width and depth than the inside of the finished column, to allow the finished pieces to join together and be scribed to the wall.

Seat structure

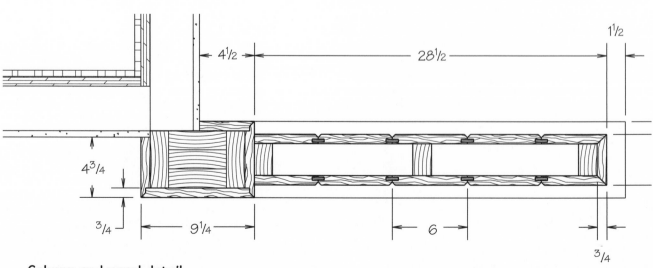

Column and panel detail

FIREPLACE WITH BOOKCASES

In an April 1907 article in *The Craftsman* Gustav Stickley wrote, "In most well planned rooms, the main feature of structural interest is the fireplace, which, by reason of being the natural center of comfort and good cheer, not only dominates the construction of the room, but gives the keynote for the entire scheme of decoration and furnishing." Bookcases were frequently shown next to fireplaces in living rooms, libraries, dens or bedrooms, and similar cabinets occasionally were seen in dining rooms that had fireplaces.

In this example the brick fireplace is capped by a wooden mantel supported by two wooden corbels. The line of the top of the mantle extends to the top of the bookcases, carrying this strong horizontal the entire length of the wall. This line would often be carried completely around the room in the form of a chair rail, or the top rail of wainscot. In this case, it also provides for an extension of the mantel as a display area, adding interest to the entire wall rather than just to a portion of it.

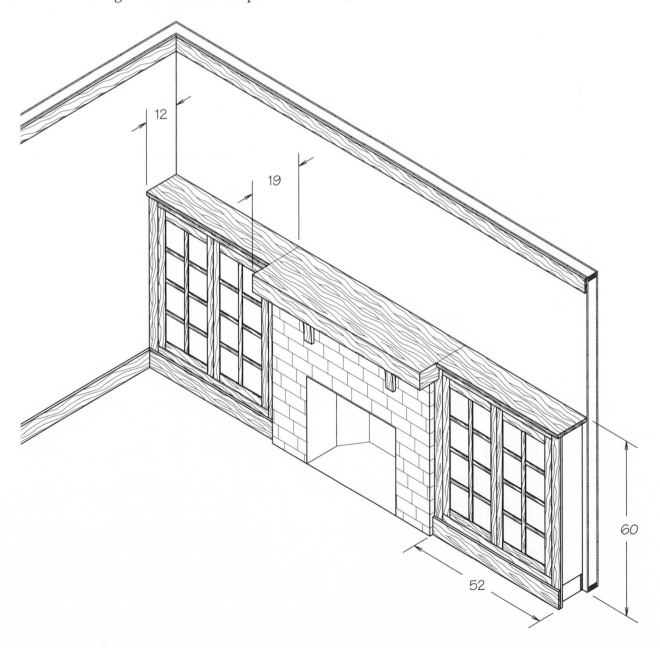

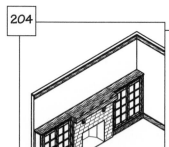

FIREPLACE WITH BOOKCASES (*continued*)

Construction of the bookcases is the same as other bookcases shown in this book, planned to ensure that the bookcases are equal in width and in proportion to the fireplace. The 60-inch height shown is in the middle of the range of period examples, and could easily be 6 inches higher or lower. Installation is tricky, since the cases butt against brick or stone and must also fit neatly to the walls and mantel. For a first-class job scribe the stiles to the masonry. The depth of the cabinets can be increased if the fireplace is deep, but it will look best if the face of the

cabinets is kept back a few inches from the face of the fireplace. The tops of the cases should also be scribed to the walls at the back and end, and should be made oversized so they can be fit neatly both to the walls and to the mantel. If possible, match the grain on the cabinet tops and the mantel ends, so the finished installation looks continuous. Note that the mantel extends beyond the brickwork, and returns at its full height to the face of the bookcases.

The wall space above the mantel should be kept plain, since visual interest will come from the items displayed there.

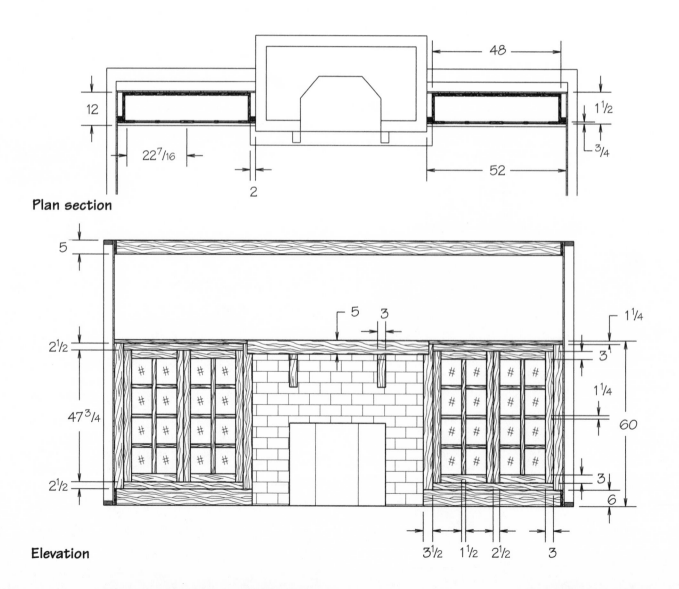

Plan section

Elevation

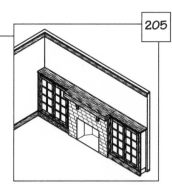

FIREPLACE WITH BOOKCASES (*continued*)

The section drawing below details the cabinet construction, and it should be noted that the width is nearly as wide as is practical to span a shelf or build a glass cabinet door. The cabinet is shown as being entirely out of solid wood, which would be authentic to the period, but may not be the most practical choice. Since it is unlikely that much of the interior of the cabinet will be seen, consider using plywood for the back, sides, top and bottom.

The small detail at right is looking down at a corbel, with the face of the brick represented by the wide horizontal line. If a groove is run down the back of the corbel as shown, a mounting cleat may be anchored to the masonry, and the corbel may then be fastened to the cleat with trim-head screws or long finish nails.

The mantel itself is shown constructed from veneered plywood, with the bottom of it returning to the face of the brick, and both the bottom and finished ends returning to the face of the bookcases. It would be wise to fit this piece to its neighbors first, and then assemble the various parts of the mantel. The blocking for attaching the mantel should be a framework of 2x material that will rest on and extend from the masonry, with the front edge of the mantel sliding over the blocking.

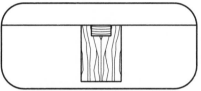

Corbel: plan section

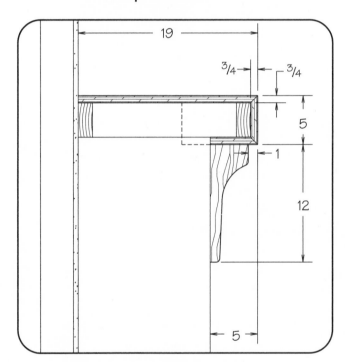

Mantel and corbel detail

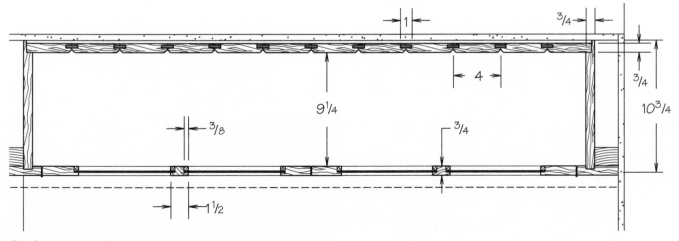

Bookcase section

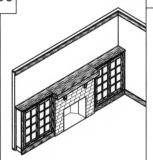

FIREPLACE WITH BOOKCASES (*continued*)

The side section shows the remaining details of the cabinet construction, detailed as being out of solid wood. The thickness of the shelf boards depends on the width of the cabinet, using $3/4$ inch or $13/16$ inch stuff for shelves up to 36 inches long, and $7/8$ inch or 1 inch thick material for distances up to 48 inches. If plywood is used for the shelves, it should be $3/4$ inch thick with a $1 1/4$ inch or $1 1/2$ inch thick solid-wood edge across the front. If tongue and groove boards are used for the cabinet back, they should be secured with one centered screw per board at the top rail, and at the cabinet bottom. Cases of the period were often made without a back, in which case nailers should be added between the case sides at the top, bottom, and centered vertically. My preference is to include a back with the cabinet, because it greatly strengthens the structure of the cabinet, and reduces the risk of racking the cabinet by attaching it to an uneven wall surface.

The depth of the cabinet is less than generally made today, but is actually quite serviceable for all but oversized books. If there is a more modern purpose intended for the cabinet, such as the housing of audio equipment, the depth of that equipment must be considered when designing the cabinets. If the cabinet is intended for display, the shelves could be made of glass, and lamps could be added inside at the top.

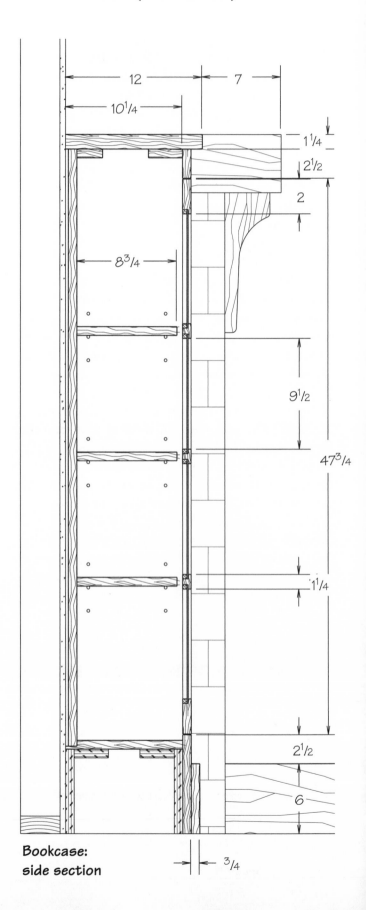

**Bookcase:
side section**

FIREPLACE WITH FLANKING CABINETS

In October 1909, *The Craftsman* featured this fireplace in an article about a small, two-bedroom country cottage. The 14 foot by 19 foot living room takes up most of the first floor, the balance being a 14 foot by 9 foot kitchen. The chimneypiece was specified as being of split fieldstone, and the hood was to be iron. Hoods, a common device in Stickley's fireplaces, were usually constructed of hammered copper, often with a motto inscribed in large letters across the face. The cabinet hardware was also specified as iron, and as *The Craftsman* described it, "The wooden paneling in these bookcase doors, and the finish of iron locks and handles, give them an unusually solid appearance, and, indeed, the whole house has a sturdiness about it that gains an added charm in a building of such small size" (*Craftsman*, Oct 1909). The balance of the room was finished with typical vee-grooved paneling up to the height of the upper cabinet doors, which align with the top of the door jambs elsewhere in the room. The cabinets anchor this end of the room, contributing to the solidity that Stickley described.

The cases are shown as being constructed in an upper and lower section, to make installation more manageable. Notice in the section and plan views that the cabinet itself is considerably smaller than the opening provided for it. This too simplifies installation. The stiles that abut the stone should be scribed to it, and could be left loose from the cabinet until this task was complete. At the opposite end of the cabinet, the stile should be scribed to the wall if paneling is not used. If the panels are present, the paneling can be put in after the cabinet, with the edge of the first panel plank covering the joint between the cabinet stile and the wall.

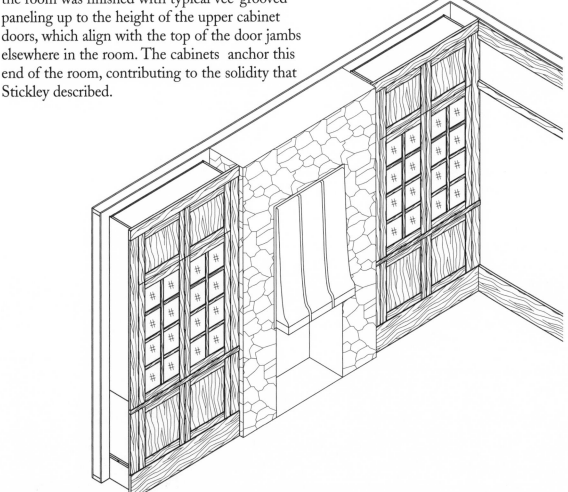

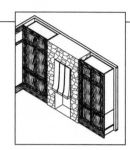

Fireplace with Flanking Cabinets (*continued*)

Here are details of the original bookcase. Setting the cabinet on a separate base, as shown below, will make installation easier because the cabinet stiles sit directly on the thicker baseboard. The bottom edge of the baseboard should be scribed to the floor, or else a small shoe molding will be needed. The large detail below shows how the cross rail covers the joint between the upper and lower cabinets.

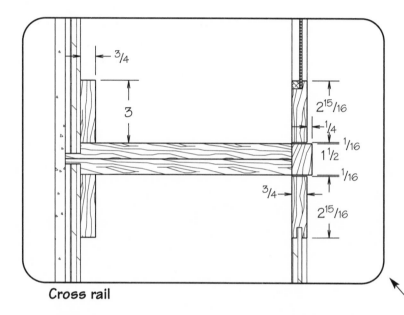

Cross rail

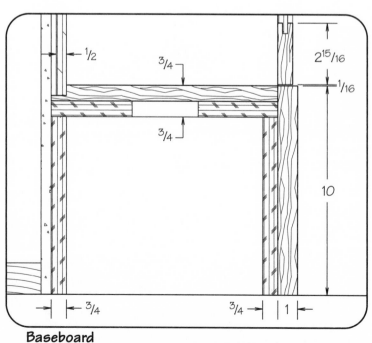

Baseboard

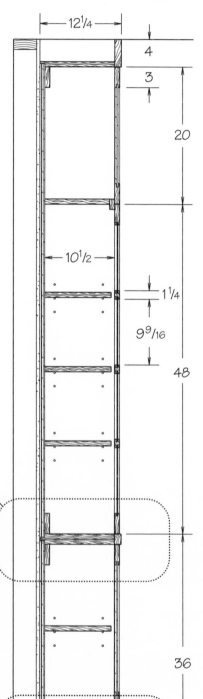

Side Section

FIREPLACE WITH ENTERTAINMENT CENTER

One of the most common forms of built-in cabinets seen today, the entertainment center simply didn't exist in the early Twentieth Century, so I have included a deeper adaptation of the fireplace cabinets to serve this purpose. These cabinets could be built in to a wall without a fireplace by substituting finished end-panels. A low cabinet in between the two tall cabinets might be added in that case.

The elevations on the next page show both versions, as do the section drawings. The large doors are shown as pocket doors that retract into the cabinet space, with vertical dividers to support shelves below the television and to hide the doors and hardware in the retracted position. Be sure to check the clearances required for the pocket-door hardware, and for any electronic equipment.

In building the deeper cabinet, it makes sense to use plywood with a $^3/_4$ inch thick back to brace the construction at the large opening required by the television set. The exact dimensions will need to be adapted for both the room and the equipment the cabinet is to house. As with the period example, build the cases as an upper and lower unit, separated by a rail 36 inches above the floor.

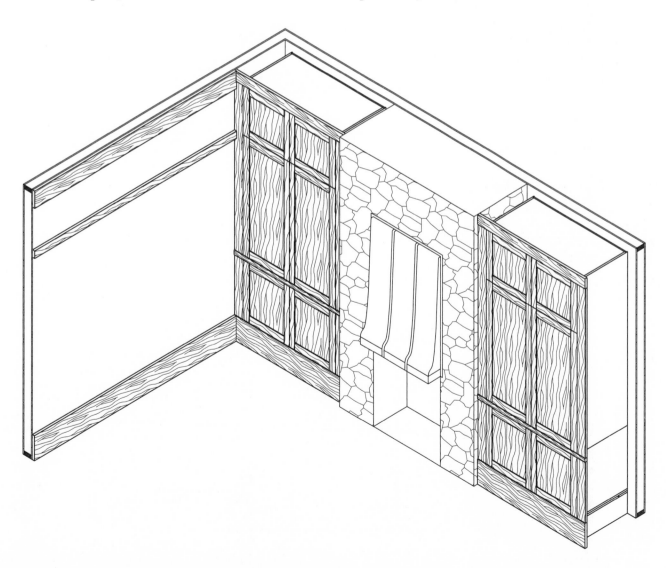

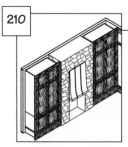

Fireplace with Entertainment Center (*continued*)

Cabinets constructed as modern entertainment center

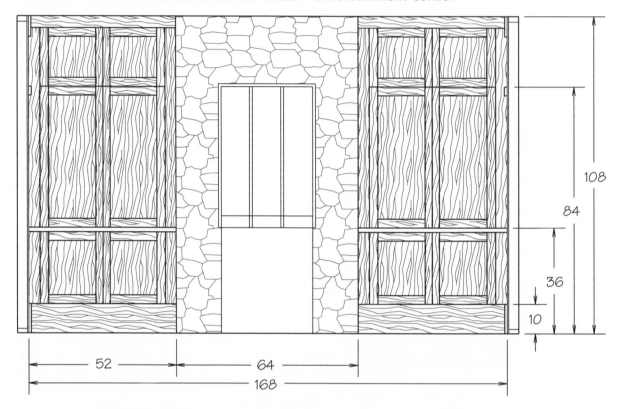

Cabinets constructed as period bookcases

FIREPLACE WITH ENTERTAINMENT CENTER (*continued*)

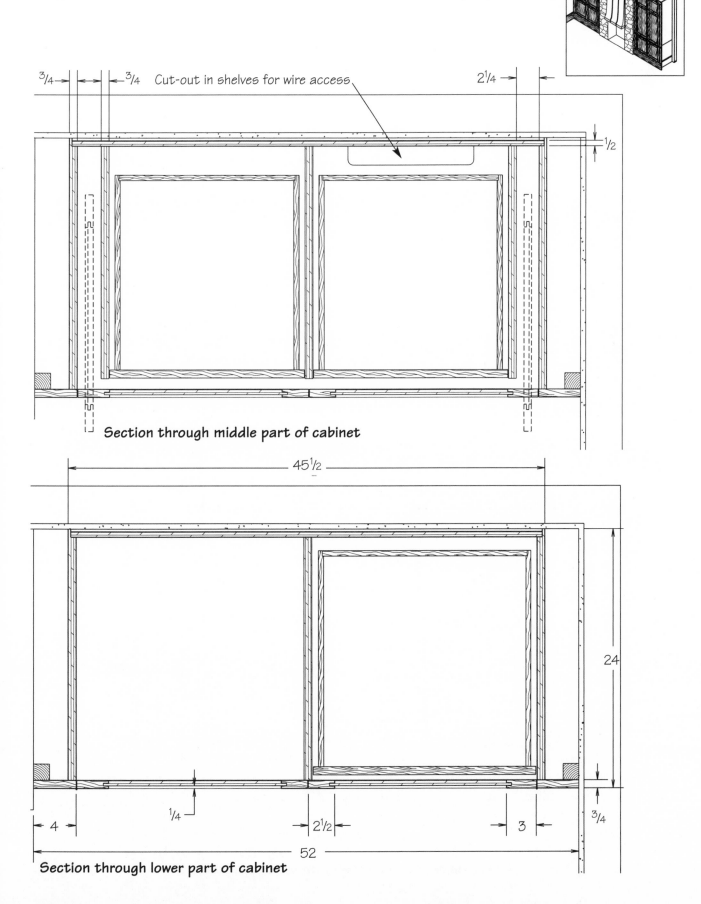

¾   ¾   Cut-out in shelves for wire access   2¼

½

Section through middle part of cabinet

45½

24

¾

4   ¼   2½   3

52

Section through lower part of cabinet

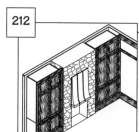

FIREPLACE WITH ENTERTAINMENT CENTER (*continued*)

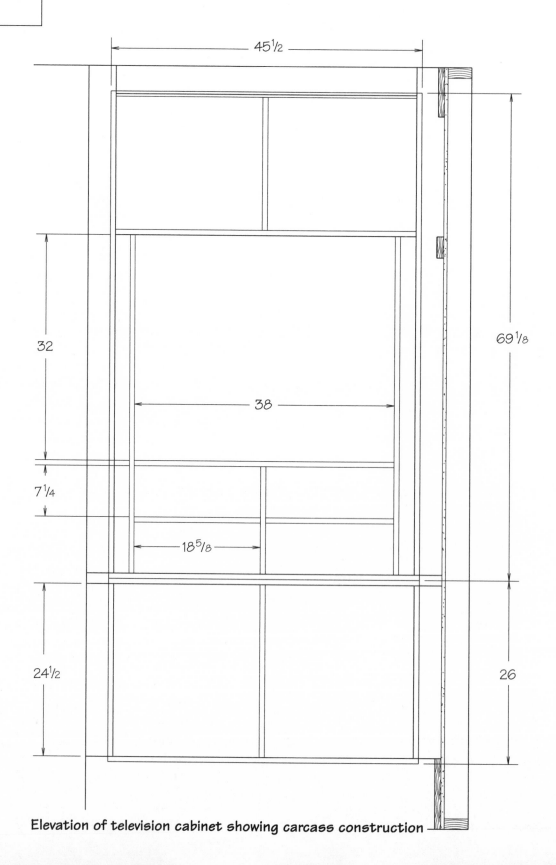

Elevation of television cabinet showing carcass construction

FIREPLACE WITH ENTERTAINMENT CENTER (*continued*)

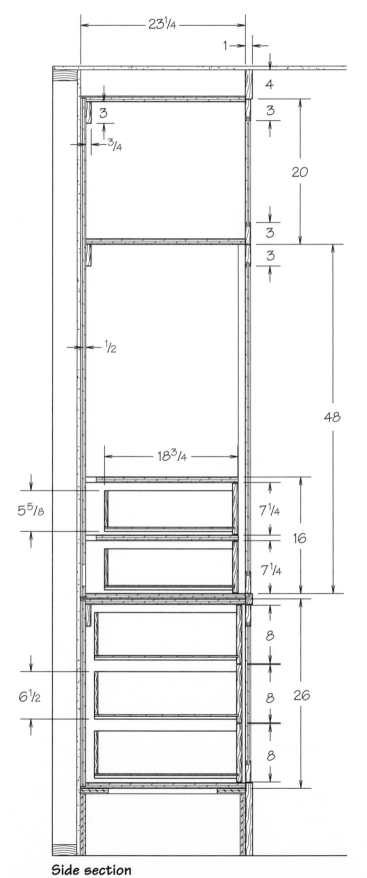

Side section

This vertical section illustrates the remaining details of the television cabinet, keeping in mind that the sizes of the specific electronic devices should be verified before building. Drawers are shown both in the lower cabinet, and in the middle cabinet below the shelf for the television. The area directly below the TV can be replaced with shelves for other electronic equipment. These drawers stop short of the back of the cabinet, to allow for wiring. There should also be cutouts in the back of the cabinet, and in the back of the fixed shelves, for cables and wires. During planning, remember to provide an electric outlet that will be accessible from inside the cabinet, as well as access for cable and audio wiring.

The drawers in the lower cabinet are meant for CDs and videos. The panels in the doors of the upper cabinet could be replaced with grille cloth for speakers. The rail that covers the joint between the cabinets must be attached to the upper cabinet before installation. When the upper cabinet is slid in place, the rail will cover the raw plywood edge of the lower cabinet.

Pocket doors can be intimidating the first time you build them, but they are not difficult. I recommend Accuride hardware, with a system of cables to retract the doors. If the doors and their opening are square, the cabinet is set level, and the hardware manufacturer's instructions followed, then this installation is simple. The cabinet on the opposite side of the fireplace, like the upper and lower doors, can be hung on conventional butt hinges. With all the doors closed, the only difference in appearance will be the absence of visible hinge barrels on the pocket doors.

STAIRS WITH FLAT BALUSTERS

This stairway is from a house designed for a private client in 1914, and the one on the next page is from a house featured in *The Craftsman* in July 1905. They share a common form of baluster, which was similar to that used in Stickley's New Jersey home. They differ in the stringer construction and the type of posts, which are the two common types seen in Stickley's designs.

Stairways were prominent in nearly every Craftsman home, often integrated with other elements such as seats at landings or the base of the stairs. In planning any stairway, local codes should be checked to make sure the design complies with current standards.

Lights on the newel posts were manufactured by Stickley, and added an interesting contrast to the surrounding wood. In Stickley's home at Craftsman Farms, the baluster were quite a bit wider, and the cut-out was in the form of a stylized S. Unfortunately, they were so wide that seasonal wood movement caused the rail above to bow significantly. To avoid this problem, keep the balusters to a width of 5 inches or less, and be certain that all of the materials are at equilibrium moisture content with the interior of the house.

Elevation

Stairs with Flat Balusters: Newel

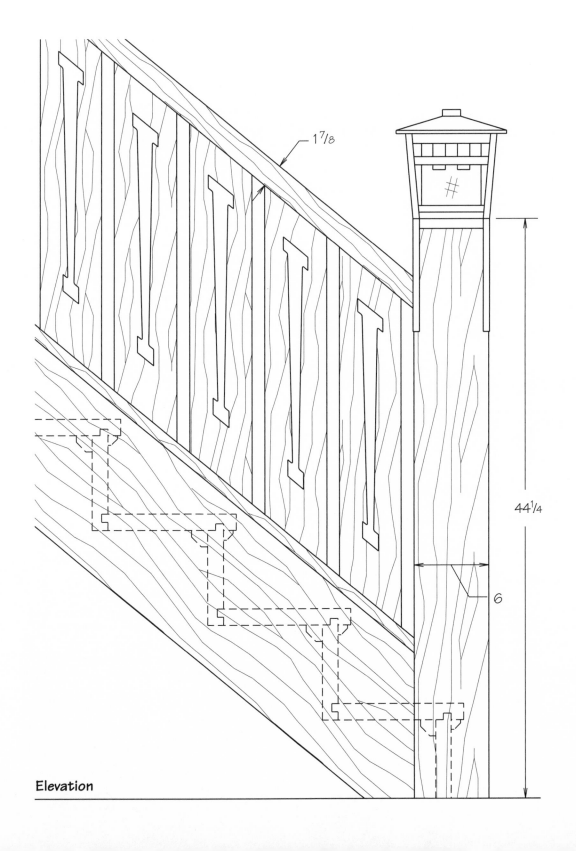

1⁷/₈

44¹/₄

6

Elevation

STAIRS WITH SIMPLE NEWEL

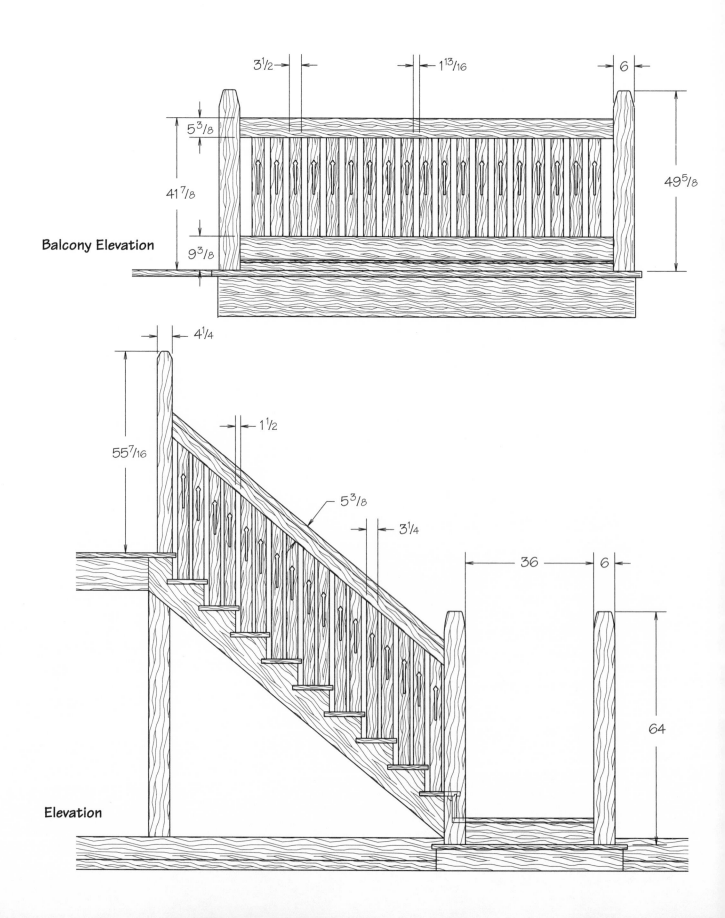

Balcony Elevation

Elevation

Stairs with Simple Newel (*continued*)

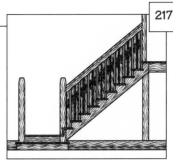

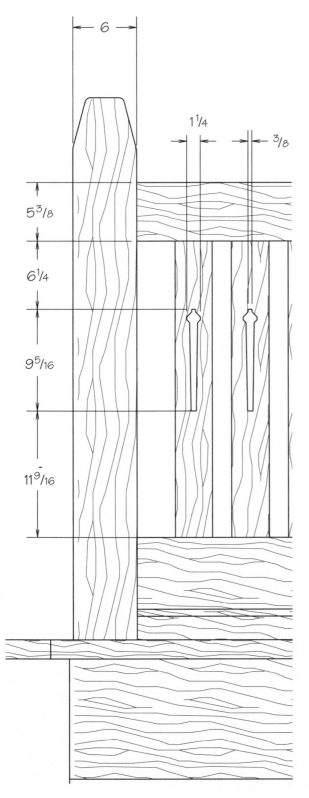

Newel: elevation

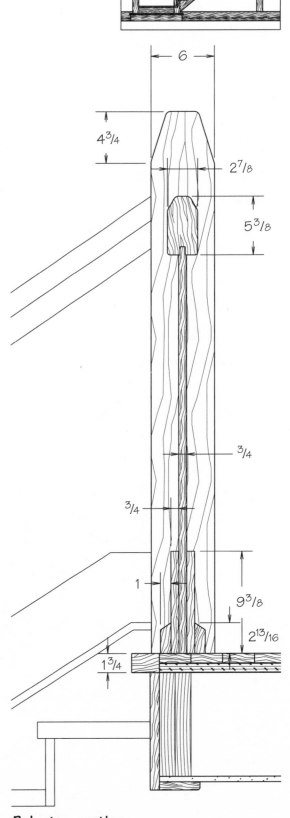

Baluster: section

STAIRS WITH SQUARE BALUSTER

This stairway was from magazine house #106, which appeared in *The Craftsman* in January 1911. It features a simple, square baluster. The balusters were specified as 2 inches square, but this could be reduced to 1³/₄ inch square in order to make use of 8/4 material. The posts could be laminated to form the finished thickness, but it is also feasible to join four pieces with rabbeted miters to form a hollow post, with a square filler piece inserted at the top. The rail will also likely need to be built up from two or more pieces of thinner material.

In this example the stair treads return over the open stringer, compared to the enclosed stringer shown in the first example. Both methods were shown in original designs. The wall below the stair stringer was often paneled, and open landings at the top of the stairs were common, making the stairwell an open transition between floors.

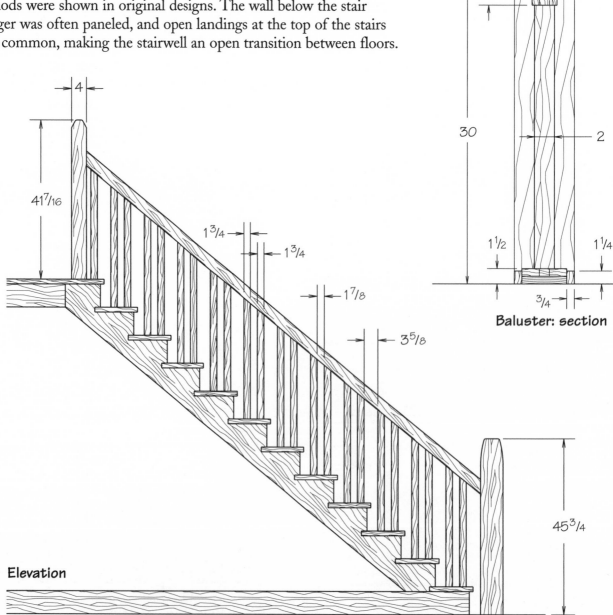

Baluster: section

Elevation

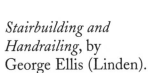

STAIRS: TREAD AND RISER

This tread and riser detail was seen throughout Stickley's architectural drawings, and was typical for the period. Space in this book doesn't permit an in-depth look at stair construction, there are many techniques and layout methods specific to the stair-building trade that are extremely important for quality work. Rather than make this book twice as long, I will recommend some others. Two period books that are considered classics are available in reprinted editions: *A Treatise on Stairbuilding and Handrailing*, by Alexander Mowat, (Linden Publishing) and *Modern Practical*

Stairbuilding and Handrailing, by George Ellis (Linden). Methods have changed since the early 1900s, but not necessarily for the better. One of the things that impressed me most about my visit to Stickley's home at Craftsman Farms was my walk up the stairs—nearly one hundred years old, and not a creak or a shake. Like anything else, the time taken to learn proper methods and techniques will pay off in quality results.

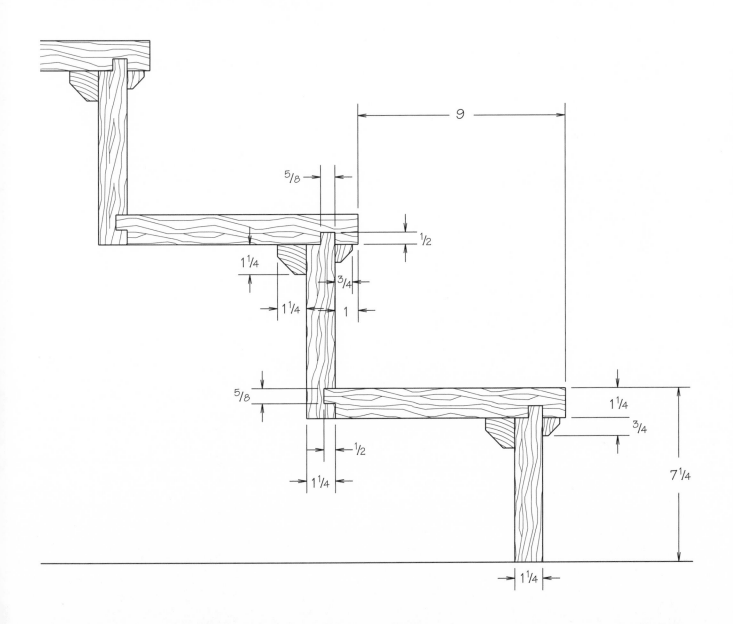

FURTHER READING

Architectural Woodwork Quality Standards Illustrated; 7th edition, 1999. Architectural Woodwork Institute

Bungalow Bathrooms, Jane Powell, photo Linda Svenson, 2001, Gibbs Smith

Bungalow Kitchens, Jane Powell, photo Linda Svenson, 2000, Gibbs Smith

Craftsman Homes, Gustav Stickley

More Craftsman Homes, Gustav Stickley

"The Craftsman" magazine, 1901-1916, Gustav Stickley, editor.

The Forgotten Rebel, Gustav Stickley and his Craftsman Mission Furniture, John Crosby Freeman, 1966, Century House

Gustav Stickley, the Craftsman, Mary Ann Smith, 1983, Syracuse University Press

The Beautiful Necessity: Decorating with Arts & Crafts, Bruce Smith and Yonhiko Yamamoto, 1996, Gibbs Smith

Old House Measured and Scaled Detail Drawings for Builders and Carpenters, William A. Radford, 1911

Gustav Stickley's Craftsman Farms, A pictorial History, The Craftsman Farms Foundation, David Cathers, editor, 1999, Turn of the Century Editions

Gustav Stickley, His Craft, A. Patricia Bartinique, 1992, Turn of the Century Editions

Furniture of the American Arts and Crafts Movement, David M. Cathers, 1996, Turn of the Century Editions

Stickley Style, Arts and Crafts Homes in the Craftsman Tradition, David Cathers, Alexander Vertikoff photo, 1999, Simon and Schuster

The 1912 and 1915 Gustav Stickley Craftsman Furniture Catalogs, Gustav Stickley, Dover reprint, 1991

Homes and Interiors of the 1920's, Lee Valley Tools, 1987

Drawings of the Craftsman Homes by the Craftsman Architects, 1904-1914, Collection of the Avery Architectural and Fine Arts Library, Columbia University

INDEX